Que's Computer Programmer's Dictionary

Conrad Weisert

Contributing Authors

David S. Linthicum
Greg Perry
Richard Stack

Que's Computer Programmer's Dictionary

Copyright © 1993 by Que® Corporation

Library of Congress Catalog Number: 93-83298

ISBN: 1-56529-125-5

95 94 93   6 5 4 3 2 1

Interpretation of the printing code: the rightmost double-digit number is the year of the book's printing; the rightmost single-digit number, the number of the book's printing. For example, a printing code of 93-1 shows that the first printing of the book occurred in 1993.

Publisher: David P. Ewing

Director of Publishing: Michael Miller

Managing Editor: Corinne Walls

Marketing Manager: Ray Robinson

About the Author

Conrad Weisert is a Chicago-based consultant specializing in software development tools and methodologies. As a representative of SHARE, the user group for large IBM computers, he made significant contributions to the design of third-generation operating systems and programming languages. As an early advocate of structured programming, structured analysis, and data administration, he promoted the integration of those disciplines into a results-oriented life cycle framework. His current interests include object-oriented design, client-server architecture, and expert systems.

Publishing Manager
Joseph B. Wikert

Acquisitions Editor
Sarah Browning

Production Editors
Lori Cates
Kezia Endsley
Linda Seifert

Copy Editor
Jill Bond

Technical Editor
Discovery Computing Inc.

Book Designers
Amy Peppler-Adams
Scott Cook

Cover Designer
Dan Armstrong

Production Team
Angela Bannan
Danielle Bird
Brad Chinn
Karen Dodson
Brook Farling
Tim Montgomery
Shelly Palma
Caroline Roop
Dennis Sheehan
Tina Trettin
Susan VandeWalle
Donna Winter
Michelle Worthington
Lillian Yates

Editorial Assitant
Jill Stanley

Composed in *ITC Garamond* and *MCPdigital* by Que Corporation

Trademark Acknowledgments

All terms mentioned in this book that are known to be trademarks or service marks have been appropriately capitalized. Que cannot attest to the accuracy of this information. Use of a term in this book should not be regarded as affecting the validity of any trademark or service mark.

Screen reproductions in this book were created using Collage Plus from Inner Media, Inc., Hollis, New Hampshire.

Introduction

Welcome to Que's Computer Programmer's Dictionary. This book is intended for everyone who has ever uttered, under their breath, "What's that mean?" It seems that such a phrase is more and more likely to be heard, because computers, data processing, and programming continue to evolve at such a breakneck pace.

Who Needs This Book?

Primarily, *Que's Computer Programmer's Dictionary* is a reference book for *programmers*—programmers from a broad range of backgrounds and experience levels, including the following:

- Practicing professionals who already make their living by developing and maintaining computer software

- Newcomers to the field who plan to become professional programmers

- Computer users in all fields who occasionally want to develop software for their own use

- Students of computer science or information systems

- Hobbyists and others who enjoy the challenge of working with computers

In addition, technically oriented systems analysts, managers, and end users will find many parts of this book helpful.

What Do You Need This Book for?

You'll look up terms in *Que's Computer Programmer's Dictionary* for two reasons:

- To gain a general understanding of a concept, method, technique, or term with which you're unacquainted

- To check some specific point of usage of which you're unsure

You may also enjoy just browsing or reading the dictionary sequentially, either to refresh your memory or just to discover interesting and useful things.

Many of the terms you'll look up are relatively *new*. The programming field continues to grow at a pace that outstrips anyone's ability to keep abreast of important developments. Terms unheard of a few years ago have now become indispensable tools in the repertoire of a software developer.

Some of the terms you'll look up are *old*. Programmers who have recently entered the field sometimes feel bewildered by traditions that older colleagues seem to take for granted, but seldom are explained in courses and manuals oriented to current technology.

Old or new, these terms cover what you can reasonably expect *any* professional programmer to know about. Although no one ever masters such a broad range of topics in detail, the successful practitioner needs to be aware of the purpose and broad nature of most of the concepts, methods, techniques, and other terms presented here.

What Kind of Information Will You Find?

Although this book is called a *dictionary*, many entries are much more than simple definitions. You'll find practical advice and informative background material, the sort of information you would expect to get from a knowledgeable colleague. Many times this material is presented, along with other practical tidbits, in the form of Notes, Tips, Warnings, or Cautions. This information, and its unique presentation, will help you understand not only *what* a term means, but *why* it's important and *how* to start making use of it.

In areas that are considered controversial, we've tried to provide a balanced point of view that fairly conveys responsible opinions held by knowledgeable professionals. Although we never endorse any product or proprietary methodology, we don't hesitate to offer our views on issues of good practice, especially where they coincide with a consensus of enlightened opinion.

Which Operating Platforms Does This Book Cover?

An *operating platform* is a combination of the following:

- A specific hardware architecture (Intel, Motorola, MIPS, and so on)

- An operating system that runs on that hardware (MS-DOS, UNIX, System 7, and so on)

- Other major system software that defines an environment for application software, such as a telecommunications monitor, a database management system, or major utility programs

Entries in *Que's Computer Programmer's Dictionary* fall into three categories:

- Concepts, techniques, and methods that are independent of any specific operating platform. Most of the content falls in this category. You'll find these entries useful in working not only with the full range of platforms currently in common use, but also with new platforms that will surely appear in the next decade.

- Keywords and other specialized nomenclature oriented to one or more platforms in widespread, current use. You won't find every platform-specific term here, of course; *Que's Computer Programmer's Dictionary* is not a substitute for a good vendor's manual or a specialized platform-oriented publication. This book focuses on those terms that are so fundamental to the very nature of a given platform that you can expect to encounter them in discussions and documentation. In this edition, these platforms include desktop and workstation platforms (such as MS-DOS, UNIX, OS/2, Windows, and Macintosh), networks (such as NetWare and Windows for Workgroups), and current minicomputers (such as VAX/VMS and AS/400).

- Certain terms that currently describe general notions but that originated in connection with some platform that has significantly influenced the state of modern technology. Programmers whose background is largely on such a platform tend to use that platform's terms generically. Therefore, even if you don't expect to use such platforms, you must be aware of the widely used terms you're likely to encounter.

In addition to the platforms previously listed, this category includes the major mainframe systems (such as OS/MVS, VM, and DOS) that are still supported and widely used.

This book doesn't include terms that are no longer in general use, that deal with obsolete techniques, or that occur mainly in connection with specialized products or application areas that most programmers don't encounter.

What about Programming Languages?

Most of the entries in *Que's Computer Programmer's Dictionary* are language-independent concepts and techniques. However, the book also includes certain terms specific to important programming languages. The languages we consider important for the modern practicing professional include the following:

- General-purpose procedural languages that are

  Available and supported on modern operating platforms

  Commonly used among organizations developing either software products or application systems

  Standardized and portable among different platforms

  Nonproprietary: either in the public domain or licensed for reasonable fee to any vendor or user.

These languages include Ada, BASIC, C/C++, COBOL, FORTRAN, Pascal, and PL/I.

- The language of spreadsheets, as supported by today's leading spreadsheet processors.

- The major languages of artificial intelligence and symbol manipulation, LISP and Prolog.

In addition, this book sometimes briefly refers to other languages—such as APL, Algol, Modula-2, RPG, and SmallTalk—that have either introduced important innovations or significantly influenced the tools and techniques that modern programmers use. However, the dictionary doesn't include highly specialized languages or proprietary products that do not fall into one of the preceding categories.

This book includes a few references to assembly languages in general, but none to any specific assembly language. Except in extremely specialized areas, the modern programmer has little need for assembly language and manages nicely using commonly available higher-level languages. Because the assembly language for each hardware architecture is unique, you must consult the appropriate vendor's manuals or specialized books if you're considering programming in an assembly language.

Some entries include examples of actual program code. For each such example, we've chosen either an intuitive pseudocode or a real language that most directly illustrates the concept or technique being explained with a minimum of linguistic peculiarity. If you're comfortable with *any* procedural programming language, you should easily understand these program fragments.

There are some constructs (such as a comment delimiter) for which almost every programming language provides a different, specialized construct. For such constructs, this dictionary provides a table showing the equivalent construct in the major languages.

A Word of Advice

This introduction started by indicating that we work (and sometimes live) in a fast-moving, ever-changing industry. Because of this, you may notice that some terms don't appear in this dictionary. Please don't take that as a sign of a lack of completeness or a deliberate slight to any portion of the programming community. Instead, such an occurrance can more likely be traced to the fact that the industry changes so fast, and new terms are coined so prolificly, that it is nearly impossible for any author or group of authors to keep abreast of them all. Rest assured, however, that the terms included herein represent the widest possible cross-section of the industry and will provide you with a firm and sure footing regarding what we lovingly refer to as "computerese."

286, 386, 486, 80×86, 80286, 80386, 80486, 8080, 8086, 8088

See *Intel CPU.*

3270 terminal

An IBM terminal consisting of a CRT (cathode ray tube) and keyboard. The 3270 terminal was widely used in online systems of the 1970s and 1980s and is still emulated in many desktop computer telecommunication applications.

See also *VT-100 terminal.*

ABEND—abnormal end

Termination of a task or job step in some manner other than a normal return.

An ABEND is triggered by an interrupt or other condition that the program is not prepared to handle. It implies a loss of control.

See also *completion code* and *crash*.

absolute cell reference

A reference in a spreadsheet formula to a cell or range to be exempt from being automatically adjusted if the formula is copied or replicated. The example that follows illustrates the difference between relative and absolute cell references.

In most spreadsheet processing programs, a dollar sign ($) specifies that a cell reference is absolute, as in $RATE_TABLE. When you don't use a symbolic range name, you can specify absolute referencing separately for the following:

- The column ($D6)
- The row (D$6)
- Both the column and the row (D6)

Thus, if you enter into cell G6 the formula

D6+$D6+D$6+D6

and then copy cell G6 to cell H7, cell H7 contains the formula

+D6+$D7+E$6+E7

A common error made in spreadsheet models is to omit the dollar sign in references to tables or constants, especially those defined by symbolic range names. Programmers should make a habit of including the dollar sign in such references.

absolute constant

A constant that arises naturally in a mathematical or algorithmic relationship.

Absolute constants include pi and many occurrences of 0, 1, the null string, the null pointer, and the Boolean constants true and false. For example, in the BASIC expression

```
SQR(1.0 - VELOCITY^2)
```

both constants are absolute. Redefining their values would make no sense.

Unlike fundamental constants, coding absolute constants as inline literals is usually considered good practice. The preceding example is more clear and less error-prone than the following:

```
SQR(ONE - VELOCITY^TWO)
```

However, for constants like pi that have many digits, defining symbolic names is customary, to avoid errors and to localize the number of digits.

absolute value

The magnitude of a number, disregarding its sign.

In mathematical notation, the absolute value of a quantity, x, is denoted by

$$| x |$$

Formally:

$$| x | = x \text{ if } x \geq 0$$

$$| x | = -x \text{ if } x < 0$$

Many programming languages and spreadsheet processing programs provide an equivalent function (such as abs, ABS, @ABS, and ¦) as part of the standard mathematical function library.

accelerator board

A pluggable circuit card added to a desktop computer to enhance its speed, either generally or in some area such as video (screen) or floating-point operations.

The growing use of graphical user interface (GUI) systems with their high overhead has created a market for accelerator boards designed to enhance the performance of high-resolution video operations.

accelerator key

A key or combination of keys you can press to perform a particular function quickly.

Operating systems, application programs, and other software provide accelerator keys to enable experienced users to perform certain program functions more quickly than they can by selecting a series of menu options. In some Windows applications, for example, pressing the F12 function key quickly executes a File Save operation. Accelerators are also known as *shortcut keys.*

acceptance test

A process or test performed on a new software product, hardware component, or complete system to demonstrate to the sponsoring users (or customers) that the product meets its specifications.

Acceptance testing is normally the last testing stage in a project. When the users have engaged an outside firm to develop a system, the acceptance test is also used to validate formally that the developers have met their contract obligations.

See also *integration test, stress test, system test,* and *unit test.*

Access

Microsoft's relational database management system (DBMS) for Windows.

Access includes a broad repertoire of facilities—including a dialect of BASIC similar to Microsoft's own Visual Basic—for developing applications that take advantage of the graphical user interface (GUI).

accessor function

A function that gives programmers access to private data items from code outside the module or object class definition in which they are encapsulated.

In object-oriented programming (OOP), a designer-programmer who creates a class definition rarely wants to give user-programmers unrestricted ability to examine or change the values of data items internal to objects of that class. Instead, for each internal data item, the designer-programmer can choose one of the following options:

- To hide the internal data item completely, permitting no external access. This is the usual choice for control fields or items that depend on internal representation. Examples of such functions include `next_item_pointer` and `usage_count`.

- To provide read-only access. This choice is common for data items that the application program needs but that, once correctly set, should never be changed. Examples of such functions include `date_of_birth` and `author_name`.

- To provide read-write access. This choice is appropriate for database fields that an application program may update. Examples of such functions include `quantity_on_hand` and `street_address`.

By providing only the appropriate accessor functions, the designer-programmer can control exactly how user-programmers must refer to each internal data item.

accumulator register

A high-speed storage circuit that holds the results of arithmetic operations. On most desktop computers, the accumulator register is internal to the microprocessor chip.

The accumulator register in the Intel 8086 family is called AX. Instructions such as MUL or DIV for multiplication or division require one operand in AX, and the result is stored in AX.

ACM—Association for Computing Machinery

The oldest professional society (founded in 1948) for people in computing.

ACM has local chapters in major cities, student chapters at many colleges and universities, and many special-interest groups. Its many publications include books, journals, and newsletters. It conducts conferences at various levels, including an annual Computer Science conference.

ACM members repeatedly have rejected proposals to change the society's name to something more descriptive of its present scope.

active directory

The directory in which the operating system looks for and stores files that are referred to without an explicit directory qualifier; also called the *current directory*.

In MS-DOS, for example, after you issue the command

```
C:>CHDIR \LETTERS\SMITH
```

the active directory on disk drive C becomes the SMITH subdirectory of the LETTERS directory. The operating system then interprets references to simple file names on drive C as references to files in that directory, so that the command

```
C:>\PRINT C:PROPOSAL
```

has the same effect as

```
C:>PRINT C:\LETTERS\SMITH\PROPOSAL
```

The active directory applies not only to data files but also to executable programs. If you then enter the command

```
C:>WP
```

the operating system looks for the program WP.EXE or WP.COM in the LETTERS\SMITH directory. (If that's not what you want, you can use the MS-DOS PATH command to establish one or more directories the operating system will search, in addition to the active directory, to find executable programs.)

See also *active drive*.

active drive

The disk drive on which the operating system looks for and stores files that are referred to without an explicit disk drive qualifier; also called the *current drive*.

In MS-DOS, for example, if drive C is the active drive and you issue the command

```
C:>A:
```

the active directory becomes disk drive A, and the next prompt you see is

```
A:>
```

The operating system then interprets names of data or program files as references to files on drive A unless another drive is explicitly specified.

See also *active directory*.

Ada

A procedural programming language aimed at ensuring the high reliability necessary for embedded systems and other critical military applications.

In the spirit of Pascal, Ada was designed in response to initiatives by the United States Department of Defense in the mid-1970s. Despite the language's specialized objectives, Ada is a true general-purpose language suitable for a wide range of business and scientific applications. Although Ada doesn't support the full inheritance required of a true object-oriented language, it does provide good encapsulation capabilities, and many of its supporters claim that it is a suitable vehicle for implementing object-oriented designs.

During its design, Ada was known as the "green language," merely to distinguish it from two other finalist candidates. After being chosen, it was renamed in honor of Ada Lovelace, who, as assistant to Charles Babbage in his unsuccessful attempts to build a programmable machine, is credited with being the first programmer.

address

A number that identifies a unit of memory.

Each byte or word of memory has a unique address. The computer uses addresses both to designate the next instruction to be executed and to designate one or more operands of such an instruction. In assembly language, the programmer refers to addresses by symbolic names.

Certain auxiliary storage devices, such as disks, also use addresses, but usually to identify larger units of storage (tracks) rather than individual bytes.

address, port

See *port address*.

addressability

Property of an area of memory into which an instruction can store data or from which it can fetch data. *Addressability* is a general term that can refer to either of the following:

- The range of memory cells an instruction can address.

- The unit of storage addressed by an instruction. In a byte-addressable computer, each byte has a unique address, and an instruction can refer to any byte within the range of possible addresses.

See also *address, address space, indirect addressing, paged memory,* and *segmented-memory model.*

address space

The range of main memory addresses accessible to a program for storing instructions and data.

In real mode, these addresses are a subset of the actual, physical machine addresses. In virtual memory mode, a larger range of addresses can be mapped onto machine addresses dynamically.

See also *address, paged memory,* and *segmented-memory model.*

ALGOL

One of a family of procedural programming languages designed to facilitate expression of numeric algorithms and specified originally by international working groups chartered for that purpose.

ALGOL-58 spawned several dialects, including MAD, JOVIAL, and NELLIAC, that were widely used on second-generation computers for academic and military applications.

ALGOL-60 was one of the earliest practical languages to incorporate block structure and recursion. It was more widely used in Europe than in America, where it was known mainly as a preferred publication language for algorithm specifications.

ALGOL-68 resulted from an attempt to define a highly recursive language of much greater power and wider scope. However, it was not widely used, for the following reasons:

- The difficulty of implementing efficient compilers
- Terminology and manuals perceived as inaccessible to rank-and-file programmers
- Lack of upward compatibility from ALGOL-60
- The availability of the competing languages PL/1, Pascal, and eventually Ada

algorithm

A procedure consisting of a finite sequence of well-defined steps for producing one or more outputs from a set of inputs.

The analysis of algorithms is a central focus of computer science from two points of view:

- General theory of algorithms:

     The classification of strategic approaches

     The impact of choices of data representation and structures

     The techniques for measuring efficiency (time and space) as a function of the dimensions or values of one or more inputs

- Specific analysis of major problem areas, such as the following:

     Searching and matching

     Sorting

     Optimizing

     Game playing

     Numerical methods

align

1. To position data or instructions according to restrictions imposed by the hardware or programming language design.

2. In typography, to line up type. You can align type so that the base of each character rests on the same horizontal line (base aligning), along

the left margin so that the first character of each line begins in the same position (left align), or along the right margin so that the last character of each line ends in the same position (right align).

See also *justify.*

allocate

1. To assign to a job the temporary use of some resource (such as an area of memory, disk space, or a device).

2. To establish during program execution a correspondence between a data item and an area of memory. See also *instantiate.*

Allocate is a transitive verb used in both directions; for example, using the second definition, you can refer either to allocating memory or to allocating the data item.

See also *automatic allocation.*

alpha

Slang abbreviation for "alphabetic" or "alphabetic character."

See also *alphanumeric character.*

Alpha AXP architecture

A high-performance RISC machine developed as a successor to the VAX series.

alphanumeric character

Any of the following:

*   The alphabet (A–Z)

*   The digits (0–9)

*   Spaces or whitespace characters

*   Special characters used in editing numeric data: the dollar sign ($), decimal point (.), plus sign (+), and minus sign (–).

Alphanumeric sometimes is misused to refer in a more general sense to any character data—for example, not just the characters in the preceding list, but also any punctuation or other printable special characters. The term *character,* however, is more precise than *alphanumeric* in describing arbitrary character string data.

The form "alphameric" was once promoted in vendors' manuals and course materials, and is occasionally still used.

See also *ASCII* and *EBCDIC*.

ALU—arithmetic logical unit

See *CPU*.

A-margin

In COBOL programming, positions 8 through 11 of a line of code; used for the beginning of division, section, and paragraph names, and level-1 data declarations.

Rigid margins are a relic of COBOL's early punched-card orientation and its catering to the convenience of compiler writers rather than programmers. See also *B-margin*.

American National Standards Institute

See *ANSI*.

American Standard Code for Information Interchange

See *ASCII*.

analog signal

A continuously variable wave form, whose amplitude or frequency is varied to represent data.

A familiar example of the use of analog signals is in data transmission by modem. Digital data is converted (modulated) by the modem to a form suitable for transmission over standard telephone lines. The analog signals are converted back (demodulated) to digital form at the receiving end.

See also *digital signal* and *modem.*

and

1. A binary logical operator that is assigned the value *true* only if both of its operands are true.

2. A machine instruction that applies the AND operation bit by bit to two bytes or words, producing a result of the same type.

ANSI—American National Standards Institute

An organization consisting of members from the business, industry, and academic communities that develops voluntary standards. ANSI is the United States' representative to ISO, the International Standards Organization.

ANSI has standardized specifications for the most widely used storage media, data representation, data communication, programming languages, and escape sequences.

ANSI.SYS

In MS-DOS, a driver that defines the standard escape sequences that define the appearance of the screen and functions of the keys on the console.

API—Application Program Interface

A collection of lower-level functions provided by an operating system or operating system extension. These routines have well-defined interfaces, and are used by application programmers to manage or obtain system resources or perform system functions.

APIs have existed since programming systems have had macro assemblers and the support tools to access libraries of source and compiled code. With the increased use of graphical user interfaces (GUIs), APIs have become powerful and complex.

Learning some modern APIs is much more difficult than just learning the hardware and operating system. The cost of mastering a new API may be so high as to make it impractical to port application software to multiple platforms.

APL—A Programming Language

A programming language proposed by Kenneth Iverson in the early 1960s as a rigorous tool for both specifying and implementing algorithms, and later implemented on various computers in a modified and extended form.

APL is based on extremely concise notations derived from mathematics. These notations require a much expanded character set not directly supported on standard keyboards, screens, and printers. Although somewhat hard to learn, APL is extremely powerful in manipulating data structures such as arrays and trees. Once mastered, APL can be effective in implementing complex processes quickly and reliably. Applicable to a wide range of business and scientific applications, APL is also useful as a teaching language. You can also use APL to develop and analyze algorithms that you can then implement in a different language.

Because of APL's highly dynamic data structuring, an APL compiler may generate object code that is inefficient compared to that of other languages. APL is often implemented as an interactive interpreter.

APPC—advanced program-to-program communication

A protocol within IBM's System Network Architecture (SNA) for communication among programs running on different computers.

append

To add elements to the end of a sequentially organized data structure such as a character string, a list, a queue, or a sequential file.

See also *concatenate*.

application software

Programs, data definitions, and other computer-based components intended to be used in a specific application system.

Some writers and software product manuals have begun to apply the term "application software" to almost any program—such as a word processor, a database management system (DBMS), or a spreadsheet processor—that isn't either a software development tool or part of an operating system. Because such products are independent of any application area, they are more properly classified, depending on their size and scope, as system software, utility programs, or productivity tools.

application system

A set of files (or databases), programs, equipment, and procedures to support a set of related functions suited to the user organization's needs. Such functions might be related to business, engineering, science, and so on, depending on the user organization's particular focus.

An application system is much more than just application software. Application software can successfully meet users' needs only if it is integrated into the larger framework of a well-designed system.

architecture, application system

1. The overall arrangement of a system into building blocks.

2. For third-generation languages, the allocation of functions to modules structured between those modules.

3. Distributed systems; for example, in a distributed database system, the data and processes are distributed over a local or wide-area network.

See also *distributed database, distributed processing,* and *generations, programming languages.*

architecture, computer

See *computer architecture.*

archive file

A file that is saved but never used again in under normal circumstances.

The following are reasons for archiving a file:

- As backup to reconstruct a database if necessary
- For reference in a system or financial audit
- To comply with legal file-retention requirements

For economy, large archive files (or collections of such files) are often stored either on magnetic tape or on microfilm (or another optical medium). To save space, archive files may be the output of a compression algorithm.

argument

Data item input to a function or operator.

An argument can be a constant, a variable, or an expression. (Some programming languages restrict arguments in some contexts.) It can usually be of any data type for which the function or operator is defined.

Examine, for example, the following expression:

```
sqrt(max(0, (1 - B) * C))
```

The two arguments of the binary operator - are 1 and B.

The two arguments of the binary operator * are (1 - B) and C.

The two arguments of the function max are 0 and (1 - B) * C.

The single argument of the function sqrt is max(0, (1 - b) * C).

See also *domain, operand,* and *parameter.*

arithmetic logical unit

See *CPU.*

array

A collection of data items (scalars or composite data items) in which the following are true:

- All items are of the same type and have the same attributes or properties.
- The location or position of each element or item within the array is uniquely designated by one or more integer subscripts.

21

The increasing size of available address spaces has led to a growing use of arrays for purposes that might formerly have called for small files. Such uses of arrays eliminate the need for explicit input-output (I/O).

See also *address, bound, scalar, table,* and *vector.*

AS/400

A series of mid-range IBM computers, targeted for "departmental computing."

A successor to the earlier System/3x, the AS/400 is incompatible with both IBM mainframe systems and desktop computers. Nevertheless, it has enjoyed success for business applications both in stand-alone configurations and in distributed processing networks.

See also *distributed processing, mainframe computer, minicomputer,* and *personal computer.*

ASC function

A BASIC language function that converts the first letter in a character string to its ASCII value. In the following example:

```
X = ASC("ABC")
```

X is set to 65, the ASCII value of the letter A.

ASCII—American Standard Code for Information Interchange

A widely recognized assignment of numeric codes to printable characters and certain device control codes.

In standard ASCII, unique seven-bit codes represent the following:

- Each letter of the Roman alphabet in both upper- and lowercase

- Each numeric digit

- The punctuation characters (including blanks) that occur in written English

- The special characters that occur in popular programming languages

- Control codes commonly used in data communication or output devices

The eight-bit bytes used in almost all modern computer systems and data-handling devices make it natural to extend ASCII to include an additional 128 characters. These extended ASCII codes include the following:

- Letters of the alphabet with diacritical marks used in European languages, such as the umlaut (ä), accent (é), tilde (ñ), and cedilla (ç)

- Straight and intersecting line segments for drawing rectilinear figures

- The Greek letters most often used in mathematics

These extended code assignments, however, are not standard, and may vary both among hardware implementations and among different language groups.

Note that alphabetic sorting of ASCII data items usually requires special auxiliary key fields, because the upper- and lowercase codes for the same letter are not adjacent and the diacritical letters do not collate in the sequence most people expect.

Appendix A presents a chart of ASCII codes.

See also *EBCDIC*.

ASCII file

A file in which the records contain only data represented in ASCII codes.

ASCII files, also called *text files,* can be printed or viewed directly on-screen.

ASCIIZ character string

A string terminated by a null character (a byte containing all zero bits).

By using a unique null-character terminator that never appears in ASCII character data, the ASCIIZ standard avoids any need for programs to store and keep track of a string's length in a separate field.

ASCIIZ is the usual string representation in *C.* The programmer must specify a string length one character greater than actually needed, as in the following example:

```
char month_name[10] = "September";
```

Now month_name contains ten bytes: the nine letters in "September" followed by the null character terminator.

Note that the term simply denotes the fact that the individual characters in the string are ASCII codes. ASCIIZ has not been sanctioned as an industry-standard data representation.

.ASM

The MS-DOS file name extension conventionally indicating that the file contains assembly language source code.

ASM—Association for Systems Management

A professional society for systems analysts and other information systems professionals, formerly called the SPA (Systems and Procedures Association).

The ASM has local chapters in most metropolitan areas. It is especially active in offering short courses in systems analysis and related areas.

aspect ratio

The ratio of width to height for a computer display or, more generally, for any projected image, including television and movie screens. A 20 by 15 screen, for example, has a 4:3 aspect ratio.

Graphics devices use different aspect ratios. Programmers working with graphics must be aware of these differences and, if necessary, use appropriate conversion routines to avoid distorted images.

assembler

A program that translates a source program coded in a specific assembly language into the corresponding machine language.

An assembler performs the same function on assembly language source code that a compiler performs on higher-level language source code. However, the task of an assembler is somewhat simpler than that of a compiler, because an assembler can usually process one statement at a time without regard to its relationship to the rest of the program. Nevertheless, some assemblers are extremely sophisticated, especially in their handling of macros and addressability.

assembly language

A symbolic form of machine language for a particular computer, in which the programmer codes the following:

- Standard mnemonics for operation codes

- Symbolic data names for operands

- Instructions in a convenient, readable format

- Pseudo operations that don't correspond to machine instructions, but rather help in organizing the program

Most assembly languages also support a macro facility to help subordinate the extreme amount of detail required in assembly language programming.

Because of the high cost and difficulty of developing and maintaining programs in assembly languages, and the availability of flexible, efficient, and machine-independent higher-level languages, assembly languages are used rarely in applications programming, and are used increasingly less frequently in systems programming. However, using assembly language in a low-level module may be justified in the following circumstances:

- When the module must access a hardware component that higher-level languages do not support; for example, when writing a device driver.

- For actions in which efficiency is critical; for example, during a high-volume search.

See also *macro.*

assignment statement

An executable statement causing a variable to be set to a specified value. The previous value of the variable is lost. Assignment is a fundamental operation in procedural programming languages.

In the following table, v represents the variable to be set, and *expr* represents a value compatible with the data type of v:

Language	Statement Form	Notes
Ada, Pascal	$v := expr$;	
APL	$v \leftarrow expr$	
BASIC	LET $v = expr$	Most modern BASICs omit LET.
C, PL/1	$v = expr$;	C considers assignment an expression operator rather than a statement.
COBOL	COMPUTE $v = exp$	COBOL's assignments also include the specialized statements MOVE, ADD, SUBTRACT, MULTIPLY, and DIVIDE.
FORTRAN	$v = expr$	
LISP	setq(v $expr$)	Using local binding with the keyword "let" is better practice than using this assignment statement.
PROLOG	Not possible directly	

Association for Computing Machinery

See *ACM*.

Association for Systems Management

See *ASM*.

associative addressing

A method of selecting an operand in memory based not on its address but on the value of a portion of its content.

Efficient associative addressing requires hardware that can examine a large number of memory cells in parallel in order to select the one(s) matching a specified key field. Popular computers (mainframe, mini-, or desktop) do not support associative addressing, but it remains a feature of special computer architectures intended for high-speed retrieval of information.

asynchronous transmission

A data transmission method that does not require an external clocking signal to maintain synchronization between the sending and receiving equipment.

Asynchronous transmission is sometimes called *start-stop* transmission because each character transmitted contains its own start and stop "clocking" bits.

Most modem transmission utilizes asynchronous techniques.

atom

An *elementary data item.*

Atom is the usual term for an elementary item in LISP, where the term refers to anything that isn't a list. A common symptom of bugs in LISP programs is an attempt to apply to an atom a function that requires a list argument.

atomic

Incapable of being decomposed into components; a synonym for *elementary.*

The term *atomic* is commonly used in two contexts:

- An atomic operation or atomic process is a process that cannot be interrupted or left in an incomplete state under any circumstance—for example, in case of a power failure.

- An atomic condition is a Boolean expression or condition that contains no Boolean operators (such as *and, or,* or *not*).

attribute

Any property of a data item.

For entities and other composite data items, attributes include the lower-level component data items. Thus, DATE HIRED and NUMBER OF DEPENDENTS would be attributes of EMPLOYEE. Other attributes may include the dimension of an array or the storage class of a structure.

Most attributes of elementary data items depend on the data type. See *data representation, data type, discrete data item, discrete data type,* and *numeric data type.*

attribute, typeface

See *typeface attribute*.

AUTOEXEC.BAT

The reserved name of an MS-DOS batch file invoked automatically on system startup.

An AUTOEXEC.BAT file should contain the commands needed to do the following:

- Initialize the environment by setting MS-DOS options and parameters
- Verify that the fixed disks are undamaged and have sufficient free space for normal operation
- Invoke any permanently resident utility programs
- Establish any linkage to the local area network (LAN)
- Transfer control to any control program such as DOSSHELL, Windows, or DesqView

See also *CONFIG.SYS*.

Many setup or install programs make assumptions about what must be in the user's AUTOEXEC.BAT and CONFIG.SYS files, and may even modify those files. Although many such modifications are helpful, some may conflict with local operating practices or with other software on the same computer. Prudent users save a copy of their AUTOEXEC.BAT and CONFIG.SYS before installing any new software product. After installation, they review the contents of AUTOEXEC.BAT and CONFIG.SYS to make sure that any changes are acceptable.

automatic allocation

In a procedural programming language, the on-the-fly allocation and freeing of memory for data items without explicit action by the program. Usually memory is allocated on entry to a block (or module) and freed on exit.

See also *bind* and *instantiate*.

auxiliary device—AUX

An input or output device reserved under MS-DOS. Standard Auxiliary (STDAUX) is by default COM1 and is accessed by using the reserved name AUX or Interrupt 21h, functions 03h and 04h. Several debugging utilities use AUX for output. Under DOS version 2 and above, COM1 (AUX) defaults to 2,400 bps, 8 data bits, no parity, and 1 stop bit.

auxiliary storage

Any storage medium or device except the main memory of a computer system. Compared to main (RAM) memory, auxiliary storage provides the following:

- Much higher capacity
- Much lower cost
- Permanence

Auxiliary storage is used for permanent files and databases that are retained at the end of program execution, as well as large temporary (scratch or work) files. However, because of the trend toward very large address spaces, program designers are now using main memory for many work files that would once have been restricted to auxiliary storage.

Most auxiliary storage media use magnetic recording technology, such as tape reels, tape cartridges, fixed disks and drums, and removable disks. Many very high capacity media, such as laser disks, use optical recording technology.

See also *tape*.

awk

A powerful file- and text-processing language used to manipulate data and to gather information from text files. You can invoke this UNIX utility directly from the command line, or by using a program file option. The program file contains the awk statements that are interpreted by awk. The text data processed by the awk program is provided in the file(s) supplied as an argument to awk. If no file is specified, awk accepts the text information from standard input.

For example, the following awk program prints the number of words in a file:

```
function cntwords(file, string) {
    string="wc " fn
    string | getline
    close(string)
    return ($2)
}
BEGIN {
        for (i=1; i<ARGC; i++) {
        fn = ArGV[i]
        printf "In the file %s I found %d.",
         fn, cntwords(fn)
        }
}
```

backdoor

A software facility that provides unauthorized access to a system.

During development, programmers sometimes place backdoors into programs. Then, after the system is installed in production status, the programmers can bypass normal security checks. Although such backdoors may have legitimate benefits in maintenance programming, they can compromise system integrity, especially if they are kept secret from managers and auditors.

backspace

1. To delete the character immediately to the left of the cursor (or to the left of the last character typed) by pressing the Backspace key located in the upper-right corner of most keyboards.

2. To reposition a sequential file to the beginning of the last record that was read or written.

3. The operation of backspacing, especially in the sense of the second meaning.

backtracking

Returning to an earlier point in searching for a problem solution, especially where the search strategy involves successive branching in a tree of possibilities.

Backtracking is a basic tool in algorithms that must make many successive choices among alternatives. Such applications include games, expert systems, and programs that understand or translate natural languages like English. Because backtracking is built into many inference engines as well as the programming language PROLOG, these tools are often more attractive for such applications than languages in which the programmer must explicitly program complex backtracking logic.

backup file

A copy of one or more master files, databases, or entire disk volumes created as a precaution in case the original file is later damaged.

See also *archive file.*

Backus-Naur form—BNF

A meta-language for describing the syntax of formal languages.

Named after John Backus and Peter Naur, BNF is a valuable notation for precisely and compactly specifying the rules for forming legal program constructs in a programming language. By recursively applying just these three elements, you can describe most elements of any formal language:

- Metalinguistic variables, enclosed in angle brackets to distinguish them from elements of the language being described. Example: <assignment statement>

- The equivalence symbol (::=)

- The alternative operator (¦)

Here, for example, is part of a BNF definition of a Boolean (conditional) expression in a hypothetical programming language:

```
<cond expr>      ::= <truth value>
                 ¦   <rel expr>
                 ¦   (<cond expr>)
                 ¦   NOT <cond expr>
                 ¦   <cond expr> <bool operator> <cond expr>
<bool operator> ::= OR   ¦ AND   ¦ EXOR
<truth value>   ::= TRUE ¦ FALSE ¦ <boolean variable>
<rel expr>      ::= <num expr> <rel operator> <num expr>
<rel operator>  ::= = ¦ < ¦ > ¦ <= ¦ >=
```

Leaving aside the missing specification of <num expr>, this example indicates that the following is a legal Boolean expression:

```
((x < 1.0) AND NOT (y = x)) OR (x >= 1.0)
```

Some compilers use modified forms of BNF to automate parsing and syntactic analysis of source programs.

.BAK

The MS-DOS file name extension used by many software products to identify a backup file.

Most editors, as well as many word processors, spreadsheet processors, and other productivity tools, create .BAK files automatically whenever the user saves a new version of a file. This automatic backup feature is intended not so much to guard against physical file damage as to guard against the user's own mistakes in making subsequent changes to the file.

See also *generation data group*.

.BAS

The file name extension used in MS-DOS and some other platforms to identify a BASIC source program.

See also *BASIC*.

base class

In object-oriented programming (OOP), a class used to create other (derived) classes. A base class is sometimes called a *parent class*.

Derived classes inherit the member data and member functions of the parent (base) class.

For example, suppose in a hotel reservation system the base class room contains member data items room_number, bed_type, and rate, and the member functions reserve, check_in, and check_out. A derived class deluxe_room can inherit those members of hotel_room and add to them a data item whirlpool and a function upgrade, and override the default values of bed_type and rate.

See also *member function*.

BASIC

A programming language developed by John Kemeny and Thomas Kurtz as a vehicle for teaching the stored-program concept and elementary programming in an interpretive time-sharing environment.

BASIC was originally a very small language that an inexperienced student could learn in a couple of hours. The language was suitable for implementing very small programs with little internal structure. However, its use for larger programs was inhibited by the following:

- Single-character variable names

- Global scope for all names

- Lack of subroutine linkage with parameter passing

- Weak input-output (I/O) facilities

Because of its small size, BASIC was implemented on most early desktop computers, and a BASIC interpreter was often bundled into the price of those machines. It quickly became the most widely used programming language on small machines.

BASIC's popularity, however, soon changed its nature. Software vendors began to compete in offering extensions to the language, which eventually became much larger, more powerful, and consequently no longer trivial to learn. Today BASIC competes with C and Pascal as a language for serious programming on desktop computers, and is superior to those languages in a few areas, such as string handling.

Proprietary extensions to support graphical user interfaces (GUIs) are now available, such as Visual Basic.

basic input/output system

See *BIOS*.

BASICA

An interpreter for BASIC developed by Microsoft and bundled into sales of MS-DOS in the 1980s.

Because BASICA was "free" and required only 64K bytes of memory, many owners of Intel computers chose BASIC as the language in which to write their programs. To overcome some of the inefficiencies of interpretive execution, BASICA relied on proprietary microcode in the IBM computer. A purely interpretive compatible version, GW-BASIC, was available for compatible computers from other manufacturers.

Starting with MS-DOS Version 5, BASICA was replaced in MS-DOS bundles by QBasic.

.BAT

A common file name extension used in the MS-DOS operating system. A .BAT file is a type of command file, consisting of a series of operating system commands that are executed as if the user typed them from the command line.

See also *command language.*

batch processing

A mode of data processing in which input data is collected in streams and periodically is processed in sequence by one or more jobs. Batch processing provides no opportunity for user interaction with the system during a job.

Compared to online or interactive processing, batch processing is often more efficient for high-volume, routine operations, such as payroll or customer billing. Many batch jobs are run at night on mainframe computers. Before networks of terminals became economical, almost all commercial data processing and scientific computing was done in batch mode.

Batch jobs can be run either on demand or on a regular production schedule, the latter being more common for business applications. The frequency at which regularly scheduled jobs are run (daily, weekly, monthly, and so on) is determined by the requirements of accounting or other business activities.

baud

The number of state changes that can take place in a second on a communications line; the most common measure of the speed or capacity of data transmission.

Note that, generally, baud is not the same as bits per second. Baud and bits per second are equal only at low transmission speeds. Modern modems and communications techniques can produce more than one data bit per state change.

The term is derived from the name of French engineer Jean-Maurice-Emile Baudot. The baud rate was originally used to measure the transmission speed of telegraph equipment.

BCD—binary coded decimal

An encoding of decimal digits as printable characters.

The original BCD was a six-bit coding scheme used in first- and second-generation computers and their auxiliary storage media. When extended to include uppercase alphabetic characters and punctuation, this scheme was called BCI (binary coded information).

With the introduction of third-generation computers such as the IBM System/360 in 1964, the eight-bit byte replaced six-bit characters as the industry standard. BCD and BCI were extended as EBCDIC to include lowercase letters and additional punctuation.

See also *ASCII* and *EBCDIC*.

before method

In object-oriented programming (OOP), a function to be invoked before the execution of an inherited method that has the same name.

A before method is useful when the corresponding primary method associated with the parent class does most of what is necessary, but a particular subclass requires additional initial setup.

benchmark test

A controlled demonstration of some hardware or software components to evaluate their performance or efficiency, usually to confirm their capability to handle a given workload.

Benchmark testing commonly occurs in the late stages of evaluating an application software product, after the product is found to provide the functionality needed by the users. Some organizations also conduct benchmark tests of hardware configurations, especially larger mainframes and networks. However, the difficulty of setting up a realistic simulation of dozens or hundreds of online users often makes benchmarking of whole configurations costly and impractical.

Independent testing organizations, such as trade journals, often conduct comparative benchmarks of competing products that are functionally similar, and publish the results as a service for prospective buyers.

See also *stress test.*

beta version

A test version of a software package.

A software vendor may make a beta version available to selected beta testers. Beta testers are end users who volunteer to evaluate the software before it is officially released, in return for advance access to its capabilities.

The purpose of beta testing is to subject the software to heavier and more varied use than is practical in the vendor's internal testing procedures.

BGI—Borland Graphics Interface

A graphics library (a collection of data structure and functions) developed by Borland International.

The library enables programmers to reference commonly needed graphics functions and fonts used to develop graphics applications.

big endian

See *little endian*.

big red switch

Slang term for the computer system's main power switch, which is usually red, but sometimes another color. "Red" denotes the serious consequences that may occur if the power is turned off.

binary

Having two possible values or states.

These two states have no inherent value until interpreted, either by people or machines. Depending on the context, they may be interpreted in different ways: 0/1, on/off, true/false, yes/no, closed/open, positive/negative.

See also *bit*.

binary number

A number expressed in base 2. Binary numbers use 1's and 0's to indicate the presence and absence of powers of 2. Each position is called a *bit* (for *binary digit*). Here's the equivalent of 181 as a 10-bit number:

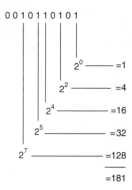

```
0 0 1 0 1 1 0 1 0 1
```

$$2^0 \longrightarrow = 1$$
$$2^2 \longrightarrow = 4$$
$$2^4 \longrightarrow = 16$$
$$2^5 \longrightarrow = 32$$
$$2^7 \longrightarrow = 128$$
$$\overline{}$$
$$= 181$$

Binary is the natural base of digital computers built from switching circuits and magnetic memories. It is therefore of central importance in internal data representation and in the architecture of registers and memory devices.

Because binary numbers are long and hard to read, the shorthand notations octal and hexadecimal are commonly used to represent groups of three and four binary digits, respectively.

binary operator

An operator having two arguments.

Most binary operators are written in infix operator form, that is, between their arguments. The operators supported by most programming languages include the following:

Operator Name	Symbols Commonly Used	Properties*
Numeric Operators		
Addition, plus	+	A, C
Subtraction, minus	−	

Operator Name	Symbols Commonly Used	Properties*
Multiplication, times	*, ×	A, C
Division, divided by	/, ÷	
Exponentiation	**, ^,	
Boolean (Logical) Operators		
And, conjunction	&, &&	A, C
Or, disjunction	|, ||	A, C
Exclusive or	< >	A, C
Relational Operators		
Equality, equals	=	S, T
Inequality, is not equal to	< >, /=, ≠	S
Less than, precedes	<	T
Greater than, exceeds	>	T
Not less than, greater than, or equal	>=, , ≮	T
Not greater than, less than, or equal	<=, , ≯	T
String Operator		
Concatenation	||, +, &	A
Set Operators		
Element of	∈	
Union	U	A, C
Intersection	∩	A, C

*Important properties of the preceding binary operators:

Property	Meaning (O Representing the Operator)	
A: Associative	x O (y O z) = (x O y) O z,	for all x, y, z
C: Commutative	x O y = y O x,	for all x, y.
S: Symmetric	if x O y then y O x,	for all x, y.
T: Transitive	if x O y and y O z then x O z,	for all x, y, z

binary relation

1. Formally, a set of which each element is an ordered pair of objects.

2. Informally, a binary operator that yields a truth value result, such as is-less-than (<) or is-a-member-of (∈).

3. Also informally, a predicate with two arguments, such as X likes Y (likes(X,Y)).

These three definitions are conceptually equivalent, differing mainly in the notations.

The notion of a binary relation is easily extended to an n-ary relation, a set whose elements are all ordered *n-tuples* (or predicates with n arguments). Such relations, also called *tables,* are the foundation of the relational database model.

In object-oriented programming (OOP), a programmer who defines a new class in which the objects have some natural ordering may have to implement special versions of the usual ordering relations (=, <, >, and so on) to ensure the intended behavior. For example, for a class day-of-week, we would like Monday < Thursday to be true and Saturday < Thursday to be false. See also *overloading.*

binary search

An algorithm for locating in an ordered array the item that matches a specified argument.

Taking advantage of the sequence of items, a binary search eliminates half the remaining table with each comparison. The maximum number of comparisons to find a match (or determine that there is none) among N items is $LOG_2 N$, considerably faster than a linear search, but slower than hashing.

Here is the algorithm in pseudocode:

```
L  = 1;                    /*    Start boundaries at each end  */
H  = DIM(TBL);             /*        of the array              */
DO WHILE (L <= H)          /*                                  */
    M  = (L + H) / 2;      /*    Locate current mid-point      */
    IF   TBL [M] = ARG     /*    Test for match                */
    THEN RETURN M;         /*    Found -- return result        */
    IF   TBL [M]  > ARG    /*    Determine which half          */
```

```
THEN H  = M - 1;        /*   Lower -- drop upper limit    */
ELSE L  = M + 1;        /*   Upper -- raise lower limit   */
END;
RETURN (-M);            /*   No match -- return error     */
```

binary tree

A tree in which each node has at most two child nodes. Binary trees are useful in implementing fast table searching.

See also *heap* and *B-tree*.

bind

To connect a value to a parameter or variable.

For example, binding occurs when a Microsoft Windows program connects the resource file—the file used to store the information pertaining to dialogs, menus, windows, and icons—to the executable program. Once that binding is made, the functions in the executable file have direct access to the information in the resource file.

See also *instantiate*.

bindery

A database, maintained on the file server by Novell NetWare, containing information about all resources and authorized users of the local area network (LAN). The bindery contains detailed information about users, user groups, passwords, accounting information, access restrictions, other servers, and other applications that can utilize the bindery.

Network applications, such as electronic mail systems, can read the NetWare bindery directly. Using this capability, the network administrator can examine all of the user data in the bindery. This can simplify the installation of "LAN-aware" software that requires a list of active users.

The bindery is critical to NetWare security. Access rights are usually protected through a NetWare utility called SYSCON.EXE (system configuration). SYSCON.EXE enables users to make changes to their portion of the bindery, but does not enable them to modify the properties of other NetWare users.

BIOS—basic input-output system

The set of semipermanent routines on Intel 80×86 microcomputers that gives the computer its basic operational characteristics, and supports the transfer of data between system components such as RAM, floppy and hard disks, and monitors.

BIOS is semipermanent because it is usually implemented in removable ROM (read-only memory). You can update the BIOS to include devices that were not anticipated when it originally was designed.

Programmers can access the BIOS routines by using assembly language or the low-level interfaces provided by some high-level languages.

bit

The smallest information-carrying element in computing, either a 0 or a 1. The term is a contraction of *binary digit*.

bit mask

See *mask.*

bitwise operators

The set of machine instructions or programming language facilities designed to manipulate bit-oriented data. These include the logical operations (*and, or, xor,* or *not*), shift and rotate instructions, and masking instructions.

See also *Boolean operator.*

block

Any well-defined section of programming code. A block may also be known as a *module* or *subroutine.*

block name

A logical name assigned to a section of programming code. Block names must follow the syntax or rules defined by the language that the programmer is using.

block structure

A hierarchical organization of a program into blocks, sections of code that correspond to the scope of identifiers and storage.

The concept of block structure originated as a distinctive feature of ALGOL-60, and was adopted in most newer procedural languages, including PL/1, ALGOL-68, Ada, and, with certain restrictions, Pascal and C. Although block structure has not been a part of FORTRAN, APL, COBOL, or BASIC, it has recently been added or proposed as enhancements to those languages.

A block can be either of the following:

- A subroutine, procedure, or function, which itself can be either of the following:

    External and compiled separately from the rest of the program

    Internal and nested within another block (C does not support functions defined within the body of another function)

- A compound statement, that is, a sequence of statements bracketed by a pair of delimiters. This type of block is also used for controlling flow—for example, in delimiting the code to be executed in each branch of an if-then-else construct.

Within each block, the programmer can declare data items (identifiers). Those data items will be known to the code within that block, overriding any items of the same name in any outer block. However, code outside the block will not know about or be able to access those data items. This capability to localize the scope of variables helps the programmer avoid many kinds of errors.

By default, storage for local data is allocated on entry to a block, and freed on exit. This is useful not only in conserving the amount of memory tied up at any one time, but also in allowing a program to allocate arrays and strings of the exact dimension required. (However, C and Pascal require constant dimension specifications.) This relationship between block structure and dynamic storage allocation is a key element in being able to write recursive functions easily.

blocking, record

See *record blocking.*

B-margin

In COBOL programming, positions 12 through 72 of a line of code; used for executable statements, subordinate data item declarations, and other coding.

See also *A-margin*.

.BMP

The file name extension for a bitmap graphics file associated with Microsoft Windows.

A .BMP file is used in Windows as the graphics format for the wallpaper or background pattern. You can create a .BMP file by using the "Paint" program that comes with Windows.

bookmark

An identifier that marks a position within a text file to which the user can return quickly.

For example, while using an editor to develop a program, you might want to examine another portion of the source code, then return to your original place and continue where you left off. You can do so, usually through menu commands, by defining a bookmark at the present position and then later returning to it by name.

Boolean data type

A data element that can assume only a true or false value. BASIC, C, and COBOL do not have a Boolean data type, but implement the concept by using integers to represent true and false. Usually zero represents false and any nonzero is taken as true.

Because different compilers and versions of the same compiler may test these integer surrogates in subtly different ways, programmers should avoid performing arithmetic operations on them, and should define constant values (true and false) in an implementation-independent way. For example, in BASIC, you could define testing values as follows:

```
TRUE = (0 = 0): FALSE = NOT TRUE
```

Boolean expression

An expression that evaluates to either true or false, combining Boolean operators (*and, or, xor,* and *not*), relational operators (usually greater than, less than, equal, and not equal), and Boolean variables or constants. Boolean expressions are the primary method of controlling program logic flow in if-then-else and loop control statements.

In evaluating a Boolean expression, a compiler or query processor may or may not apply optimization techniques to avoid evaluating terms that cannot affect the result. If P is true and Q is false, for example, then:

P   OR   *any-expression* must be true.

Q   AND   *any-expression* must be false.

Such Boolean optimization may lead to incorrect results if the programmer is depending on side effects from functions invoked within *any-expression*. Programming language manuals usually specify precise rules for the order of evaluation in such situations.

Boolean operator

One of a set of operations performed on logical variables (variables which are true or false). Boolean operators are *and, or, xor* (exclusive or), and *not*.

See also *bitwise operators.*

boot, cold

A hardware-defined full reset and startup of a PC system, which you can initiate either by pressing the Reset (or equivalent) key, or, less desirably, by turning off the system, pausing for several seconds, then turning on the system again.

See also *IPL.*

boot, warm

A hardware-defined partial reset and startup of a PC system, which you can initiate by pressing the Ctrl, Alt, and Del keys simultaneously.

See also *bootstrapping.*

boot sector

On a hard or floppy disk, an area reserved for a program that begins loading an operating system from other locations on the storage device. A system's initialization routine reads the boot sector into a fixed location in random access memory (RAM) and branches to a predetermined instruction location within that area to continue reading in the remainder of the operating system.

bootstrapping

The process of bringing an operating system to a ready state.

This term is derived from the computer system's need to "pull itself up by its own bootstraps." The process usually requires some hard-coded instructions in a system's ROM and a simple program loaded in the boot sector of a floppy or hard disk.

See also *boot sector.*

Borland Graphics Interface

See *BGI.*

Borland Pascal

See *Turbo Pascal.*

bottom-up

In design or development, beginning with the lowest level components and then using them to build the next higher level components. In pure bottom-up programming, each module is developed before any of the higher-level modules that invoke it.

Until the "structured revolution" of the early 1970s, most programmers who practiced modular programming at all followed a bottom-up development sequence. No module could be tested until all the lower level modules it used were developed. To test a module, the programmer would have to write a temporary test driver program that called the module being tested with various sets of test data. The weakness of a purely bottom-up approach was that it depended on the insight and inspiration the programmer, and that there was no systematic way to ensure that the process would lead to a workable complete program.

Although top-down development is now recognized as a simpler and more disciplined strategy, situations arise in which critical modules must be identified, designed, and developed before anyone knows which other modules will invoke them. Such bottom-up modules typically include the following:

- Error handling routines
- Data structures and the functions that operate on them
- Object-oriented class definitions
- Database interface routines

The programmers developing the rest of the application system in top-down fashion can then use these modules wherever they're needed.

See also *integration test, test driver, top-down,* and *unit test.*

bound

In an array, a maximum or minimum value of a subscript, usually specified in an array declaration.

Each dimension of an array has a lower bound and an upper bound. In some programming languages, the lower bound is fixed—0 in C, 1 in FORTRAN and COBOL—and the programmer can specify only the dimension or upper bound. In other languages, the programmer can specify both the lower and the upper bounds; for example, the Pascal declaration

```
var scores[1988..1997,-5..5]
```

declares a 10 by 11 matrix.

Some languages (such as C and Pascal) permit only constant bounds. However, others (such as PL/1) permit any numeric expression as an array bound:

```
declare scores (start_year:end_year, min_score:max_score);
```

Bourne shell

The standard UNIX shell, named after its developer, Steve Bourne. The function of this shell is to submit UNIX commands entered by the user to the kernel for processing. For example, if you want a listing of the files in the current directory, you need only enter the following command at the Bourne shell prompt:

```
$ ls
```

This UNIX shell is characterized by the distinctive $ prompt. The user can enter UNIX commands at the shell prompt one at a time, or a shell script can be created. A shell script is a file that contains a programming language which is very similar to C. The language consists of a mix of UNIX commands and standard program logic statements. The commands are interpreted by the shell and executed line by line. Complex systems can be created with the powerful shell-scripting language.

See also *Korn shell.*

branch

1. A departure from the sequential execution of consecutive statements in a program.

2. An instruction in some assembly languages to reset the computer's instruction counter.

   Many branch instructions are conditional. If some specified condition is not met, the branch is not taken, and the computer proceeds to the next instruction in sequence.

The term is synonymous with *goto, jump,* and *transfer.*

breakpoint

A marker or special programming instruction that causes the suspension of program execution at a statement or instruction address designated in advance by the programmer. Breakpoints are usually used as a debugging technique.

Breakpoints are commonly supported by interpreters. When the flow of control reaches a designated breakpoint, interpretive execution stops.

The programmer can then examine the values of variables, change some of those values, and, in some programming environments, even change statements in the program before resuming from the point of suspension.

Implementing breakpoints with compiled programs is much more difficult, because the required symbolic information from the source code—data names, types, formats, and so on—is not easy to access during execution. However, debugger programs associated with some compilers can maintain that information and thereby support a limited breakpoint facility.

 Breakpoint is conceptually the same as a feature on many early computers that enabled the operator to set an address in "address stop" dials on the console. Then when the instruction counter matched that address, the machine would stop, and the operator could examine the various console indicators and register contents. With the advent of multiprogramming and the diminishing use of assembly languages, demand for such a hardware feature faded away.

The use of breakpoints for debugging is often a last resort after more conventional testing methods have failed to diagnose the cause of a problem. Breakpoints are especially useful in diagnosing a loss-of-control situation, in which the program never reaches the output statements that would display the information of interest. By setting breakpoints successively closer to the point at which the program loses control, the programmer can examine what is happening just as the flow approaches that point.

B-tree

A tree structure, often used for efficient file indexing, in which

- Every node contains a list, in ascending sequence, of key values for records in the file (along with either the records themselves or, more commonly, a pointer to the corresponding record).

- Except for leaf nodes (which have no children), every node has $k+1$ child nodes, where k is the number of key values in the node.

- The key values in each node define the range of keys covered by the corresponding child node.

For example, the following 10-node B-tree of depth 3 indexes the 26 letters of the alphabet:

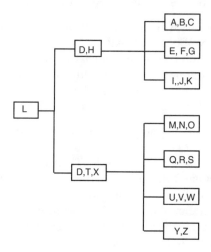

bubble

A function or process, especially on a data-flow diagram, in which the elliptical shape of process symbols resembles a bubble in some versions of structured analysis.

Bubble is an slang term best avoided in precise communication.

bubble sort

A naive method of internal sorting.

The scheme is to compare adjacent elements and swap them if they are out of sequence. At the end of the first pass, the largest item is in the last table position; at the end of the *k*th pass, the *k*th largest item is in its correct position. The following BASIC code demonstrates how to sort the array NAME$:

```
FOR  PASS.CTR% = 1 TO UBOUND(NAME$)-LBOUND(NAME$)
     FOR  NX% = LBOUND(NAME$) TO UBOUND(NAME$)-PASS.CTR%
          IF   NAME$(NX%) > NAME$(NX%+1)
          THEN SWAP NAME$(NX%), NAME$(NX%+1)
          NEXT
     NEXT
```

The bubble sort is sometimes used in teaching beginning programmers about nested loops and array indexing. Because it's so easy to remember, experienced programmers occasionally code it when no efficient sorting routine is readily available. However, in a bubble sort, the running time to sort N elements is proportional to N^2, and therefore it's an impractical approach for large arrays.

bucket

An area of a disk or other storage medium that can hold multiple records.

Buckets are sometimes used with hashing or other direct access mapping techniques as well as external sorting algorithms. Instead of associating a unique key with each record, a key is associated with a group of records to be stored in the same bucket. This may result in fewer clashes that require chaining to separate overflow areas. To obtain high performance, buckets are sometimes chosen to correspond to physical tracks on a disk.

buffer

A portion of memory used for short-term intermediate storage of data. Programs use buffers to hold information being transferred to or from a disk drive, a printer, or other device.

Buffers also are used for temporary storage of data. A print buffer, for example, can be used to accept a print stream from a program, enabling the program to continue even though the printer has not yet completed printing. The information in the buffer is moved to the device when the device is no longer busy.

bug

Any behavior of a program that deviates from the program's specifications.

Symptoms of bugs range from a drastic loss of control (see *ABEND* and *crash*) to subtle, slightly incorrect results. Their impact on users range from making software completely unusable to causing mild annoyance.

Many organizations regard a bug as any shortcoming a user perceives in application software. Thus a program that conforms perfectly to a specification, but doesn't reflect a user's wishes, is still seen as a bug that the programmer is obliged to repair.

See also *system test, unit test,* and *validation.*

bulletproof program

A program for which the code is so well-written that it does not fail during normal or intense use.

Software vendors often proclaim that their products are bulletproof.

bundling

The practice of selling a complete package of hardware, software, and support services for a single price.

In the era of first- and second-generation computers, software and services provided by computer vendors were usually bundled into the hardware rental or purchase price. Customers came to think of vendor-supplied software, training, consulting, and maintenance services as "free." As a result, it was nearly impossible for an independent software vendor or services firm to compete successfully, and major hardware vendors enjoyed a near monopoly in many areas.

The major shift occurred in 1968 when IBM—responding to pressure from the user groups SHARE and GUIDE, and to the threat of antitrust litigation— agreed to price some of its software and services separately from hardware. This unbundling by the largest vendor led quickly to the growth of an independent software industry.

Today, vendors often sell bundled packages, especially of closely related software products. Many desktop computers are now sold with an operating system already installed.

bus mastering

A high-performance bus design enabling special boards to process independently of the processor, gaining access to memory and peripherals without bothering the central processing unit (CPU). This type of technology is associated with some advanced PCs.

A network adapter, for example, can provide bus mastering capability, processing network communications without accessing the CPU. This enables the system to operate more quickly, because the CPU can perform software operations without first servicing requests from the network adapter.

button

In a graphical user interface (GUI), an object on the screen that the user can select, either by a mouse click or by an equivalent keyboard operation, to trigger a specified action or response by the software.

Program designers use buttons to give an effect like pushing a physical button on a control panel. Typically, graphics are used so that buttons being chosen appear to be physically pressed. Some buttons may include special text or pictures (icons) that make them easy to recognize.

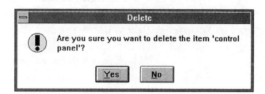

A typical use for buttons.

byte

A sequence of eight bits. A byte is the unit of the following:

- Addressable data storage in most computer architectures

- Printable characters recognized by printers, display devices, and other hardware

With the introduction of third-generation computers in the mid-1960s, the standard eight-bit byte replaced both the earlier six-bit character codes and the (usually longer) addressable word. The eight-bit size has proved to be appropriate, for the following reasons:

- Its 256 possible values accommodate the full range of printable characters in European languages, plus a useful set of control characters for data transmission and printing.

- Its 256 possible values accommodate a wide range of operation codes in the machine language of many computer architectures, allowing an instruction format in which a single byte contains the operation code.

- A length that is an exact power of 2 facilitates the use of multiple bytes for a variety of numeric data formats, including *binary, packed decimal,* and *floating-point.*

C

A procedural programming language developed at AT&T Bell Laboratories. Originally associated with UNIX, C has now become the most widely used language for software products on many other platforms.

C, as augmented by libraries of standard modules, combines high-level functions, such as screen painting, with low-level functions, such as interrupt control. One of C's original objectives was to provide a high degree of portability, and C applications that avoid implementation dependencies can usually be moved from one platform to another with few if any modifications.

See also *C++*.

C++

An object-oriented programming language originally based on the C programming language. C++ features many of the same strong points that made the C language popular, yet implements stronger type checking and essential object-oriented concepts such as classes, inheritance, encapsulation, and polymorphism.

cache

A portion of memory used as temporary storage to improve device performance. A cache can reside in memory or on the disk controller, and usually is associated with a fixed disk drive.

When a program requests a transfer of information between memory and disk, a copy of that information is saved in the cache. The cache contents can then satisfy later requests to read the same information, avoiding a physical input-output (I/O) operation.

Because a cache has a limited capacity, later references to other areas of the disk may cause the oldest or least-frequently accessed information in the cache to be discarded. Therefore, caching is most effective where a program frequently rereads the same small areas of the disk, such as a file directory or a database index.

See also *buffer* and *paged memory*.

CAD — computer-aided design

Automated tools for design of real-world objects, often generating the actual control of machine tools to manufacture the objects. When the control of machine tools is linked with the design of what those tools are supposed to create, the appropriate acronym is CAD/CAM (computer-aided design/computer-aided manufacturing).

CAD and CAD/CAM are used extensively in research and development efforts for consumer items such as automobiles, electronics, or virtually any other item you can think of. Also, many architects use CAD to facilitate the design of buildings and the development of other output, such as blueprints.

call

1. To invoke a subroutine or procedure.

2. A statement in many programming languages to invoke a subroutine or procedure.

Call is the most common verb for invoking a module that is not a function, that is, one that does not return a value. The verb originated in FORTRAN and appears in COBOL, PL/1, BASIC, and the MS-DOS command language. The term is commonly applied also in discussing or documenting the equivalent operation in other languages, as in the invocation of a void function in C.

callback

A security feature of systems that permit dial-up access, to ensure that users call from authorized telephone numbers. To gain access, the user dials into the system, then is requested to hang up (some implementations add an additional layer of security by requesting that a special password be entered on telephone's touch-tone keypad). The system then calls the user, using a list of authorized numbers.

In addition to providing increased security, callback is a convenient way to "reverse the charges" so that communications costs for employees or clients are limited to the cost of the initial call.

calling sequence

A standard block of code that effects linkage to a subroutine. A calling sequence consists of instructions that accomplish the following:

- To pass (or identify) the parameters, if any
- To branch to the subroutine
- To establish in the calling program a return address to which the subroutine branches on completion

Each platform includes a calling sequence standard. Such a standard includes conventions for the following:

- The choice of hardware instruction(s) for effecting the branch
- The use of registers, descriptors, and so on for locating parameters
- The use of a specific register for locating the return address
- The list of any registers or status indicators that a subroutine must not change. If the subroutine must use those registers, it must first save them on entry and later restore their original content on exit.

Some programming languages extend the platform-specific calling sequence standard to support their own special requirements for data structuring, dynamic storage allocation, interrupt handling, and so on.

car

A primitive LISP function that returns the first element of a list. For example

(car '(A B C)) is A

(car '((A B) C)) is (A B)

The names of car and the related cdr function did not originate from what they do, but rather how they were implemented on the first-generation IBM 704 computer. They stand for, respectively, the contents of address register and contents of decrement register. Although newer versions of LISP, such as Common LISP, provide equivalent meaningful names first and rest, some programmers prefer to use the original names.

card image

An 80-byte record, especially when used as input to a program.

Although punched-card technology is all but obsolete, its influence will continue to be felt for another decade or two. The common 80-position width (in character mode) of display terminals and printers is a direct consequence of the punched-card tradition. Manuals and course materials still occasionally refer to a line of input as "the next card" or a card image.

 In the heyday of punched cards (before the mid-1970s), designers sometimes devised ingenious data compression schemes to stuff an entire input transaction onto one card. Some of those schemes may persist today in files descended from those card-oriented systems. In particular, watch for "overpunched" signs, that is, a minus sign superimposed on a digit so as to conserve one position. The constraint of punched-card input also explains some of the highly encoded, user-unfriendly input formats used in older systems.

carriage return-line feed

Two distinct ASCII characters, commonly used together to end a printed line or a data record. In ASCII, carriage return (CR) is 13 decimal, and line feed (LF) is 10 decimal.

CASE—computer-aided software or systems engineering

The use of automated tools to aid in the analysis, design, and development of an application system. Most CASE tools are developed and sold as products by software vendors.

For the systems analysis phases of a development project, some CASE products provide a range of tools to automate the preparation and maintenance of the materials normally produced in structured analysis. These tools typically include a data dictionary system and diagramming facilities for data-flow diagrams and entity-relationship diagrams. They not only reduce the work of preparing and modifying such documents, but also keep track of the complex linkages and relationships among the elements in a structured specification.

For the design and programming phases of a development project, CASE tools range from sophisticated editors, debuggers, and integrated development environments (IDEs) to complete application generators that, for some systems, can avoid the need for programming altogether.

See also *lower CASE* and *upper CASE*.

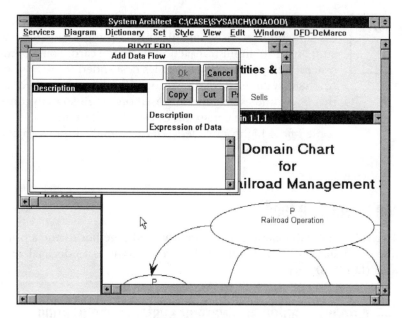

A CASE screen.

case-sensitive

A characteristic of programs and operating systems that determines whether uppercase (capital) letters are treated differently from lowercase letters.

UNIX commands are case-sensitive. However, MS-DOS commands are not, so that, for example, to display a directory, you can enter **dir**, **DIR**, **Dir**, and so on. Some text editors and word processors offer case-sensitivity as a user-selected operating mode.

For some programming languages, such as C, the case of data names and keywords is significant. Other languages, such as BASIC, recognize case only within string constants.

casting

Explicit conversion from one data type to another.

The C language provides a casting operator: the name of a data type enclosed in parentheses. In the following example, casting avoids integer truncation:

```
long total;
int  n;
float avg;
.
.
avg = (float) total / (float) n;
```

Other languages provide similar conversion functions.

See also *coercion,* and *conversion, data type.*

catalog

An inventory of data sets (or files) giving their names, physical locations, and important attributes.

A directory (or VTOC) always resides on the same volume with the data sets it describes, whereas a centralized catalog lists files stored on other volumes. A centralized catalog is essential in managing a library of magnetic tape reels. It is therefore supported by many mainframe operating systems, such as OS/MVS.

cataloged procedure

A packaged sequence of job control language (JCL) or other control statements.

The term used to refer to this important concept varies, depending on the operating platform:

Platform	Term
IBM OS/MVS	Cataloged procedure
IBM TSO	CLIST
VAX VMS	Command file
MS-DOS	Batch file
UNIX	Script

Whatever it is called, a library of such packaged control statements is important in establishing standard and disciplined ways of invoking useful operating system functions. In addition, it is essential in supporting the operation of batch processing components of application systems.

cathode ray tube

See *CRT*.

CCP—certified computer programmer

An individual who has completed the requirements to earn a Certificate in Computer Programming from the Institute for Certification of Computer Professionals (ICCP). This certificate is awarded for the successful completion of an examination in programming concepts.

CD-I—compact disc-interactive

A compact disc format and hardware/software standard developed by Philips and Sony. CD-I material includes audio, video, and text information. This format is not compatible with other CD-ROM standards.

CDP—certified data processor

An individual who has completed the requirements for the Certificate in Data Processing from the Institute for Certification of Computer Professionals (ICCP). This certificate is awarded for the successful completion of an examination in computer-related concepts such as hardware, software, programming, systems analysis, and management.

cdr

A primitive LISP function that returns a list with the first element removed, as in the following examples:

```
(cdr '(A B C)) is (B C)

(cdr '((A B) C)) is (C)

(cdr '(A)) is nil
```

See also *car.*

CD-ROM—compact disc, read-only memory

An optical storage medium identical to the compact digital discs used for musical recordings. A CD-ROM disk can store about 650M of data.

See also *auxiliary storage* and *disk.*

ceiling function

A standard integer function returning the smallest integer not exceeded by its argument.

ceil(3.2)	is 4
ceil(3.0)	is 3
ceil(–1.5)	is –1

The ceiling function is useful for computing the number of containers or buckets needed to hold some number of items.

APL, PL/1, and C provide a built-in ceiling function. In languages that don't provide such a function explicitly, you can express it in terms of integer truncation. For example, in a spreadsheet language, you can express a ceiling function as follows:

```
@INT(X) + (X > @INT(X))
```

See also *floor function, truncation,* and *round.*

cell

The unit of storage in a spreadsheet; the intersection of a column and a row.

central processing unit

See *CPU.*

CGA—color graphics adapter

An IBM low-resolution video standard for text and graphics display, comparable in quality to television.

CGA was the first graphics standard developed for the IBM PC, but is no longer widely used, having been eclipsed by EGA, then VGA.

See also *EGA, RGB,* and *VGA* .

chained records

A sequence of records stored in noncontiguous locations (usually on a disk or other direct-access medium, but sometimes in main memory), in which each record contains a pointer to the next record.

Chained records are often used with hashing schemes to resolve clashes (when two or more keys yield the same disk address or when a bucket overflows). A database management system (DBMS) or other general input-output (I/O) support routines usually handle chaining, so it usually is not visible to the application program. However, the programmer may need to be aware of the behind-the-scenes chaining if it should degrade performance, and to take corrective tuning action.

chaining of rules

The strategy for drawing inferences from a knowledge base. Two basic strategies are used: forward chaining and backward chaining.

A rule base is a collection of rules of the form

```
IF condition THEN conclusion
```

Many expert systems and the language OPS5 use forward chaining. The user gives the system a set of facts. The system then finds rules in the rule base for which these facts imply the condition part, then asserts the corresponding conclusion parts as new facts. Using those facts, the system continues until no more conclusions can be drawn. The final conclusions are the results. Medical diagnosis based on input symptoms is an example of such an application.

Other expert systems and the language PROLOG use backward chaining. The user gives the system a conclusion or goal (or an inquiry based on a goal), and the system finds rules in which the conclusion part implies that goal. The system then uses the corresponding condition parts as new goals, continuing until it either finds facts that make the conclusion true or discovers that there are no such facts—in other words, that the goal is false. Theorem proving is an example of such an application.

Some expert systems use a combination of forward and backward chaining.

In either case, to make a rule true, the system may have to substitute values for variables. Such values—the set of data for which the conclusion or diagnosis is valid—are included in the results or output.

change control

The process of keeping track of and controlling changes made to successive versions of software.

Formal change control disciplines are essential for large software products or application systems being developed or maintained by a large team of programmers. Such disciplines may be supported and enforced by a software change-control (change management, version control) system. A change-control system, whether manual or automated, should ensure the following:

- For every executable program, there is a record of which version of each of its component source-code modules was used in creating it. Furthermore, the system ensures that the source-code modules for the entire program can be rebuilt.

- For every executable program, there is a record of the test plan, including all test data, that was used in the integration test that validated that program. Furthermore, the system ensures that the results of that test can be reproduced.

- For every change that affects the behavior of any program module, there is a documented record of who made the change, when it was made, and why it was made.

character set

A collection of letters, numbers, punctuation, codes, and special characters. ASCII is an example of a character set.

check digit

A digit in an identifier field (such as an account number) derived mathematically from the other digits in that field.

When a number containing such a check digit is entered, an editing program can check its validity immediately without accessing a database of valid numbers. The following is a simple algorithm for computing a check digit:

1. From the original number, form two numbers consisting of the digits in odd and even positions. For example, if the original number is 5732583, the two numbers will be 5353 and 728.

2. Multiply the second of these numbers by 2 ($728 \times 2 = 1456$).

3. Sum the digits in both numbers: $(1+4+5+6) + (5+3+5+3) = 32$.

4. Divide that result by 10 and use the remainder as the check digit. Thus the self-checking number for the example is 57325832.

When the self-checking number is later entered, the program can recompute the check digit and reject the input if it does not agree. The reason for multiplying every other digit by two is to ensure detection of adjacent transposition errors, such as 1324 for 1234, which is a common error in high-volume data entry. To improve the chances of detecting other common kinds of data entry error, some check-digit algorithms are much more sophisticated than the simple one shown in the example.

checkpoint

Information describing the status of a program at a given instant during execution. This information can be saved in a file and used later to restart the program from that point.

A noninteractive program that runs for a very long time, say more than an hour, can initiate checkpoints from time to time. If a power failure or hardware malfunction then occurs, only the time that elapsed since the last checkpoint is wasted.

For programs that do not create or update files, checkpointing is simple: at worst, a copy of the program's address space is written for possible reloading and restart. However, if a program changes the contents of a file, the checkpointing process must also include some way of keeping track of updates and the original file contents so that the file can also be restored.

See also *log file* and *transaction file*.

checksum

A sum formed during the creation of a data block to be transmitted over communication lines or to be written to permanent storage.

As the data is received, the sum is recomputed and checked against the original value. If there is a disagreement, the receiving program raises an error condition.

chief programmer

A role within a software development project team, combining responsibility for overall design with the assignment of programming and clerical tasks to other team members.

The "chief programmer team" approach to large-scale software development projects was popularized in the early 1970s by Harlan Mills, Terry Baker, and others. Its success depends both on other well-defined project team roles and on its integration with a highly structured methodology for design, coding, and testing.

The position of chief programmer is not usually considered permanent, but rather a role existing only for the duration of a project. The same person who acts as chief programmer on one project might play a different role in another project.

See also *designer* and *lead programmer*.

chmod

A UNIX utility that modifies the attribute mode of specified files or directories. For example, the following code changes the mode of a shell script from nonexecutable to executable:

```
ls -l go.ss
-rw-r--r--  1 root     other        11 Mar 18 23:17 go.ss
$ chmod +x go.ss
ls -l go.ss
-rwxr-xr-x  1 root     other        11 Mar 18 23:17 go.ss
```

Note that an x is added to the extended listing, denoting that the file is known to the operating system as a file that can be executed. Other attributes that can be modified include read permission, write permission, user or group identification, and locking procedures.

See also *attribute*.

CICS—customer information control system

A widely used teleprocessing monitor for online application systems on IBM mainframes.

With interfaces to popular programming languages, database management systems (DBMS), and CASE tools, CICS plays a central role in the typical high-performance online system that supports many user terminals. Compatible products from various vendors are also available on other platforms, including IBM minicomputers, MS-DOS, Windows, and OS/2.

clash

In hashing, two or more keys that yield the same address or bucket.

Clashes are an inevitable occurrence with hashing schemes. When a new record being added to a file or table yields an address that is already occupied by another record, some strategy must be provided to resolve the clash. Among the common strategies are chained records and computing a second hashing function.

class

In object-oriented programming (OOP), a defined structure for a set of objects having specified components or members, which may include the following:

- Member data items (possibly including other objects of the same or a different class)
- Member functions that define the operations or functions that can be performed on objects of that class

See *object-oriented programming* for an explanation of specialized object-oriented terminology.

See also *base class* and *derived class*.

clause (COBOL)

A standard part of a COBOL sentence or statement.

For example, in the statement

```
SELECT  TRANSACTION-FILE  ASSIGN TO 'SYSIN'.
```

the last three words are commonly referred to as the "ASSIGN clause of the SELECT statement."

clause (PROLOG)

A PROLOG rule of the form

head <- body

For example, note the following definition of an ancestor predicate:

```
ancestor(X,Y) <- parent(X,Y).
ancestor(X,Y) <- parent(X,Z), ancestor(Z,Y).
```

The definition consists of two clauses: a base clause and a recursive clause.

click

The action of pressing and quickly releasing a button on a mouse or similar pointing device.

Clicking is always directed at some object shown on the screen. The usual terminology is to "click on" the object; that is, to click while the mouse pointer on the screen is touching that object.

By convention in many graphical user interface (GUI) systems and applications, a single-click simply selects an object, whereas a rapid double-click activates an object.

See also *double-click, drag and drop,* and *mouse.*

client process

See *client-server architecture.*

client–server architecture

A network configuration in which decentralized client processes request services from centralized server processes. Usually the client processes run on single-user desktop computers or workstations, whereas the servers can run on a desktop computer, a minicomputer, or a mainframe computer.

Specialized server processes, running on the same or different computers in a network configuration, may include the following:

- Database servers that provide and control access to the database of an application system

- File servers that provide and control access to all files stored on a central facility

- Print servers that handle SPOOL requests from multiple users, directing output to a pool of printers

- Telecommunications servers that handle the interfaces between a local application and remote locations

Client-server architecture is increasingly seen as a desirable vehicle for implementing an application system, because it potentially combines the following:

- The economy of desktop computers

- The central control and integrity of a mainframe

- Shared access to common facilities

Offsetting these desirable characteristics, however, is much more complex software development.

By extension, the terms *client* and *server* are sometimes used in a non network context. In object-oriented programming (OOP), for example, a program (client) requests services from objects of some class (server).

See also *LAN*.

clipboard

A special memory resource or buffer that enables users to use cut or copy operations to store information (such as text or graphics), and later use a paste operation to place the stored information into another file or another portion of the same file.

A clipboard is a standard feature in many word processing programs, desktop publishing systems, and graphical user interface (GUI) operating systems.

See also *cut and paste, DDE,* and *OLE* .

clipping

In computer graphics, the process of finding whether a line or polygon is intersected by another polygon. There are two major applications for clipping:

- To determine whether certain constructs fall within a display window.

- To solve object visibility problems. Deciding whether one object obscures another requires that you first determine whether the objects intersect one another.

CLIST

See *cataloged procedure.*

clock speed

The speed of the central processing unit (CPU) clock, usually measured in megahertz (millions of cycles per second) as a frequency of clock ticks or in MIPS (millions of instructions per second).

The IBM PC introduced in 1981 had a clock speed of 4.77 MHz. By the early 1990s, desktop computers operated at speeds up to 66 MHz.

clock tick

The smallest unit of time recognized by the processor. Also called a *CPU cycle.*

A computer executes its simplest instructions in a single clock tick. On modern computers, a clock tick is typically just a fraction of a microsecond.

CLOS—Common LISP Object System

A standard package of definitions extending Common LISP to support object-oriented programming (OOP).

CLOS provides LISP with full support for almost all aspects of OOP, including multiple inheritance, keyword accessor functions, before methods, and after methods.

close (application window)

An operation informing a program that the user has finished using a program running in a window. An application window can be closed in either of two ways:

- Externally, by the user invoking some standard way of forcing termination, such as a mouse double-click on the control-menu box

- Internally, by normal termination of the process running in the window

In either case, the program, after closing its files and completing any other cleanup operation, returns control to the operating system, which then frees any resources assigned to the window and removes the window's display from the user's screen.

close (file)

An operation informing the operating system that the program has (at least temporarily) finished using a file.

When a program closes an input file, this is what happens:

- Any attached buffers are discarded and the memory they occupied is freed.
- If the input file is a temporary file that will not be used again, the disk space (or device) allocated to it is released.

When a program closes an output or update file, this is what happens:

- Output buffers are drained; that is, the buffers' contents are written to the file.
- If the output file is a permanent file, the appropriate catalog or directory is updated with the name, size, physical location, creation date, and so on, of the new or modified file.

closing

A processing cycle, usually monthly or quarterly, that includes a cut-off of normal input transaction processing before running one or more batch processing jobs. Closing is fundamental to accounting systems.

Computer centers may experience a corresponding workload peak for a few days each month during the closing cycle. To accommodate these peak demands, they might have to maintain excess capacity the rest of the time.

cluster

1. A group of disk sectors treated as a single entity by either a disk controller or an operating system.
2. A group of computer terminals connected to a single controller or computer system.

COBOL

The most widely used programming language for business applications, especially on mainframe computer platforms. Originally an acronym for *co*mmon *b*usiness-*o*riented *l*anguage.

Despite its name, COBOL is no more business-oriented than many other procedural programming languages. It provides no built-in support for functions or processes central to accounting, manufacturing, marketing, or other business application areas. What COBOL does provide is a capability to manipulate the wide range of files, databases, and input transactions encountered in traditional business data processing.

COBOL was specified in the late 1950s by CODASYL (Conference on Data Systems Languages), a group chartered by the United States Department of Defense with participation from equipment manufacturers and major user organizations. CODASYL's main objective was machine independence, so that application software could be, for the first time, portable among different platforms. The vigorous backing of the Department of Defense assured COBOL's eventual status as the language of choice for most business applications.

COBOL is criticized for lacking various modern facilities, and especially for the following:

- Extreme verbosity, making some common coding tasks tedious to perform manually

- Encouraging monolithic program organization, making maintenance programming unreasonably expensive

- Not allowing (until 1985 improvements) direct use of structured coding constructs

Nevertheless, COBOL continues its dominant role in large-scale business data processing, and is now making impressive inroads into midsized, client-server, and desktop computer platforms as well.

CODASYL—conference on data-systems languages

An organization responsible for specifying, enhancing, and standardizing COBOL. CODASYL's membership includes participants from the U.S. Department of Defense, major computer vendors, and other volunteers.

code

1. One of the permitted values of a discrete or enumerated data item.

   In traditional business data processing, the term *code* was often appended indiscriminately to the name of nearly every discrete data item, as in "area code," "customer code," "department code," "product code," and "state code." Today's careful writer limits such use of the term to specific references to an item's internal data representation. In modern practice, a programmer should use a simple data name, such as "product," and then, if necessary to distinguish between an entity and its key, append _id (which stands for "identifier"), as in product_id.

2. Any data resulting from encryption. See also *encrypt.*

3. Any sequence of statements in a program.

   The cryptic nature of the machine language used by early programmers probably accounts for the origin of this usage, which persists today to denote statements in any programming language. See also *statement* and *program.*

4. To write statements in a programming language; that is, to prepare code.

   Note the important difference between the terms *coding* and *programming*. Programming denotes the entire process of implementing a computer solution to a problem, and includes at a minimum program design, coding, and unit testing. See also *coder.*

coder

A programmer who specializes in low-level coding. Today the position is nearly obsolete.

Before the introduction of structured programming in the early 1970s, some organizations tried to develop massive amounts of application software by parceling extremely detailed assignments to large numbers of semiskilled coders, who had little input to the creative process. That approach demanded that systems analysts develop detailed flowcharts, record layouts, and so on, and rarely led to high-quality results. The acceptance of structured design, the chief programmer team, and other modern approaches has led enlightened organizations to abandon totally the use of pure coders to develop software.

code segment

An area of memory reserved for executable instructions; that is, an area not used for data. For background and explanation, see *data segment*.

CodeView

A debugging tool developed and marketed by Microsoft. CodeView is intended to be used with other languages and development tools marketed by Microsoft.

CodeView features a user interface based on multiple windows, each offering a different view of the program code or data. The tool enables you to do the following:

- Set and manage breakpoints
- Monitor the contents of named variables
- View source code along with the executable code for a module
- Modify data in memory as the program executes

coercion

Automatic (compiler-generated) conversion of a data item from one type to another.

Items of two different types are compatible if well-defined rules exist for converting from one to the other. Conversion among the various numeric data types, for example, is well understood and taken for granted by many programmers. Other conversions, however, can lead to unexpected results. For example, when a numeric item is converted to a character string, assumptions are made about left or right adjustment, padding with blanks, and so on.

In object-oriented programming (OOP), conversion between objects of a base class and a derived class is often trivial. However, the programmer who defines such classes sometimes must define such conversion rules explicitly or, in some cases, to prohibit automatic conversion between objects of such classes.

In a language with strong typing, the programmer may have to code explicit casting to accomplish type conversion.

cold boot

See *boot, cold.*

collate

To merge two or more sorted (on some key field) files to form a single file sorted on the same key field. The term is synonymous with *merge.*

color graphics adapter

See *CGA.*

.COM

1. MS-DOS file name extension to identify an executable program that fits in one 64K segment of memory. The contents of the program file are identical to the image loaded into memory and executed. See also *.EXE.*

2. VAX/VMS file name extension to identify a file of commands; similar to MS-DOS's .BAT extension.

COM file

A packaged sequence of VMS commands. See also *cataloged procedure* and *VMS.*

combo box

In a graphical user interface (GUI), a dialog box that combines the features of a list box and a text box.

A combo box is useful when the programmer wants to present a list of suggested alternatives to the user, such as a list of files in the current directory. The user can either select one of those items (using the mouse or the cursor keys) or type some other response.

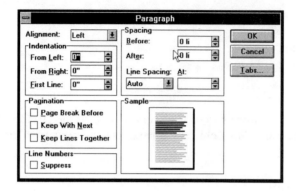

A combo box.

COMDEX—Computer Dealers Exposition

The largest American trade show for computer hardware, software, and related products and services, held biannually. In the spring, COMDEX is held in Atlanta, and in the fall, COMDEX is held in Las Vegas. Of the two annual shows, the fall COMDEX is the larger.

Vendors often use COMDEX as an occasion for introducing new products.

command

An instruction to a program, especially an operating system specifying an action to be taken.

The most common form of command is similar to a statement in an assembly language:

```
label operation  parameter-list
```

where

- The optional *label* is used mainly in cataloged procedures (or batch files) to enable one command to refer to another for branching or localization. In IBM mainframe JCL (job control language), it also specifies the name of the file or process associated with the command.

- The *operation* is the command name; that is, it designates the operation to be performed. In many operating systems, including MS-DOS, this often corresponds to the name of a program.

• The *parameter-list* can contain variable data (such as file names) or coded options, usually in a sequence the command-processing program expects.

command, spreadsheet processing

A spreadsheet processor operation initiated either by a user at the keyboard or by a macro program.

In most spreadsheet processors, the command language is separate from the language of formulas in spreadsheet cells. Facilities available to one are not directly available to the other.

The user specifies the operation and fixed parameters of a spreadsheet command by selecting options from a hierarchical menu structure. In a traditional spreadsheet command language, the user follows these steps:

1. Initiates a command by doing one of the following:

    Typing a reserved "command" character; in many older spreadsheet processors, this character is the slash (/)

    Selecting an option from the main menu by pressing the Alt key and a highlighted letter

    Placing the mouse pointer on the main menu

2. Selects each level in the hierarchy of options by doing one of the following:

    Typing the single-character (conventionally the first letter unless more than one item in the same menu begins with the same letter) of the desired option shown on the menu

    Moving the cursor with the arrow keys until the desired menu item is highlighted

    Clicking on the desired menu item

3. Provides variable information in response to prompts by doing one of the following:

    Typing the information (for example, a file name)

    Selecting something (such as a block or range) by using the arrow keys or the mouse

By the mid-1980s, the conventional use of the first character of each menu option had led to rather cumbersome and illogically structured command menus, as new features were added to leading spreadsheet processors that still had to support full compatibility with earlier versions. More recent products, especially those for graphical user interface (GUI) platforms, have sacrificed some compatibility with earlier versions in return for a more consistent and logically organized user interface. However, modern spreadsheet macro languages continue to support the old command structures.

command language

The syntax and rules defining the repertoire of commands recognized by a program, especially an operating system.

Some operating systems give a special name to their command language, as in the following examples:

IBM mainframe: JCL (job control language)

DEC VAX/VMS: DCL (digital command language)

A command language that has many different specialized commands or operations, each with a small number of options, is said to be highly "vertical;" UNIX and MS-DOS exemplify vertical command languages. In contrast, a highly "horizontal" command language has only a few commands, each of which has a large number of options; IBM JCL exemplifies a horizontal command language. Each style has advantages and disadvantages: Vertical command languages are usually more flexible for adding new features, whereas horizontal ones may be more consistent and easier to learn thoroughly.

The trend toward graphical user interfaces (GUIs), menu systems, and other higher-level ways of communicating with an operating system is reducing the importance of command languages. Today many computer users never see the underlying command-level interface, and some operating systems, such as System 7, don't even provide a traditional command processor.

command line

See *command prompt.*

command-line switch

An option parameter passed to a program invoked by a command.

For example, using the MS-DOS DIR command, you can enter the following:

DIR A: /P a:

The /P is passed to DIR as the switch. (This particular switch tells DIR to pause when the screen is full.)

command prompt

A standard sequence of characters displayed on-screen and indicating that the operating system (or other control program) is ready for the user to enter a command.

MS-DOS issues its default command prompt by displaying C> at the left edge of the current input line and positioning the cursor immediately to the right (if C is the current default disk drive). For example, after typing a DIR command but before pressing the Enter key, the user would see the following on the current line:

C>DIR

Many MS-DOS users override the default command by using the PROMPT command, which enables the user to customize the command prompt to display such information as the time of day or the current directory. This capability has become less important with the emergence of higher-level menu systems or graphical user interface (GUI) systems that make it unnecessary to enter commands in normal operation.

Other operating systems that support interactive command entry have their own style of command prompt.

comment

A piece of documentation within program source code or a command language file.

Comments in a program fall into two categories:

- Introductory comments at the beginning of a module or major section of code to explain what the module does, how it is used, and the strategy or algorithm it employs.

- Line-by-line comments interspersed with source code statements to explain the purpose or effect of each statement.

Good programmers write introductory comments for every nontrivial section of code. Such comments, of course, greatly facilitate future maintenance programming. In addition, programmers sometimes write introductory comments before they write the actual code as a way of strengthening their own grasp of the problem or algorithm.

Line-by-line comments are most useful in low-level languages, such as assembly language, in which the relationship between an individual statement and its purpose or effect is rarely obvious. An instruction that adds one register to another, for example, might be explained by the comment "Advance buffer position."

commentary

A set of related comments.

The terms *comment* and *commentary* are used almost interchangeably. *Commentary* is more common when used collectively or generically; *comment* is more often applied to a particular instance or fragment of commentary.

comment delimiter

A unique token separating source code from commentary.

Some programming languages provide a line-oriented comment delimiter, such as those listed in the following table. Any source text to the right of such a delimiter is a comment.

Language	Delimiter	Special Rules
Ada	--	
BASIC	'	Older BASICs use the keyword REM as a statement keyword.
C++	//	Also allows the C bracketing convention (see the following table).
COBOL	*	Appears in position 7. Older COBOL uses NOTE as verb.
FORTRAN	C	Appears in position 1.
LISP	;	Special conventions exist for multiple semicolons.
PROLOG	%	

Other languages provide a bracketing pair, as shown in the following table. Any text between a left and right comment delimiter is a comment, and may extend over multiple lines.

Language	Left Delimiter	Right Delimiter
C, PL/1	/*	*/
Pascal, Modula-2	(*	*)

comment out

To nullify a portion of a program by putting comment delimiters in front of or around it, without actually deleting it from the source code. A programmer may do this to suppress compilation of such code as the following:

- Debugging statements in production versions of a program

- Statements needed in some but not all special program versions

- Unfinished code fragments in a program under development

- Obsolete code in an old program

- Unwanted code in a custom or one-time run

COMMON

The keyword for designating external or global data in FORTRAN and in BASIC.

Unlike external data in other languages, COMMON items in FORTRAN are identified not by their names but by their position in a list. Therefore, programmers working on large programs with many separately compiled modules must be very careful that the lists of COMMON data are identical in every module.

Common LISP

A standard version of LISP, specified in the early 1980s by a consortium of vendors and academic institutions in reaction to a proliferation of incompatible versions on various platforms.

COMP

Abbreviation for the COBOL keyword COMPUTATIONAL.

compatibility

See *downward compatibility* and *upward compatibility.*

compile

To convert source code written in a high-level language such as COBOL or C into machine language.

The object modules produced by a compiler are seldom directly executable. Modern systems generally require that a linking loader be executed to bind library code to the object module and resolve references to external modules.

compile-time binding

Defining in source code a value or other characteristic of a program that cannot be changed without recompiling the program.

For example, a C program might contain the following definition:

```
#define max_items    20
```

The program could then use `max_items` many times—as an array dimension, in a loop termination specification, in an error message, and so on. To increase this limit to, say, 24, the programmer must change the `#define` statement and then recompile all modules in which it appears.

Compile-time binding is more flexible than hard-coding, but less flexible than runtime binding. Because it carries no runtime overhead, compile-time binding is often considered a good trade-off between flexibility and efficiency.

compiled

An attribute of an executable program produced by a compiler that translates code into executable machine language.

In contrast, some language processors, including popular versions of APL, BASIC, and LISP, generate code that must be interpreted line by line.

See also *interpreter*.

compiler

A program to translate source code written in some programming language to object code for a particular computer.

See also *procedural language*.

compiler directive

A command or option embedded in a source code file that instructs a compiler to take some action.

Depending on the programming language and the specific implementation, a compiler may handle two kinds of directives:

- A parameter that determines some option in compiling. For example, such a parameter may determine whether to optimize the object code or whether to print macro expansions in the listing. Many of these directives can alternatively be specified as parameters when the compiler is invoked.

- A command that directs the compiler to take some action immediately. The most common example is the include or COPY facility, which inserts code from a source code library.

Other statements in a macro (or preprocessor) language are usually not considered compiler directives.

complement

A quantity derived by subtracting a number from the radix of the number system being used. For example, the nine's complement of 3 is 6.

Many computers use complements to represent negative numbers, so that subtraction is accomplished by adding the complemented number. For PCs, the two's complement is used to represent negative numbers.

complete program

The set of all modules needed for execution; a main program and all the modules it uses directly or indirectly.

See also *linking loader*.

completion code

Numeric value returned as the result of a job or process that has terminated abnormally, usually due to loss of control caused by an unrecoverable error.

Completion codes are fundamental to the abnormal end (ABEND) processing in IBM mainframe operating systems. After encountering an ABEND, the user or programmer can consult a manual explaining each of the possible completion codes.

See also *ABEND, condition code,* and *crash.*

complex number

A superset of the real numbers, with a real and imaginary component. A complex number is written as a + bi, where i is defined as the square root of -1.

Some programming languages, such as FORTRAN and PL/1, include a complex data type. In languages like Ada and C++ that let you define data types (or classes) with operator overloading, you can define a complex data type and the usual mathematical operations on items of that type.

composite data item

A data item made up of other (either composite or elementary) data items.

Composite data item is a neutral term. More specialized terms such as *entity, record, structure,* and *data flow* imply something about how the data item is used or interpreted.

All entities, data flows, and records are composite data items, but a given composite data item need not be any of these more specialized structures.

 Avoid "false composites": data items that can be decomposed, but only into components that aren't really independent data items. A common example is a date, which may have a mixed-unit representation (that is, <year, month, day>), but is almost always entered, stored, and processed as a single data item. Components of such false composites can clutter up a data dictionary and make an application system look more complicated than it really is.

See also *data item definition* and *data representation.*

compression algorithm

A class of mathematical transformations for text data to minimize storage requirements or transmission time.

Data compression can be implemented either in software (such as PKZIP and most backup utilities) or in hardware (such as MNP modems).

compute

To execute a sequence of operations that yield a well-defined result.

Both *compute* and its near synonym *calculate* usually refer to numerical operations. The term *computer* was established when early machines were used almost exclusively for such operations, and now applies to hardware systems that do far more than just compute in the original sense.

COMPUTATIONAL

A COBOL data attribute specifying that a declared item is to be represented in the computer's internal numeric form rather than as a character string (DISPLAY). Here's an example:

```
1   RECORD-COUNTER  PICTURE 9(7)  COMPUTATIONAL.
1   ACCOUNT-NUMBER  PICTURE 9(7)  DISPLAY.
```

On most computers, RECORD-COUNTER would be stored as a full-word (31 bits and sign) binary integer, whereas ACCOUNT-NUMBER would occupy seven 8-bit (ASCII or EBCDIC) characters. On many computers, COBOL implementations extend this keyword as follows:

Attribute	Internal Data Representation
COMPUTATIONAL-1	Single-precision floating point
COMPUTATIONAL-2	Double-precision floating point
COMPUTATIONAL-3	Packed decimal

Because DISPLAY is the default, omitting COMPUTATIONAL results in the data item being represented as a character string. Neglecting to specify COMPUTATIONAL when its use is appropriate can impose costly and hard-to-find conversion overhead for any data item that is used in many calculations.

In all contexts, you can use the abbreviation COMP, as in COMP-3. If you prefer verbose coding, you can write USAGE IS COMPUTATIONAL.

computer-aided design

See *CAD*.

computer architecture

The characteristics of a computer system that determine its behavior, in particular how it interacts with both programs and human operators.

Among the details of a particular computer's architecture are the following:

- Data types and their representations: character coding (ASCII or EB-CDIC), sizes of binary integers, representation of negative numbers, format and lengths or floating-point numbers, and availability of packed decimal

- Registers: how many there are, how many bits are in each one, what their purposes are, and how their contents are manipulated

- Memory addressing: the unit of addressability (byte, word), the range of such units that can be directly addressed, and how addresses are formed from their component parts (segment, offset)

- Instructions: their format, length, and repertoire of operation codes

- Input-output: channel and device addressing, interrupts, and exceptions

- Sequencing paradigm: traditional sequential instruction processing or any of several models of parallel processing

Special computer architectures are employed to develop machines suited to specialized functions, such as database servers or support of a particular programming language (especially LISP and APL).

See also *parallel processing* and *stored program computer.*

computer system configuration

The set of hardware options chosen for a particular computer system, usually including the following:

- The amount of memory attached to the computer

- The clock speed (or model) of the central processing unit (CPU)

- The type, capacity, and addresses of auxiliary storage devices, such as fixed disks, disk drives, CD-ROM, and tape drives

- The type of console, monitor, or attached local terminals

- The type, speed, and communication protocol of remote terminals or network connections

- Any optional features, such as a coprocessor or a cache

This term sometimes also includes operating system options, especially those that depend on hardware, such as the choice of device drivers, the use of spoolers, and the size of various tables or stacks.

See also *maximum supported configuration, minimum required configuration,* and *platform.*

CON

In MS-DOS, a reserved word for the console. In most programming languages, CON can be used as a file name.

concatenate

To combine two sequential data structures into a single data structure, by appending the elements of the second to the first. The data structures that can be concatenated include strings, lists, and sequential files.

File concatenation is useful for bringing together components of a larger entity, such as separate chapters of a book. The MS-DOS COPY command facilitates such concatenation, as in the following example:

```
COPY   CH1+CH2+CH3+CH4+CH5   THE-BOOK
```

The preceding technique works for text files, but generally not for files that have internal structure, such as those produced by a spreadsheet processor or an advanced word processor. However, those software products usually provide their own internal commands for file concatenation.

String concatenation is frequently needed in all areas of text manipulation and in the support of user-friendly interfaces. Programming language designers have chosen a wide variety of structures for the concatenation operator, including the following:

Language	Concatenation
BASIC:	`FULL.NAME$ = FIRST.NAMES$ + SURNAME$`
C:	`strcpy(full_name,first_names);` `strcat(full_name,surname);`
COBOL:	`STRING FIRST-NAMES SURNAME INTO FULL-NAME;`
PL/1:	`FULL_NAME  = FIRST.NAMES ¦¦ SURNAME;`
Spreadsheet:	`+FIRSTNAME & SURNAME (in the FULLNAME cell)`

condition

A logical or Boolean value or expression.

The term *condition* is more common than *logical* or *Boolean expression* in the context of a test conducted in a program. Programmers commonly speak of "testing a condition" or "checking for a condition." Many conditions contain a relational operator, as in the following example:

```
IF BALANCE > 0 . . .
```

A simple condition is one that contains no Boolean operators (and, or, not); a compound condition contains at least one Boolean operator.

See also *Boolean expression, Boolean operator, condition name, do while,* and *if-then-else construct.*

conditional

See *branch* and *if-then-else construct.*

conditional compile

A feature of many compilers that provides a preprocessor pass before actual compilation, with variables that the programmer can set to specify which parts of source code to pass on to the compiler.

This feature provides an elegant way to produce different versions of an executable program from a single source code file. Among the common applications of this technique are the following:

- To customize versions of a software product to run on different operating platforms

- To include extra diagnostics statements while a program is being tested but eliminate them from the final version released to the users

See also *macro*.

condition code

A numeric value, often associated with an error-severity level, returned as the result of a program or process; also called a *return code, exit code,* or (in MS-DOS) *errorlevel.*

In IBM mainframe operating systems, job control language (JCL) statements can test the condition codes returned by earlier job steps to determine which subsequent job steps should be executed. Many utility programs and compilers as well as application programs observe the following conventions for the meaning of their resulting condition code:

0	No errors encountered
4	Trivial (warning) errors encountered
8	Serious errors encountered
12	Terminal error encountered

In newer operating systems, it is more common to use consecutive values 0, 1, 2, and so on.

See also *completion code.*

condition name

A COBOL data name used as shorthand for a relational expression.

In the DATA DIVISION, level number 88 is reserved for declaring a condition name subordinate to an actual data name. For example:

```
10    MARITAL-STATUS      PICTURE X.
      88    SINGLE        VALUE   'S'
      88    MARRIED       VALUE   'M'.
      88    DIVORCED      VALUE   'D'.
      88    WIDOWED       VALUE   'W'.
```

Now in the PROCEDURE DIVISION

```
IF    SINGLE  .  .  .
```

is equivalent to

```
IF    MARITAL-STATUS = 'S' . . .
```

This feature helps the programmer to localize dependencies on coding schemes. For instance, if you later wanted to adopt a numeric encoding of MARITAL-STATUS in the preceding example, you would have to change only the DATA DIVISION entries. In PL/1, C, and some other languages, the programmer can implement this technique with macro variables.

See also *COBOL*.

CONFIG.SYS

An MS-DOS ASCII file containing parameters and commands that specify the physical or logical configuration of the computer and certain options chosen by the user.

Some software products require specific CONFIG.SYS values, and their install (or setup) programs may actually modify the user's MS-DOS CONFIG.SYS file. Although this practice relieves the user from having to know about and enter these values, it can occasionally lead to conflicts.

configuration

See *maximum supported configuration, minimum required configuration,* and *network configuration.*

configuration, computer system

See *computer system configuration.*

cons

A primitive LISP function that constructs a new list by pushing an element onto an existing list.

For example:

```
(cons 'A '(B C))   is      (A B C)
(cons '(A B)')     is      ((A B) C)
(cons 'A nil)      is      (A)
```

The term also refers to the pair of cells used to represent internally the result of a cons function.

console

The control panel or main controlling terminal connected to a large, multiuser computer system. Using the console, the operator controls major system operations such as backups, user administration, and system shutdown.

In MS-DOS, the word CON is a reserved device name that a program can use for access to the keyboard for input and to the screen for output. The file handle is the console.

constant

See *absolute constant, fundamental constant, derived constant, symbolic constant,* and *figurative constant.*

constructor

An object-oriented programming (OOP) function that creates a new object belonging to a specified class. Destructors are used to delete the object when it is no longer needed. In C++, constructors and destructors are defined in the class definition.

In C++, constructors have the same name as their class, and destructors have that name preceded by a tilde, as in the following example:

```
class hotel_room {
    ...
public:
    ...
    hotel_room();      // constructor declaration, no parameters
    hotel_room(rate);  // constructor declaration, one parameter
    ~hotel_room();     // destructor declaration
};
```

See also *destructor*.

container

A dynamic data structure, the elements of which are arbitrary data items whose type is not known when the program is written.

One of the most general containers is the LISP programming language's list structure. The elements of such a list can be items of any type, and lists can be built and changed dynamically without restriction. Libraries of container classes are available for object-oriented programming (OOP) in C++.

See also *array, list, queue, set, stack,* and *tree.*

context-sensitive help

Any help facility that takes note of what the user was doing just before asking for help and attempts to provide information relevant to that situation.

This term differentiates a help facility from the more general online documentation, which simply presents the user with a table of contents and a way of moving (navigating) through a chain of related topics.

Designing user-friendly context-sensitive help is extremely challenging because of the difficulty of anticipating hundreds of possible situations. After accidentally making the wrong menu choice, for example, a user doesn't want to see an explanation of all the things he or she can proceed to do with that choice. Instead, that user wants to know how to get back to the original menu without doing any further damage. If the designer of the context-sensitive help facility didn't anticipate such a situation, the frustrated user may become more dissatisfied than if the system had provided no help facility at all.

context switching

In a single-user operating system, the activation of a new or previously inactive job in response to a user request.

Context switching does not require multiprogramming. Under the DOSSHELL, for example, the user can suspend one program in the middle of execution to run another. Under Windows or a multiprogramming operating system, however, the first program may continue to run in the background.

To effect context switching, the user must have some way of interrupting an executing program. In a windowing environment, the user can usually click the mouse outside the area of the active window. In a full-screen environment, the operating system usually reserves some hot-key combination, such as Alt-Esc, for initiating context switching.

control block

A composite data item (or record) containing related data items associated with some process or entity.

The purpose of a control block is to simplify the passing of status information among different modules by providing a standard structure that any module can access or update appropriately. Control blocks are especially useful in operating systems, which typically contain such structures as the following:

- A task control block
- A device control block
- A file control block

In object-oriented programming (OOP), you can achieve similar advantages by encapsulating the related data items within a class.

control break

A point within a sequential input file (or spreadsheet, or other sequentially processed data) at which a group of related data ends.

In report-generating programs, a control break may trigger such actions as printing subtotals, starting a new page, or changing the page heading. For example, in a mailing list sorted by postal ZIP code, you might have two levels of control break: a change in ZIP code and a change in state.

control card

An obsolete term for *control statement,* reflecting the almost universal use of punched cards for input before the late 1970s.

control module

A module that makes decisions and invokes lower-level modules, but doesn't actually operate on data. Many main modules are control modules.

control panel

In graphical user interface (GUI) systems, a screen that simulates the elements of an actual control panel, including buttons, dials, and switches. The user manipulates the elements of a control panel with a pointing device, such as a mouse.

 Industry observers have pointed out an interesting circular phenomenon:

- Second-generation computers had elaborate control panels that demanded a highly skilled operator. One of the benefits of third-generation computers was to be a simpler operator's console that uses a keyboard and a display. The operator no longer had to deal with a complicated array of buttons and switches, but could communicate with the system in plain English and well-structured commands.

- Enthusiasts now point out that a major benefit of modern GUI systems is a simpler interface. The user no longer has to deal with error-prone English and complicated commands but can communicate with the system through intuitively obvious buttons and switches.

See also *desktop.*

control program

The part or parts of an operating system that manage the execution of application programs. These parts were formerly called a monitor program.

control statement

1. In a command language for an operating system, a statement used to request a service or to set a parameter.

2. A similar statement directing the actions of a utility program, such as a linking loader, an external sort utility, a spooler, or a data compression algorithm.

3. An input to an application program, established by the designer for setting parameters or selecting run options. Control statements are especially convenient in situations where a program normally uses default values but users may occasionally specify overriding values.

See also *command language, JCL,* and *statement.*

control total

A precomputed sum of a field in a batch of transactions, used to verify that no transactions are missing or duplicated.

The use of control totals is strongly recommended wherever batches of data are subject to a procedure—such as manual handling of input documents or transmission of files—in which an error may occur. You should also consider using control totals for purely automated processes, such as external sorting, in which abnormal conditions may be encountered, such as insufficient disk space.

See also *checksum.*

conversion, data type

A function, either explicit or implicit, in which the input is a data item of one type, and the result is a data item of a different (but compatible) type that has the corresponding value.

For example, suppose the following are true:

X is an integer variable, and its current value is 201.

Y is a real (floating-point) variable.

Z is a complex variable.

S is a character string having fixed length of 8.

B is a Boolean (logical) variable.

Then, if the programming language supports implicit conversion (coercion), the following assignment statements would produce the designated results:

```
Y = X;    /*  Y is now 2.01E+2 in floating decimal notation   */
Z = X;    /*  Z is now (2.01E+2,0) or 2.01+0i                  */
S = X;    /*  S is "   201 " (depending on conversion rules)   */
B = X;    /*  illegal statement; incompatible data type        */
```

In object-oriented programming (OOP), the programmer who defines a new class often must explicitly specify the rules for converting objects of that class to other compatible classes. See *overloading*.

See also *casting, coercion, data type, numeric data type,* and *strong typing.*

conversion, file

The creation of a file having the same contents as an existing file, but in a different format.

File conversion is required whenever a file created on one platform, database management system (DBMS), productivity tool, or application system is to be accessed by a different platform, DBMS, productivity tool, or application system.

One-time, permanent file (database) conversion occurs as part of the startup of a new application system, often on a platform that differs from the old system.

Recurring, temporary file conversion occurs in the interfaces among different application systems, especially in distributed processing environments that have multiple operating platforms.

A file that must be converted typically has the following attributes:

- Representation of individual data items (see *data representation*)
- Internal pointers, counters, and control information used by a DBMS or other program
- A physical storage medium
- Blocking factors
- Auxiliary indices

Although file conversion can be extremely complicated, especially with the proprietary formats used in many software products, software vendors often provide conversion programs.

See also *import*.

conversion, operating platform

The conversion of all jobs running on one operating platform to jobs that yield equivalent results on another platform, often performed to transfer a workload from an obsolete computer to a modern one.

Operating platform conversion is often expensive and error-prone. In the worst case it involves changes to every application program, conversion of all databases and permanent files, and changes to the users' procedures for entering data and obtaining results. Because the operational philosophies of platforms may differ significantly (for example, consider the operational differences between a large mainframe platform and a client-server distributed platform), some facilities of the old system may have no exact counterpart in the new system. Furthermore, the new system may offer attractive features, such as a graphical user interface (GUI), that the old jobs can't take advantage of without considerable reworking.

A large-scale conversion effort is usually planned and managed in detail as a project. The estimated cost of that project is a major factor in deciding whether to do the conversion.

conversion, source code

Changing the source code of a set of programs to obtain equivalent programs in a different programming language, in a different (usually more standard) version of the same language, or in the original programming language but for a different operating environment.

The more standardized the programming language and the less that programmers take advantage of implementation dependencies, the less source code conversion is required. In the ideal case, you can simply recompile the original source code without change. The worst case might be converting an assembly language program to run on a different computer.

Automated conversion aids are often available for conversion between dialects of a programming language, especially conversion to new versions that may not be strictly compatible with the old version. Using automated conversion aids between very different languages (such as PL/1 to C++, or COBOL to BASIC, or one assembly language to another) is rarely successful.

coprocessor

An auxiliary processor designed to assist a computer's main processor by handling specialized tasks.

A common example is a math coprocessor, optimized for floating-point computations. Larger systems often have highly capable input-output (I/O) channels acting as coprocessors. Examples of other small system coprocessors include graphics accelerators and signal processing interfaces.

See also *emulation*.

COPY (COBOL)

A COBOL compiler directive that causes the inclusion of text from a source code library.

COPY is similar to the include operation of PL/1, C, and other languages, but more limited. COPY files cannot be nested; that is, a COPY library file cannot itself contain instances of COPY. Parameter substitution is limited to complete tokens. No conditional inclusion is provided.

Even with its limitations, COPY is still one of the most valuable tools for organizing a COBOL program. In addition to its obvious use for localizing record descriptions in the DATA DIVISION, COPY can be used with the REPLACING option to serve as a simple macro facility in the PROCEDURE DIVISION.

Here, slightly oversimplified, is a routine to invoke a designated paragraph for every record in a sequential input file:

```
OPEN INPUT      filename;
MOVE F          TO    END-OF-FILE-SWITCH;
MOVE 0          TO    RECORD-COUNTER;
READ filename
    AT END MOVE T TO END-OF-FILE-SWITCH; END-READ;
PERFORM   UNTIL      END-OF-FILE-SWITCH = T;
    ADD  1     TO    RECORD-COUNTER;
    PERFORM   process;
    READ filename
        AT END MOVE T TO END-OF-FILE-SWITCH; END-READ;
    END-PERFORM;
DISPLAY   RECORD-COUNTER, ' records read from file.'
CLOSE filename;
```

Suppose you put the preceding routine in a source code library under the name SQFLPRCS. Now any programmer who wants to process a sequential input file need only code the following:

```
COPY SQFLPRCS   REPLACING
    filename    BY TRANSACTION-FILE,
    process     BY EDIT-TRANSACTION;
```

Because of other COBOL restrictions, this kind of inline routine is sometimes the only way of packaging a potentially reusable module. It is impossible, for example, to package the function performed by SQFLPRCS as an ordinary COBOL subroutine.

COPY (Intel)

An MS-DOS and OS/2 command that copies one or more disk-resident files. Although the newer command XCOPY and graphical user interface (GUI)-based file managers offer greater flexibility and functionality, many users continue to use this simple command.

copy library

See *source code library*.

coroutine

A program module designed to execute concurrently with another specific module, usually with internal points of synchronization in which one module waits for data or a signal from the other module.

See also *multitasking* and *semaphore.*

counter

An integer variable incremented by (usually) 1 to reflect some occurrence.

Counters occur frequently in programs written in procedural languages, keeping track of such things as the following:

- Records in a sequential file
- Character positions in a string
- Pages in a report
- Lines on a page
- Entries in a table
- Errors encountered (by an editing program or a compiler, for example)

Because errors in counting are a common source of a program bug (being off by 1 at the end), some procedural languages provide special constructs to facilitate incrementing counters, such as the ++ operator in C. In many situations, very-high-level (VHL) or nonprocedural languages relieve the programmer altogether from having to increment counters explicitly.

CP/M—control program for microprocessors

An operating system developed by Digital Research for the early desktop computer Z80.

CP/M is a forerunner of MS-DOS, which closely resembles it.

CPU— central processing unit

The part of a computer that executes instructions, performs arithmetic, and controls the computer configuration.

A CPU consists of a control unit and an arithmetic logic unit (ALU). Modern CPUs are usually a small chip inside the main computer cabinet.

See also *Intel CPU, Motorola CPU,* and *Zilog CPU.*

CPU clock

The quartz crystal used to create an even electrical frequency used to synchronize digital pulses in a computer.

crash

Termination of execution, especially of the operating system itself, by a loss of control.

Although the terms *crash* and *ABEND* are often used interchangeably, *ABEND* more commonly denotes termination of individual jobs or tasks, whereas *crash* more commonly refers to a failure of the whole operating system. A crash is, of course, an extremely serious event, especially in multiprogrammed operating systems, in which many processes may be interrupted and recovery may be costly and time-consuming.

Modern operating systems are expected to run routinely for a week or more without crashing, even if the jobs running under its control (and in some cases the hardware itself) are themselves unreliable.

See also *disk crash.*

crash, disk

See *disk crash.*

CRC—cyclic redundancy check

A logical sum computed by communications programs and disk input-output (I/O) routines and stored at the end of a physical record. As the record is read, the computation is performed again and the result is checked against the original. A disagreement triggers a request for a retry.

CRT—cathode ray tube

The vacuum tube used as a computer display (such as a PC monitor) that can display text or graphics.

This technology also is the basis for a television screen. A CRT is constructed with one or more electron beams that move in a very rapid horizontal pattern across the inside of the tube. A special material is coated on the screen that glows when hit by the beam. Many people refer to an entire terminal as a CRT.

See also *interlaced video* and *non-interlaced video.*

currency type

A data type supported by some languages, including variants of BASIC, that is optimized for dollars-and-cents computations or equivalent operations in other currencies.

current directory

In MS-DOS and some other operating systems, a directory (either the root directory or a subdirectory) that is to be taken as the default in subsequent reference (by a program or a command) to a given disk drive.

The user can change the current directory by using the CHDIR (or CD) command. Although the flexibility of being able to change the default directory is sometimes a convenience, it can also be a source of confusion or error, as in the following examples:

- Many application programs and productivity tools change the current directory during execution, then fail to restore it on exit.

- When the user changes disks in a disk drive, the system remembers the original current directory until the first attempt to reference it.

To avoid confusion, many MS-DOS users have formed the habit of coding an explicit backslash (\) in front of all file names, thus nullifying the effect of any current directory setting.

cursor

A conspicuous symbol on a computer screen showing the exact position at which the next keystroke or mouse click will take effect.

Many programs that process character input display the cursor as a blinking underline character or rectangle within the displayed text. For graphical user interfaces (GUIs), a cursor can also appear in graphical forms that convey additional information to the user. For example, many systems use the following graphical cursors:

- A clock or hourglass cursor indicates that the program is waiting for some external event, such as completion of disk input-output (I/O), and is not ready to accept input from the keyboard or mouse.

- A bidirectional arrow indicates that the mouse is positioned at the border of a displayed window and can now be used to change the size or shape of that window.

cut and paste

The process of selecting and removing a section of text or a graphics image from a file displayed on-screen and then inserting it in another file or in another part of the same file.

For most systems that support cut and paste operations, the user performs these five steps:

1. Select the area to be cut, using the mouse or appropriate keys.

2. Execute the cut operation for the selected area, either by selecting Cut from a menu or by pressing some designated key or combination of keys, often Shift-Del. The cut operation causes the information to be moved to a buffer area called the clipboard.

3. Display the desired destination on the screen, either by shifting to a different window or by scrolling the current window to a different location.

4. Place the cursor at the exact position at which the information is to be inserted, using the mouse or the arrow keys.

5. Execute the paste operation to transfer the information from the clipboard to the position corresponding to the cursor location.

cycle, processing

See *processing cycle.*

cylinder

On a disk device that has multiple surfaces, a set of all tracks at a given radius from the center; the vertical dimension of a disk device.

Most large, magnetic disk devices have a single access mechanism with a separate read-write head for each surface. To minimize movement of the access mechanism, it is customary to allocate space vertically in contiguous cylinders rather than horizontally across each surface.

Diskettes used on desktop computers generally have only a single platter that contains two surfaces. Nevertheless, the term *cylinder* still arises in some contexts—for example, in the MS-DOS FORMAT command, in which the operating system reports its progress in units of cylinders and tracks. On such devices, of course, each cylinder contains only two tracks: one on the top surface and one on the bottom.

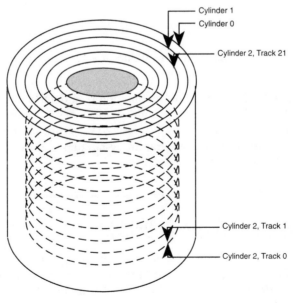

A cylinder.

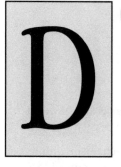

daemon

1. A program operating in the background of the operating system. Daemons normally perform certain repetitive functions, such as controlling the printer. The term, pronounced as "demon," was inspired by the guardian spirits of Greek mythology.

2. A routine of a function that is triggered as a side effect of an event, not directly invoked.

DASD—direct-access storage device

See *disk drive*.

data

Raw facts, often used as input to a program or an application system.

See also *information*.

database

The collection of permanently stored data used by one or more application systems.

A database is usually created and maintained by a database management system (DBMS). Where extremely high performance is required, a database may instead be maintained as a set of related files through the normal input-output (I/O) statements of a programming language. Many simple, small databases are maintained as spreadsheets.

See also *master file*.

database management system—DBMS

1. A major component of system software that provides an interface between application programs and databases. This type of DBMS typically does the following for one or more databases:

Handles all input-output (I/O) operations

Keeps track of the relationships, among records

Generates backup files or archive files when required

Enforces the disciplines needed for security, privacy, and integrity

2. A software product that provides a comprehensive set of tools for developing and operating application systems that build, maintain, or use databases. In addition to the functionality previously described, they typically include the following:

A query processor

A user interface for data entry

A report generator

A programming language (often proprietary) for implementing application logic, computation, and custom interfaces

See also *Access, dBASE, DB2, ORACLE, Paradox, R:Base, relational database, Revelation, SQL,* and *Sybase.*

data dictionary

A repository of data item definitions.

A data dictionary may either be maintained by a single application system development project or be administered centrally in an organization. Although most data dictionaries are computerized (see *data dictionary system*), you can manually create and maintain a data dictionary on paper or index cards.

A data dictionary is not limited to describing the components of databases. All data items used anywhere in a system or referred to in system documentation can be and usually should be defined in a data dictionary.

No standards have been set for the content or structure of a data dictionary. At a minimum, a data dictionary should contain all the information described in the entry on data item definitions.

data dictionary system

A software product for building and maintaining data dictionaries. Most recent data dictionary systems also provide the functionality of a data directory, maintaining for each data item a list of files, programs, documents, and so on, in which the data item appears.

Data dictionary systems span a wide range of capabilities and approaches to defining and managing data. Depending on the vendor's point of view and related products, such systems may be packaged as one of the following:

- A separate (stand-alone) product

- An integrated component of an associated database management system (DBMS)

- A component of a software development (CASE) tool

A stand-alone product may offer greater flexibility, appealing to a large organization that supports central data administration and decentralized application system development. An integrated product may appeal to a project team concerned with one family of application systems.

 It is possible, of course, to build and maintain a data dictionary manually without using a data dictionary system. The advantages of using a data dictionary system are that it relieves systems analysts and data administrators of burdensome work, and that it enforces standards for the form and structural completeness of data item definitions. It cannot, of course, ensure that data item definitions are either complete or correct.

See also *CASE, data dictionary, database management system,* and *stand-alone program.*

DATA DIVISION

The part of a COBOL program containing declarations of data items and files.

COBOL's rigid division structure was originally intended to enforce disciplined program organization. Today, however, many programmers who are well-versed in structured design find the division structure more an impediment to good program organization. In particular, a monolithic DATA DIVISION in which data item declarations are far away from the PROCEDURE DIVISION code that uses them makes it difficult to localize the scope of data.

The actual data declarations are representation-based rather than type-based. Newer languages such as Pascal and Ada, as well as object-oriented languages such as C++, emphasize the type or class to which a data item belongs, whereas COBOL's PICTURE attribute simply defines what a data item looks like in the computer.

See also *block structure.*

data-driven programming

A variety of structured programming in which the hierarchy of modules and the flow of control in each module are derived directly from the structure of the data on which the program operates.

data-flow diagram—DFD

A graphical representation of the relationships among the components of a system.

Data-flow diagrams are the central product of structured analysis. A DFD contains elements of four types:

- Processes: active elements (functions, activities) that transform data from one form to another

- Data stores: passive elements that hold data for an unspecified duration

- Terminators: representations of users or other interfaces outside the boundary of the system

- Data flows: composite data items that move between a process and another process, a data store, or a terminator connecting other elements

Proponents claim that a good DFD should be intuitively clear to a manager or prospective end user without any special training. Such people can then understand exactly what a proposed new system will do before they commit funds to developing or purchasing software. The degree to which people really do understand DFDs depends both on their own willingness to examine the diagrams conscientiously and on the quality of the data-flow diagrams.

In structured analysis, a "logical data-flow diagram" describes a system from an abstract point of view, showing only what occurs. A "physical data-flow diagram" also shows who performs each function, which functions are automated and which are manual, and what organizations are involved in each activity. Note that "physical" has a very narrow meaning in this context; a physical data-flow diagram specifies nothing about programs, files, or other physical aspects of an eventual implementation of the system.

Although most writers on structured analysis agree on the purpose and content of data-flow diagrams, they use several different sets of symbols for the four types of elements. Although the symbolic representation of each element may vary from set to set, most people who have worked with DFDs for any length of time will recognize and be able to interpret the diagrams.

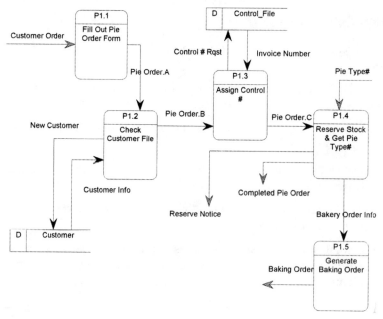

A typical data-flow diagram.

See also *decomposition* and *mini-spec*.

data item definition

An exact specification, either written or stored in a data dictionary system, of a data item.

A lack of rigor in defining of data items is a common source of serious trouble in developing application systems. In defining any data item, you must specify the following:

- A unique name.

- Its purpose or exact meaning in the real world.

- The class (the type, generic subtype, and so on) to which it belongs and from which it inherits already standardized properties. (The use of classes is mandatory with object-oriented analysis, and is always highly recommended.)

- Any security, audit, privacy, or access restrictions to be applied.

If the item is a composite data item, listing its components usually provides sufficient data item definition. Structured analysis textbooks have proposed a number of notations for listing such components, but no such notation has become standard. Some data dictionary systems provide their own standard notation.

 Some data dictionary systems and low-end database management systems (DBMS) still use a representation-based way of classifying data, rather than a true hierarchy of types. If the tool you're using insists on knowing the "length of" or "number of positions in" a numeric item rather than its range and precision, or if it classifies U.S. Post Office ZIP codes as "numeric," it probably lacks support for data classes.

If the item is an elementary data item, you must be particularly careful that its meaning is precise and unambiguous. Depending on the type of item, you may have to specify further information, such as encoding schemes, units of measure, and range.

See also *data dictionary* and *self-defining name*.

data processing—DP

1. The systematic transformation of data, usually involving a computer system, to produce a set of outputs.

2. A common name for a department or service organization supplying computer services to users within a larger organization.

This is the most general term for the running of application systems. In some circles, however, the term is now considered somewhat old-fashioned. Once-common variants emphasizing business applications, ADP and EDP (automatic and electronic data processing, respectively), are now considered dated and are rarely used.

Near synonyms include *computing, information processing,* and *information systems.*

Data Processing Management Association

See *DPMA.*

data representation

The set of choices determining how a data item (elementary or composite) is to be stored, recorded, or transmitted.

A data item used in an application system may have more than one representation in that system:

- Its internal representation appears in databases, master files, temporary files, programs, or other places where system users cannot see the representation directly.

- One or more external representations may appear on input transactions, screen displays, printed reports, forms, or other places where users of the system can see the representations.

Conversion from external representation to internal representation is done by an editing program. Conversion from internal to external representation is handled by report generators or output display modules.

The criteria for choosing external and internal data representations are very different. Designers should choose external representations that are familiar and natural to the users, traditional in the application area, and, for input, not error-prone. Internal representations, on the other hand, should be simple, easy to manipulate in program logic, and efficient to store and process.

These choices can have a significant impact on the maintainability and performance of software and large databases.

See also *data item definition, data representation standard, data type,* and *user-friendliness.*

data representation standard

A required or preferred data representation for all data items belonging to a particular class.

An organization may establish data representation standards for common classes of data in that organization. Such local standards facilitate data interchange among different application systems and platforms, simplify program and database design, and foster exploitation of reusable modules. In an object-oriented design, the internal representations are encapsulated within class definitions, thus assuring compliance and facilitating both reuse and future change.

Various industry groups and standards organizations disseminate global data representation standards to promote data interchange. Although compliance with such industry standards is voluntary within any organization, contracts or regulations may require compliance for data sent from one organization to another. A growing collection are the EDI (Electronic Data Interchange) standards.

data segment

A portion of memory reserved during execution for data; that is, memory that is not used for instructions.

First- and second-generation computers stored instructions and data in the same address space, relying only on the flow of control to distinguish between them. Indeed, the power of the stored-program concept was then attributed to a program's capability to modify itself. Programmers soon recognized, however, that dynamic modification of instructions seriously complicated program testing and was an obstacle to software reliability. Furthermore, it is impractical to implement re-entrant or recursive programs in which the actual instructions are changed during execution.

Third-generation computers' flexible use of registers for addressing rendered most self-modification by programs unnecessary (although still possible). This led some compiler designers to generate separately a code segment and data segment, with the former often protected against modification (even by itself). Later, the limited 16-bit addressability of micro-computers forced compiler designers to follow that example to enable programmers to develop programs of reasonable size. This approach is now well established and remains common practice, even with today's larger (32-bit) address spaces.

data set

A named collection of records.

Although *data set* has become a near synonym of *file,* the term was introduced to clarify a basic distinction between the following:

- A file as the generic entity seen by a program (such as a back-order file)

- A data set as a specific physical occurrence of that file (such as the November back orders for the Western Region)

Some operating systems (such as OS/360) provide a facility in the job control language (JCL) to associate (for a given run) the file name in the program with a specific data set name stored on a magnetic medium. Other operating systems (such as MS-DOS) treat the file name and the data set name as equivalent, thus contributing to an erosion of the distinction between the terms.

data set label

One or more records describing the content of a data set or file, physically recorded either at the beginning of the file or in a separate directory or VTOC. A data set label typically contains the following:

- The data set name

- The date and time the data set was created or last updated

The data set label may also specify the following:

- Password or access information

- Record format, length, and blocking information

- A retention period or expiration date

The practice of including a machine-readable label with files recorded on magnetic media became commonplace with the coming of third-generation computer systems like the IBM 360 series. The label's purpose is to eliminate run failures caused by human error in mounting tape reels or setting up jobs.

data structure

A programming structure that defines a data block.

data type

The type of data contained by a specific variable. For instance, the data type of a variable could be integer, which indicates that the variable will contain only integer values within a certain range.

Depending on the language, data types are either implicitly or explicitly declared in a program. The compiler implements implicit declaration by examining how the variable is first used, and then assumes that this usage defines which data type the variable is to use. Explicit declaration, on the other hand, is accomplished through specific declaratory statements, such as the following (from the C programming language):

```
int i, j;
```

This statement defines the data type of the variables i and j as integer.

data type conversion

See *conversion, data type.*

data validation

The process of verifying that input data items conform to their specifications.

Data entered by human operators or originating from unreliable sources, such as analog to digital conversion equipment, must be checked before being stored in a database or used in a process or calculation.

A systems analyst shouldn't need to specify routine validation rules implied by the data type and the data item definition. Experienced programmers should always include code that checks every input data item to confirm the following:

- That the syntax conforms to the data type; for example, that the input value of a numeric data item is actually numeric.

- That the value lies within the allowable range; for example, that HOURS WORKED for a given day is neither negative nor greater than 24.

- That the value is consistent with other data items from the same input transaction; for example, that a new employee has not passed retirement age.

- That the value is consistent with data in the database (if the database is online during data validation); for example, that a retired employee is not applying for maternity leave.

If the programmers are known to be competent, the systems analyst needs to specify only any custom editing rules that go beyond these standard ones.

See also *editing program.*

date representation

Any data representation used to represent calendar dates.

The representation of dates has generated confusion out of proportion to its actual difficulty. Inappropriate choices add to the complexity of programs and seriously threaten the reliability of many application systems.

The traditional mixed-base representations (MM/DD/YY, DD-MM-YY, YYMMDD, and their four-digit-year counterparts) are appropriate for external representations (as in user-supplied inputs and in reports), but seldom for internal representations (as in programs and permanent files). It is awkward and error-prone to perform arithmetic on dates in such formats, or (except for YYMMDD) even to compare two such dates. Errors in supposedly tested software are all too common in such functions as leap-year adjustments.

In particular, considerable apprehension exists regarding the behavior of application systems in which two-digit-year representations are stored in databases. Many such systems were designed many years ago by people who didn't expect them to remain in use at the turn of the century. When such systems first encounter input data with years of 00, 01, and so on, they may behave incorrectly or even lose control in an ABEND.

The simplest and most flexible internal date representation is a simple serial number, an integer (32-bit) count of the number of days elapsed since an arbitrary but standard origin. Although business application systems have been slow to adopt this representation, its use in popular spreadsheet processors and database management systems (DBMS) has recently revived interest in this form of date as a preferred representation in databases, other permanent files, and programs.

DB2

An IBM database management system (DBMS) based on the relational model. DB2 originally was implemented on mainframe computers, then later made available on other platforms, including OS/2.

dBASE

A family of database management systems (DBMS) for MS-DOS originated by Ashton-Tate and currently the property of Borland International. dBASE IV supports the relational database model.

Like many other DBMS products, dBASE also provides a proprietary procedural language for programming.

See also *Paradox* and *Access*.

DBMS

See *database management system*.

DCL—digital command language

The operating system command language for VAX/VMS.

See also *cataloged procedure* and *command language*.

DDE—Dynamic Data Exchange

A proprietary method used in Microsoft Windows and OS/2 for linking data created and maintained by one program into a file processed by a different program.

DDE is initiated by the user, but unlike the cut and paste process, it needs to be set up only once. If your word processor and spreadsheet processor both support DDE, for example, you can establish a link so that the most recent values of certain data in a spreadsheet always appear in a designated place in a word processing document.

See also *cut and paste, edition,* and *OLE.*

deadlock

A condition in which each of two (or more) concurrent processes requests a resource currently held by the other, and neither process will release the resources it already holds until its request for the additional resource is satisfied.

Deadlock may be encountered in multiprogramming situations in which resources are allocated dynamically, such as the following:

- By an operating system in assigning devices such as tape drives to jobs

- By a database management system (DBMS) in retrieving and locking records for updating

Robust software is expected to avoid or prevent deadlock, or at least to detect it after it occurs and to recover from it with minimum disruption and delay. This may require highly sophisticated techniques, and in some cases no fully satisfactory solution to the deadlock problem is known.

debug

To diagnose and correct bugs in software.

This term has been criticized for having a negative connotation: that bugs are to be expected. Many experts now prefer to describe this process of assuring correctness in software by using the neutral term *testing* or the more positive term *validation.*

debugger

A program that assists the programmer in unit testing by supporting various kinds of interaction between a programmer and a running program. A debugger is often specific to a particular compiler or family of compilers from a particular vendor.

The programming community is divided on the value of debuggers. Some programmers rely routinely on a debugger for nearly all nontrivial programming. Because debuggers can be complex and hard to learn, such programmers often invest considerable effort in mastering the capabilities of their debugger, but such a one-time effort, they assert, is amply repaid in future productivity.

Other programmers maintain that debuggers encourage sloppy habits, and that a well-structured, highly modular program should be easy to test straightforwardly without such aids. Some strong advocates of structured programming add that good programmers using disciplined methods generate very few bugs in the first place.

Debuggers are probably most useful in programs that manipulate dynamic data structures (lists, trees, and so on) or that implement highly recursive strategies with backtracking.

decimal

The common numbering system using 10 as its base.

Some languages provide a decimal data type, to avoid imprecision generated when fractional values are converted between decimal and binary.

See also *binary, hexadecimal,* and *octal.*

decision table

A technique for documenting and analyzing complex logic as a compact table of conditions and actions.

A common form of decision table has the following structure:

- The condition part on top of lists, in the leftmost column, English descriptions of the independent conditions.

- The action part at the bottom of lists, in the leftmost column, English descriptions of the actions.

- Columns at the right, one for every possible combination of conditions, specify the following:

  In the condition part, the possible combinations of true or false values for the conditions listed at the left (using Ys and Ns or an equivalent notation)

  In the action part, check marks indicating whether the action specified at the left on that row is to be performed for the combination of true or false values above in that column

This is easiest to see in a concrete example. Consider the following well-known example taken from Gane and Sarson's *Structured Systems Analysis* (Prentice Hall, 1979):

  Customers who place more than $10,000 business per year and have a good payment history or have been with us more than 20 years are to receive priority treatment.

Although this example is deliberately ambiguous (what is a "good payment history"?) and trivial (because there's only one action), it serves to illustrate several techniques for documenting decision logic. Here's the corresponding decision table:

	1	2	3	4	5	6	7	8
C1: More than $10,000 per year	Y	Y	Y	Y	N	N	N	N
C2: Good payment history	Y	Y	N	N	Y	Y	N	N
C3: With us more than 20 years	Y	N	Y	N	Y	N	Y	N
A1: Give priority treatment	*	*	*					
A2: Give normal treatment				*	*	*	*	*

After preparing such a decision table, the systems analyst may look for ways to simplify it. In this case, the analyst notices that the actions under columns 1 and 2 are the same, as are the actions under columns 4 through 8, so that the columns can be combined as follows:

	1, 2	3	4	5, 6, 7, 8
C1: More than $10,000 per year	Y	Y	Y	N
C2: Good payment history	Y	N	N	_
C3: With us more than 20 years	_	Y	N	_
A1: Give priority treatment	*	*		
A2: Give normal treatment			*	*

where the dashes signify "indifference" to a condition.

Although the main use of decision tables is for documentation and analysis, tools exist for generating source code from them automatically. In the 1960s, such "decision table processors" typically generated COBOL code that could then be embedded in a program. Today, decision table handling is integrated into some CASE tools.

Alternatives to decision tables include decision trees and structured English.

decision tree

A diagram that represents in tree form a set of interdependent conditions and actions.

The purpose of a decision tree, like that of a decision table, is to document complex decision logic. Here, for example, is a decision tree representation of the same example shown in the *decision table* entry:

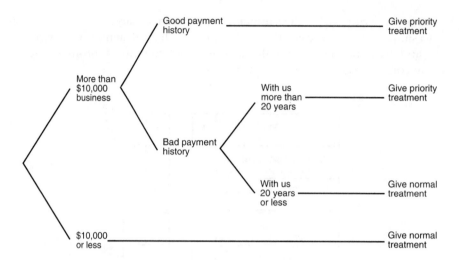

Decision trees are useful in fewer situations than decision tables, for the following reasons:

- A decision tree, unlike a decision table, specifies a sequence for testing the conditions.

- A decision tree may have to repeat some of the conditions and actions, as the example illustrates.

- A decision tree with more than three or four conditions becomes unwieldy and too large to fit on standard paper and screens.

See also *decision table*.

declaration

A programming language statement used to establish an identifier name and associate attributes with it.

Declarations are also used to describe the number and type of arguments passed to functions or subprograms.

See also *implicit declaration*.

decode

To undo, according to a known algorithm, the result of a previously applied encoding operation.

See also *encode* and *encrypt*.

decomposition

The process of subdividing a data-flow diagram (DFD) into a hierarchy of lower-level data-flow diagrams.

A data-flow diagram becomes almost impossible to grasp if it contains more than about ten processes and data stores. To keep the diagrams understandable, the systems analyst must begin by specifying processes at a very high level of detail. For each of the processes on a high-level DFD, the analyst then prepares a separate expanded lower-level DFD. This decomposition continues until the analyst reaches a level at which the purpose of each process on the lowest-level DFDs is obvious.

See also *stepwise refinement*.

default

An assumption made in the absence of explicit information. In programming, the term often refers to the values of options and input parameters.

The term *default* is often used as an adjective. For example, the default font is a font to be used when the user doesn't specify a font, and the default directory is the directory to be assumed for any unqualified file name.

default attribute

An attribute assumed by a compiler (or a data dictionary system) for a data item whose declaration is either missing (see *implicit declaration*) or incomplete.

Although many programming languages require explicit declaration of all data items, most allow a declaration to omit certain options that the language designers believe programmers would choose most of the time. Among established languages, PL/1 has by far the most elaborate structure of default attributes. A well-known example in C++ is the assumption that class members are private unless explicitly declared public or protected.

 A notorious, ill-advised choice of default attribute is COBOL's assumption that all numeric data items are to be stored in external-character (DISPLAY) representation if the programmer omits the keyword COMPUTATIONAL. When the programmer forgets to specify this attribute explicitly, the program still works, but often with severely degraded performance due to the overhead of repeated data conversion.

In object-oriented programming (OOP), the programmer who defines a class can sometimes provide for default attributes by either establishing alternative constructors to be used when certain parameters are missing, or establishing default values for one or more initialization parameters.

default value

A value assigned to an input data item when the user does not enter any overriding value.

If default values are used judiciously, a program can free the user from having to do the following:

- Re-enter options, parameters, and other data that do not change from run to run

- Enter information that merely confirms the choices that most users prefer

- Know about the existence of rarely used options

 Some people refer to "changing the default" when they simply mean overriding the default value. If you "change" a default, the new value becomes the default value for future runs. Many software products provide this second-level capability as well: a "default default" (set by the vendor), the capability to change the default (set by the installer), and the capability to override the default (set by the user).

defragment

A utility operation performed on a disk file to rewrite it as a contiguous block. This operation can significantly improve performance, especially if the file is badly fragmented or is heavily accessed. Abbreviated as *defrag*.

Some file systems do not allocate space on an as-needed basis; for such systems, space for each file must be preallocated, so fragmentation does not occur. However, most modern file systems allocate file space dynamically as the program issues requests to write new records. If you change the file contents often when using these systems, fragmentation will occur. Such fragmentation impairs performance because sequential access will require frequent repositioning of the disk access mechanism.

Popular utility packages provide defragmentation routines that determine, either for a single file or more often for an entire disk, whether defragmentation is needed and then, if necessary, perform it.

defun—define function

The LISP primitive used to define a function.

Defining a function in LISP is like defining a function or subroutine in a procedural language. You give the function a name and a list of parameters (dummy arguments), and then specify the result in terms of LISP primitives, previously defined functions, and sometimes (recursively) the function being defined.

For example, the following trivial function squares a number:

```
(defun square (X) (* X X))
```

The following example is a more interesting recursive function that raises a number X to the positive integer power N:

```
(defun power (X  N)
  (cond ((> =  0  N)          1)
        (( =  0 (mod N 2)) (square (power X (/ N 2))))
         t                 (*  X   (power X (- N 1)))  ))
```

Now the result of evaluating, for example, (power 2 5) will be 32.

delimiter

A constant, usually a single or double character, used to mark the end of a syntactic element or to separate two syntactic elements.

In text and in most programming languages, blanks, parentheses, and other punctuation marks are delimiters. In many programming languages, operators and various bracketing symbols are also delimiters. Note that many symbols (such as the plus sign in ALPHA+BETA) act both as a delimiter and a meaningful language element.

Application software often must recognize and process delimiters when processing input transactions that permit variable-length fields or variable numbers of fields.

See also *comment delimiter, parse, syntax,* and *token.*

demodulate

To sense variations in an analog signal and convert them to digital information for presentation to a computer's input-output (I-O) subsystem. A common example of a demodulator is a receiving modem (the "dem" in *modem* is an abbreviation of *demodulator*).

De Morgan's Laws

Logical identities expressing the distributivity of negation (NOT) over conjunction (AND) and disjunction (OR).

For example, if p and q are logical (true or false) expressions, then

NOT (p AND q) is equivalent to (NOT p) OR (NOT q)

NOT (p OR q) is equivalent to (NOT p) AND (NOT q)

Another form of De Morgan's laws applies to set membership rather than logical expressions. This form expresses the distributivity of the complement (~) operation over intersection (_) and union (U).

For example, if S and T are sets, then

~ (S ∩ T) _ ~S U ~T

~ (S U T) _ ~S ∩ ~T

Programmers may have to apply these laws to simplify compound conditional statements in procedural programming languages, in rule bases, and in SQL or similar database retrieval requests.

deque—double-ended queue

A dynamic linear data structure in which items can be added to or removed from either end.

See also *queue, stack,* and *list.*

dereference

To remove a level of indirect addressing; that is, to substitute a pointer with the thing to which it is pointing.

Some programming languages support implicit dereferencing as a special case of coercion. For example, suppose that X is a data item of type T, and that a data item of type T is legal. The program code, however, instead has a pointer to an item of type T. If the compiler allows this and generates object code to use the actual item X, it supports implicit dereferencing. In some cases this process can extend to multiple levels (that is, a pointer to a pointer to a data item of type T).

Most languages that provide any support of pointers also support explicit dereferencing under the programmer's control, such as the use of the C language's unary * (contents of) operator.

derived class

In object-oriented programming (OOP), a class that inherits properties from another (base) class. See the example under *base class.*

derived constant

The result of a function or formula applied to other constants.

Note the following C code:

```
#define   chars_per_line   72
#define   lines_per_page   58
#define   chars_per_page   chars_per_line * lines_per_page
```

The last constant, `chars_per_page`, is a derived constant. Its value is changed automatically whenever the programmer changes the value of either of the two fundamental constants on which it depends.

designer

An individual responsible for determining the internal structure of a program or set of programs. The term is a near synonym of *chief programmer*.

For an application system, the designer's responsibilities usually include the following:

- Establishing the project's programming standards
- Choosing or designing data structures and algorithms suited to the problems
- Specifying and perhaps developing program modules related to the use of the data structures and algorithms
- Dividing the system into individual complete programs and rigorously specifying those programs
- Decomposing each complete program into major modules, then specifying those modules

In addition, the designer may specify or propose some or all aspects of the user interface, if a systems analyst has not already done so.

device

A name representing a physical or logical hardware component to the computer system. For instance, on MS-DOS and UNIX systems, the CON device represents the console (video monitor and keyboard), and the PRN device represents the printer.

Devices can be used to designate the source of input or the destination of output from other commands or programs.

See also *redirection*.

device driver

A program, usually considered part of an operating system, that provides an interface between a particular kind of hardware device and the rest of the operating system.

Device drivers localize knowledge of the detailed characteristics of a device, so that application programs can use a wide range of functionally similar devices in a simple and standard way.

Drivers come from several sources:

- Drivers for widely used, standard devices are usually included in the operating system, as distributed by the software vendor.

- Drivers for new or unusual devices are provided by the hardware vendor.

- Software products, such as word processors, designed to operate under MS-DOS or another small operating system, may include their own drivers, especially for supporting a wide range of printers.

MS-DOS includes several standard device drivers, such as HIMEM.SYS (an XMS memory driver), EMM386.SYS (an EMS memory driver), RAM disks, and cache programs. The CONFIG.SYS file specifies which of these drivers is to be loaded and activated.

See also *device-independent*.

device-independent

Able to operate with a variety of peripheral hardware.

For example, a report generator that can print a given report on any of several different kinds of printers is device-independent.

Application programs that properly use published operating system interfaces and standard device drivers, and that avoid taking advantage of unusual features of a particular device, usually are device-independent.

See also *device driver* and *version dependency*.

desktop

A metaphor in graphical user interface (GUI) systems to suggest a correspondence between managing icons and windows on a screen and managing real objects on one's desk.

See also *control panel.*

desktop computer

See *personal computer.*

destructor

In object-oriented programming (OOP), a function that destroys or deletes an object.

See also *constructor.*

diagnostic message

A message that a program displays when it encounters erroneous input.

All programs that process input prepared by human beings should validate the correctness of that input. Such programs include the following:

- Editing programs that validate input transactions to an application system

- Compilers and assemblers that translate source code written by a programmer

- Productivity tools such as spreadsheet processors and word processors that respond to data and commands entered by the user

- Operating systems and other programs that execute commands specified by a user

The quality of diagnostic messages is an essential consideration in user-friendly software. A good diagnostic message pinpoints the most likely location of the error and describes exactly what is wrong. Vague diagnostic messages such as "syntax error," "illegal function," or "error in line 61" are a common cause of dissatisfaction among software users.

diagramming template

A stiff paper or plastic form used to draw diagrams.

Programmers and systems analysts use diagramming templates to draw flow-charts, data-flow diagrams, and entity-relationship diagrams. A template makes it easy to prepare neat and attractive graphical documentation containing standarized symbols. However, such documentation is nearly impossible to maintain manually, because you must redraw an entire diagram whenever you change anything on it. Therefore, diagramming templates are being supplanted by software CASE tools that support the same kinds of diagramming.

dialog box

A window that a program displays to prompt a reply from the user.

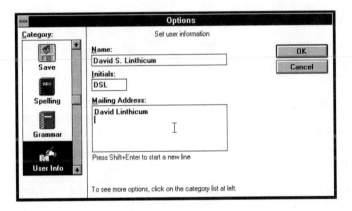

A dialog box.

Many graphical user interface (GUI) systems use the following dialog box elements to obtain input from the user:

- A command button initiates some action (or cancels the dialog box).

- A list box displays a list of alternatives from which the user must select one.

- A check box displays a list of options from which the user may check all that apply.

- A radio button displays a list of mutually exclusive options from which the user must choose only one.

- A text box solicits a free text reply.

- A combo box combines a list box and a text box.

In any of these elements, a default value may be highlighted initially, so that a user who doesn't need to override the defaults can simply press Enter or click the OK button.

See also *menu, input transaction,* and *user-friendliness.*

DIF—data interchange format

A standard representation for spreadsheet files, originally developed with VisiCalc.

digital computer

A computer that stores and processes data represented by discrete values. Almost all general-purpose computers are digital, and the word *computer* by itself has some to mean "digital computer."

The other major kind of computer is an analog computer, which represents data in the form of voltages or some other continuously variable quantity. In the 1940s, analog computers were applied to solving numerical problems. Today, however, they are applied mainly to a few specialized applications that process continuously measured input.

Because analog technology is based on approximate measurements, it is inherently less accurate than digital technology.

digital signal

A transmission signal that carries information in discrete states (usually two).

See also *analog signal.*

DIR

Command in MS-DOS and OS/2 to display a directory: the list of files and subdirectories and their attributes.

direct access device

An auxiliary storage device that can move from one location to another without having to move through all the intermediate locations.

Most modern direct access devices are disk drives. A disk read-write mechanism can move within milliseconds directly to the desired track.

See also *direct access file, keyed file,* and *sequential file.*

direct access file

A file whose records can be accessed by location within the file, independent of the location of the most recently accessed record.

The program must have a method to derive the location of a desired record, and the access method used must be capable of nonsequential access. Direct access files are almost always implemented on disk units.

See also *keyed file* and *ISAM.*

directive

See *compiler directive.*

directory

A list of file names, used in file management subsystems of operating systems.

In many operating systems (including MS-DOS, VAX VMS, UNIX, and OS/2), directories form a hierarchy. Each directory can contain both lower-level directories and file names. Some operating systems call directories *catalogs* or *folders.*

dirty bit

A hardware indicator used in paging to record that a page was modified while in memory.

The dirty bit contributes significantly to the efficiency of paging. Here's how it works:

1. When the operating system loads a new page into memory, the dirty bit for that page is turned off.

2. Whenever a program stores data in memory, hardware circuitry automatically turns on the dirty bit for the corresponding page.

3. Paging algorithms can then examine the dirty bits for any page that is a candidate for replacement in memory, as follows:

> If a given dirty bit is off, its contents must be exactly the same as the copy originally loaded from disk. Therefore, another page can safely be loaded into the same area of memory without destroying any information.

> However, if a given dirty bit is on, the operating system must first rewrite that page onto disk before loading another page into the same area.

See also *LRU*.

discrete data item

A non-numeric data item that can take on any of a finite set of possible values.

If the number of possible values is small and all the current values are known during design, a discrete data item is also an *enumerated item.* Examples of enumerated items might include the following:

- Marital status (single, married, divorced, widowed, unknown)

- Sex (male, female, unknown)

- Region (U.S. East, U.S. Central, U.S. West, Europe, South America, Pacific, unknown)

Examples of discrete data items that are not enumerated items might include the following:

- social_security_number
- ZIP_code
- product_id

See also *code, data item definition, enum,* and *numeric data type.*

discrete data type

In the C programming language, a user-defined data type that may have any of a number of values. For instance, a variable may be defined to indicate the sex of an individual. This may only have the values M, F, or U (for unknown).

See also *enumeration* and *enum.*

disinfect

To remove a virus from a computer system.

To disinfect a computer, the user can either use special software to remove the computer virus from the computer system's memory and auxiliary storage or reinstall the operating system and application software from scratch.

Software products are available that detect the presence of certain known computer viruses.

See also *infect.*

disk

The most common auxiliary storage medium for all types of computer systems. The term usually refers to a magnetic disk, but newer technologies, such as optical disks, offer even higher capacity.

As disks rotate, the read-write heads positioned over the disk can read information from any track very quickly. Like all magnetic media, disks can be read from, written to, and erased repeatedly.

The surface of each disk is divided into tracks (similar to a record album). However, each track meets to form a circle. Tracks are further separated into sectors. When you update a disk, a sector is first read into the computer's memory and altered. The operating system is responsible for maintaining the information on disk.

See also *cylinder, fixed disk,* and *floppy disk.*

disk crash

An undesirable occurrence when the head of a disk drive falls onto the rotating disk, thus destroying information on the disk.

disk drive

A storage device that contains, rotates, reads, and writes a magnetic or optical disk.

The disks can be either permanently mounted within the disk drive (a fixed disk) or removable (a floppy disk).

diskette

See *floppy disk.*

display

A monitor or equivalent output device having a screen.

The term *monitor* usually connotes a separate device, whereas a *display* can be any kind of screen. On most portable computers, the display is built-in, and is implemented in LCD (liquid crystal display), gas plasma, or electro-luminescent technology.

DISPLAY

1. The COBOL data attribute specifying internal representation as a character string. See also *COMPUTATIONAL.*

2. The COBOL verb to send data to a standard output stream.

Although standard COBOL limits the DISPLAY verb to data items declared with the DISPLAY usage attribute, some compiler vendors have removed this restriction, allowing numeric (COMPUTATIONAL) items as well. Programs can then use the DISPLAY verb for debugging output, as in the following example:

```
DISPLAY   TRANSACTION-TYPE, CHANGED-RECORD-COUNT,
          NEW-RECORD-COUNT, DELETED-RECORD-COUNT;
```

display adapter

A circuit board providing the video signal required to display or generate text and graphics on a screen. Other names for display adapter include graphics adapter, graphics card, video adapter, video card, video board, and video controller.

This device typically contains additional memory that is reserved for video use. A program can access the memory and associated video circuitry either directly or through a device driver program. Data stored in video memory is converted into signals that appear on the screen. Display adapters produce two kinds of output, depending on the type of system: digital output, such as monochrome, CGA, and EGA, and analog output, such as VGA, Super VGA, and XGA.

See also *EGA* and *VGA.*

distributed database

A database regarded conceptually as a single collection of data, but physically stored in multiple locations under the local control of different computers. Those local computers are often connected in a network, so that any user can access any record regardless of where it is stored.

See also *client-server architecture* and *distributed processing.*

distributed processing

Implementation of a single application system on multiple computer configurations in different locations, often under different operating platforms and usually connected in a network.

The goals of distributed processing are to optimize the cost, responsiveness, availability, and reliability of application systems that have users at workstations at multiple sites. In a successful implementation, a system appears to the user as a unified whole, and the user is unaware of the coordination and data transmissions taking place behind the scenes.

See also *client-server architecture* and *distributed database.*

.DLL

A Microsoft Windows file name extension for a file that contains a program to be loaded dynamically when another program invokes it.

See also *dynamic call.*

DMA—direct memory access

A microprocessor that transfers data from one portion of memory to another without using the central processing unit (CPU).

DMA is usually associated with input-output (I/O) operations related to devices such as floppy disk drives, cartridge tape drives, CD-ROM, or SCSI host adapters. One problem you might have while installing these types of devices is called a *DMA conflict.* This conflict occurs when two or more installed devices are attempting to use the same DMA channel. After the DMA-utilizing devices are moved to their own channels, the devices should operate correctly.

In many second- and third-generation computers, the corresponding facility was called a "data channel."

documentation

Written material describing an application system or software product.

Different kinds and levels of permanent documentation are addressed to different audiences:

- User documentation consists of reference manuals, tutorial manuals, and online help facilities. It should describe everything a user needs to know to understand and use all features of the software.

- Maintenance documentation consists of anything a maintenance programmer may need in order to understand the internal structure of the software and the techniques used. It may include design documents such as structure charts, file specifications, screen layouts, and commented source code listings.

- Operational documentation consists of information needed to install, configure, and efficiently operate the software. For software intended for a single-user machine (desktop computer), it is often integrated with the user documentation; for software to be run on a network or a mainframe, it is usually packaged separately for support specialists.

In addition, during the course of the system development life cycle (SDLC) certain documentation is produced that may or may not be retained permanently. Of particular importance are the detailed user requirements and the functional specification.

In a modern software product, much of the documentation may be in the form of computer-based information rather than hard copy material. Whatever medium is used, however, the reader should always be able to find relevant material quickly. A recent, unfortunate phenomenon is the lack of any accessible documentation of the processing logic or file designs generated through interaction between the programmer and certain CASE products or other high-level tools.

domain

The set of possible input arguments for which a function or module gives meaningful results. For example, the domain of a square root function is the set of non-negative real numbers.

Some experts strongly recommend that every module check its arguments before using them to make sure that their values are within the expected domain. Other experts argue that such checking demands unreasonable overhead when a program's input data items have already been validated by an editing program. Some compilers (including Ada, Pascal, and those associated with object-oriented languages) can automatically generate such checking in many situations, if the programmer has used data types or classes that exactly correspond to the intended domain.

See also *range*.

DOS—disk operating system (Apple)

The operating system for the Apple II series of desktop computers. This DOS bears no relation to MS-DOS, which is often informally referred to as "DOS."

DOS—disk operating system (IBM)

The most widely used operating system for smaller IBM mainframe computer systems. This DOS bears no relation to the later MS-DOS for Intel-based desktop computers, which is often informally referred to as "DOS."

The origin and subsequent development of DOS and its successor DOS/VSE had a huge impact on the efficiency of computer center operations in thousands of organizations.

In introducing the System/360 in 1964, IBM intended that a single operating system, OS/360, would run on models having at least 32K of memory. For very small (8K or 16K) machines, IBM provided the primitive BOS (Basic Operating System). Because the user communities for the two operating systems were thought to be separate, no one paid much attention to compatibility between them. As a result, BOS and OS, designed and developed by different groups at IBM, diverged in numerous ways.

It turned out that the full OS/360 needed 64K to run at all, and 256K to run well. Many organizations that had ordered 32K, 64K, and 128K configurations returned to BOS instead of ordering additional, expensive memory. IBM responded by enhancing BOS, splitting it into TOS (Tape Operating System), for the smallest machines with no disks, and DOS (Disk Operating System), which resides on and utilizes disk storage.

As those organizations began to outgrow the capabilities of DOS, it was natural for them to convert to OS. However, because of the incompatibilities between the two operating systems, such conversions were extremely expensive and disruptive. Rather than undergo the pain of conversion, many organizations pressured IBM to extend DOS further to support larger-scale, multiprogrammed operations.

The longer an organization using DOS delayed conversion to OS, the more jobs, programs, and files they had to convert. Many organizations never did make the transition, and ended up running DOS on machines having a megabyte or more of memory. Thus IBM mainframe users were permanently split into two incompatible communities.

DOS—disk operating system (Intel)

An informal name for MS-DOS. This DOS bears no relation to the earlier IBM mainframe DOS.

See *MS-DOS.*

DOS extender

Software that enables an MS-DOS application to use extended memory (XMS) above the Intel CPU's 1024K boundary.

DOS extenders exploit the protected mode of an 80×86 processor. They intercept requests by the application program for services from the operating system, and either pass them on to MS-DOS in real mode or simulate their effect.

Many software products use DOS extenders to increase performance and to use memory more effectively.

See also *VCPI, DPMI,* and *paged memory.*

DOS prompt

See *command prompt.*

DOS window

In a multiprogramming operating platform that supports compatibility with MS-DOS, a window running DOS emulation. Windows and OS/2 both provide DOS windows.

A DOS window gives the user access to the usual MS-DOS command prompt. The user can then invoke any of the standard MS-DOS commands as well as any application program written to run under MS-DOS. (However, some programs that violate MS-DOS conventions may not run correctly.)

dot-matrix printer

An impact printer utilizing a pattern of dots to form characters and graphics on paper.

This inexpensive device, which is still widely used, uses one or two columns of pins, striking the paper through a ribbon saturated with ink; the more pins used, the sharper the printed image. Dot-matrix printers commonly are available in 9-, 18-, and 24-pin configurations.

Laser printers provide better quality and much quieter operation than dot-matrix printers, usually at higher initial and operating costs.

dot product

An operation on a pair of numeric vectors of equal length, yielding a scalar result, the sum of the pairwise products of the elements.

If

$$X = (x_1, x_2, \ldots, x_n)$$

and

$$Y = (y_1, y_2, \ldots, y_n)$$

then

$$X \bullet Y = \_ (x_i * y_i), \text{ from } i = 1 \text{ to } n$$

For example:

$$(3,1,4,-2) \bullet (5,2,4,3) = 15+2+16-6 = 27$$

Some programming languages and spreadsheet processors provide a dot product function. If no built-in function is available, the programmer must write an explicit loop to compute the required sum.

See also *scalar* and *vector*.

double-click

To click the mouse button twice very quickly.

The double-click is used to invoke applications under many graphical user interfaces (GUIs) such as Windows. When the cursor arrow is moved over a icon representing a program, the user simply double-clicks on the icon to start that program in a new window.

Also see *click, mouse,* and *mouse button.*

double linked list

See *linked list, double.*

double precision

A floating-point number requiring two words (eight bytes). In many implementations, double precision offers precision equivalent to 16 decimal digits, instead of only 6 provided by single precision.

See also *numeric data type.*

do until

A loop construct in which the body of the loop is executed at least once; that is, the termination test follows the body of the loop.

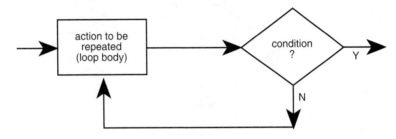

A do until loop.

This construct is used less often than do while, because it can't "do nothing," as in the event of an empty input file. Nevertheless, there are situations where a program must do something at least once regardless of the input.

Although do until is the usual term in the literature of structured programming, programming languages use a variety of terminology and syntax for the loop:

Language	Before Loop Body	After Loop Body
BASIC	DO	LOOP UNTIL condition
C	do	while (condition);
COBOL	PERFORM TEST AFTER UNTIL condition	END-PERFORM;
Pascal	repeat	until condition;
PL/1	DO UNTIL (condition);	END;

See also *do while, loop,* and *structured programming.*

do while

A loop construct in which the body of the loop is executed 0 or more times. That is, the termination test precedes the body of the loop.

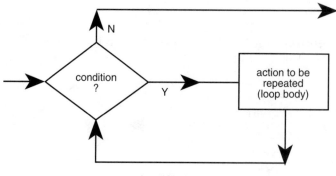

A do while loop.

This is the most commonly used loop construct in structured programming. Although *do while* is the usual term in the literature of structured programming, programming languages use a variety of terminology and syntax:

Language	Before Loop Body	After Loop Body
BASIC	DO WHILE condition	LOOP
	or	
	WHILE condition	WEND
C	do while (condition)	;
COBOL	PERFORM UNTIL NOT condition;	END-PERFORM;
Pascal	while condition do	
PL/1	DO WHILE (condition);	END;

See also *do until, loop,* and *structured programming.*

downward compatibility

1. The capability of software designed for newer computer systems to run on older models. For example, software written for an 80486 computer that can also run on an 8088 computer is downward-compatible.

2. The capability of programs, documents, or spreadsheets to be used in older versions of the software (compilers, word processors, spreadsheets, and so on). For example, if an older 1.0 version of a word processor can edit a 2.0 document, the document is downward-compatible.

Products usually provide upward compatibility, but not downward compatibility.

See also *upward compatibility.*

DPMA—Data Processing Management Association

A professional society for systems analysts, programmers, and managers interested in business applications.

In the 1960s, DPMA established the first certification program for data processors, awarding the title CDP (Certified Data Processor) in an attempt to secure a stature for data processors comparable to the CPA in accounting. This program was later turned over to the ICCP (Institute for Certification of Computer Professionals).

DPMA has local chapters in most areas.

DPMI—DOS protected mode interface

A DOS extender standard developed by Microsoft for 80×86 processors.

An application created to be DPMI-compliant can use normal DOS extender features, and can run under Microsoft Windows 3.X without conflict. However, this standard is incompatible with VCPI, an earlier DOS extender standard.

See also *real mode, protected mode,* and *VCPI.*

drag and drop

The action of using a mouse to select and move an object or icon on a graphical user interface (GUI) system. The icon representing the object moves on the screen with the mouse cursor as long as the mouse button is pressed. When you release the mouse button, the object is dropped onto its destination.

DRAM—dynamic random-access memory

A type of random-access memory (RAM) that must be refreshed periodically to retain the data it contains. See also *SRAM.*

Refreshing the DRAM is handled by motherboard support circuitry and usually is not a concern for application developers. DRAM, the more commonly used type of RAM, is typically slower and less expensive than SRAM.

driver, device

See *device driver.*

driver, test

See *test driver.*

drop

See *drag and drop.*

dump, backup

An exact copy of the contents of one or more disk-resident files (or a whole volume), to be used only for recovery if the original is damaged. The backup dump is often written to high-volume magnetic tape, but sometimes to one or more removable disk volumes.

Note that this use of the term *dump* differs sharply from both *file dump* and *memory dump.* Both of those dumps produce output that humans can read.

See also *dump, file* and *dump, memory.*

dump, file

A printed or displayed listing of the contents of all or part of a file.

File dumps have the following uses:

- To verify that the program that created the file is working correctly

- To audit an application system to detect any deviation from expected contents

- To examine a file supplied by an external source, to determine the file's format

dump, memory

A printed or displayed listing of the contents of all or part of a computer's memory or a program's address space, used most often as a diagnostic tool after abnormal termination of a process or system.

Most dumps exhibit minimal formatting, displaying memory contents in absolute octal, hexadecimal, or character form, regardless of whether the information is executable code or any of the internal data types. Some systems, however, provide symbolic dumps, using dictionary information passed from a compiler to determine the intended format of each area of memory.

For application programmers, memory dumps are less useful with current computers than they were with second-generation computers, for the following reasons:

- Modern computer architectures rely more on registers than memory cells for both addressing and intermediate results. Consequently, programs leave less of a trail that can be examined on a dump.

- Modern compilers and debuggers provide much better runtime tools for preventing loss of control and for displaying intermediate results.

- Many programs now use such huge address spaces that printing or examining the entire contents is impractical.

However, systems programmers coding in assembly languages or working on low-level components of an operating system still may need to use dumps.

duplex

A transmission channel that can send data in both directions simultaneously. The term is synonymous with *full-duplex*.

See also *half-duplex*.

dynamic array

An array that can be resized, erased, or deleted during program execution.

In BASIC, you create dynamic arrays by using the keyword REDIM, or by using the keyword DIM to dimension with a variable:

```
REDIM TEMP$(100)          'a dynamic string array

or

X% = 100
DIM TEMP$(X%)             'another dynamic array
```

dynamic call

A call to a module to be fetched from a library at runtime.

A dynamic call is in contrast to a static call, which is bound by a linking loader to a specific instance of a module embedded in the executable program.

A dynamic call allows the program to select or create the name of a called module during execution, possibly on the basis of some test or combination of conditions. Such flexibility can be useful in complex programs that process a wide range of input transactions. In addition, dynamic calls offer these advantages over static calls:

- Each program that calls a particular module always gets the latest version of that module.

- Multiple programs can share a single copy of a shared module, saving space.

On the other hand, static calls offer these advantages:

- Production programs have full control over which version of each module is to be used and when new versions are to be tested and implemented.

- Runtime overhead for finding and loading modules is avoided, saving execution time.

Invocation of modules that are part of the operating system is almost always dynamic.

See also *.DLL.*

dynamic data exchange

See *DDE.*

dynamic data structure

A data structure whose shape or size can be changed by a program during execution. Pointers are often used to implement dynamic data structures.

See also *array, graph, list, pointer, queue, stack,* and *tree.*

dynamic link library

See *.DLL.*

dynamic memory allocation

The allocation of areas of main memory (random-access memory, or RAM) from a free pool as needed during execution.

Dynamic memory allocation offers several benefits:

- In a large program, the total space needed to store arrays and other variable data structures can be minimized, because all the data items used in a program need not consume memory all at once.

- When the dimensions of an array depend on some parameter or intermediate result, the program can defer allocation until the dimensions have been computed. (Note: C and Pascal do not support adjustable array dimensions.)

- When the size of a dynamic data structure is unpredictable and highly variable, the program can allocate elements as the structure is being built.

On the other hand, dynamic memory allocation incurs an overhead cost, which can be significant when repeated allocation and freeing occur in a loop.

See also *automatic allocation.*

EBCDIC—extended binary-coded decimal interchange code

An assignment of eight-bit numeric codes to printable characters and certain device control codes. The term is pronounced "ebs'dic" or "eb'seedic."

Although EBCDIC was once the dominant character-coding scheme, it now appears mainly in large-scale IBM computers and IBM-compatible computers, devices, and storage media. Most other equipment today uses ASCII character coding.

EBCDIC retains links to very early coding schemes: the Hollerith codes used in punched cards, and the six-bit BCD (binary coded decimal) codes common in second-generation computers. Each byte consists of the following:

- A four-bit zone bits portion, corresponding to the holes in the top three rows (12-11-0) of a punched card

- A four-bit numeric portion, corresponding to the holes in the bottom nine rows 1–9 of a punched card

Thus, gaps occur in the alphabet so that, unlike ASCII, if you add 1 to the code for "R," you don't get the code for "S."

Some software products and hardware devices provide conversion between ASCII and EBCDIC. Such conversion is, of course, easy to program using a table of corresponding byte values.

See also *ASCII, byte,* and *Hollerith code.*

edge

A connection between two nodes (or vertices) of a graph.

editing program

A component of an application system concerned with the input of data from the external world, most often from people using keyboards.

An editing program performs two functions:

- Data validation, to make sure that each value entered satisfies the formatting, syntax, and perhaps context-dependent rules for that field.

- Data conversion, to transform the external, people-oriented data representation to an internal, efficient representation.

In a pure batch processing system, an editing program usually makes a pass over an entire set of input transactions before any transactions are actually processed or acted on. Transactions containing errors are rejected, and the user may correct or reenter them in the next batch run.

In an online system, however, editing modules may be interleaved with other processing modules and not thought of as a separate system component. Errors are reported to the user, who can often correct them immediately, so that the transaction will be accepted.

Many newer batch processing systems contain an online editing program. Users enter transactions throughout the day, correcting errors as they go. At the end of the day, the system processes the batch of already-edited transactions.

See also *data representation.*

edition

In Macintosh System 7, a file containing a document to which other documents can subscribe.

As in the similar Windows facility OLE, the user can choose to have a subscriber document automatically updated whenever changes are made to the edition.

editor

A utility program used to create and modify text in a structured form, especially program source code.

An editor has less flexibility than a word processor, but may know about certain specific syntax or formatting rules of one or more programming languages. It may use that knowledge to do the following:

- Detect errors in punctuation, keywords, indentation, nesting, or other easily recognized syntax elements, and prompt the user to correct them.

- Apply default formatting rules (pretty print) to promote readability.

- Assist the user in matching nested parentheses or bracketing constructs

See also *IDE (integrated development environment).*

EEPROM—electrically erasable programmable read-only memory

A memory chip that holds a computer program or other contents, but does not require power to maintain the contents of the firmware.

Programmers create firmware by using an EEPROM burner, a device that stores machine language instructions and data in an EEPROM. Many PC boards include EEPROMs that contain information or software required by the board.

See also *firmware* and *ROM.*

efficiency

Any measure of the ratio of the quantity of processing to its cost.

People sometimes use the term *efficiency* informally when they mean speed, describing an algorithm or a program as "efficient" when they mean that it is fast. Careful writers, however, distinguish between speed and efficiency.

In algorithm theory, measures of efficiency are often stated as a function of the size or dimension of the arguments. For example, the number of comparisons required for an internal sort of N items is proportional to N^2 for the bubble sort algorithm, but proportional to N log N for the merge sort algorithm.

EGA—enhanced graphics adapter

An IBM-originated graphics interface. The EGA standard supports a resolution of 640(h) × 350(v), and 16 colors drawn from a palette of 64. Importantly, the EGA adapter standard supported both older CGA (Color Graphics

Adapter) and MDA (Monochrome Data Adapter) standards, providing a transition for existing software.

See also *VGA.*

electronic mail

See *e-mail.*

element

1. A synonym for *elementary data item* or *field.*

2. A data item that belongs to or is a member of a composite data item; also the relationship between a data item and the composite item to which it belongs.

Composite data items that have elements include arrays, lists, and sets. The notation x ∈ S indicates that x is an element (or member) of S.

See also *container.*

element, table

In COBOL, the individual tables within a dimensioned data structure. Note that most COBOL documentation departs from standard terminology, in which the term *element* refers to the individual items in a table. For example:

```
2    STATES            OCCURS 50 TIMES.
     3    CAPITAL-CITY   PICTURE X(14).
     3    ZIP-RANGE      COMPUTATIONAL-3.
          4  LOWEST      PICTURE S9(5).
          4  HIGHEST     PICTURE S9(5).
     3    POPULATION     COMPUTATIONAL PICTURE S9(7).
```

The preceding structure contains four one-dimensional arrays: CAPITAL-CITY, LOWEST, HIGHEST, and POPULATION. COBOL manuals and text books typically would refer to each of these as an element of the structure STATES.

elementary data item

A data item that cannot (or need not) be decomposed into other component data items.

Near synonyms include *field* and *atom*.

 Some advocates of modern data analysis techniques (see *entity-relationship diagram*) recommend a strict top-down approach to identifying and defining data items. Such an approach is fine for systematically identifying the data items that eventually will be stored in a database. However, a systems analyst who follows only that strategy may entirely overlook those elementary items that don't belong to any higher-level entity. A prudent systems analyst is ready to define any kind of data item at any level whenever he or she first thinks of it.

else

See *if-then-else statement.*

emacs—editor macros

A UNIX editor developed by MIT to replace the hard-to-use vi editor.

This editor provides many useful features, including multiple windows. The command and function set used by the editor can also be modified and added to by the user.

See also *vi.*

embedded system

A specialized computer used to control the device in which it is contained. For instance, automotive control systems utilize embedded systems. Depending on the designed purpose of the control system and the automotive manufacturer, these control systems monitor and control everything from fuel injection to environmental systems (heating and air conditioning) to antilock brakes.

The programming for embedded systems is contained within firmware (generally ROM or EPROM); it cannot be used for general purposes.

e-mail—electronic mail

The use of a computer network by individual users to send, store, and receive messages or documents to and from other individual users.

E-mail software typically runs on mainframe computers or local area networks (LANs), and serves user populations ranging from a single workgroup to a large corporation to (via dial-up utility services) the public at large. The growing availability of terminals and desktop computers has led to rapid adoption of e-mail by many business and academic organizations.

Using a store-and-forward scheme with simulated "mail boxes," e-mail, along with FAX and voice mail, is increasingly being used to handle much business communication that formerly might have required several phone calls to establish contact. E-mail is particularly attractive to organizations whose members must communicate with individuals in distant time zones, because often in such circumstances the two parties who must communicate are rarely in their offices at the same time. E-mail is more private than FAX, more permanent than voice mail, and often less expensive than either.

EMS—Expanded Memory Specification

A method used in MS-DOS for addressing up to 32M of memory on Intel computers that normally limit a program's address space to 1M.

On the 80286 and earlier computers, EMS requires a special memory board and driver program, and defines rules regarding how a program should address the memory. Because EMS is an open standard, you don't have to pay royalties to use the specification.

Using this memory specification, a software product like Lotus 1-2-3 can store information in the memory area above the 1024K boundary. An EMS board tricks the operating system by switching segments of high memory (over 1M) to and from lower memory (under 1M). A specialized memory driver on 80386 or 80486 computers, such as 386 to the Max or EMM386, is loaded from the CONFIG.SYS file to convert available extended memory over 1M into expanded memory.

The memory area utilized by EMS is split into several blocks of memory, called *pages.* The DOS application program can allocate these pages as needed, and information (such as parts of a spreadsheet) can be stored in the pages for retrieval later. EMS typically is used when conventional DOS memory (0 to 640K) must be conserved. EMS page(s) later can be reallocated, and then the EMS memory is released.

DOS programs can take advantage of EMS only if they are programmed to do so. They do not take advantage of EMS automatically.

See also *address space, paged memory,* and *virtual memory.*

emulate

To imitate another device or program.

See *emulation.*

emulation

Programmed imitation of one type of computer, device, or operating system on a different type of system.

Here are some examples of emulation facilities:

- MS-DOS communication programs often emulate the popular DEC VT100 terminal. Therefore, the communication program can display information on a PC's screen in the same manner as the information would appear on a VT100 screen, and the user can enter keystrokes corresponding to the VT100 keyboard.

- Some UNIX computers provide MS-DOS emulation, which enables DOS programs to run under UNIX, as the DOS emulator imitates the functions and facilities of MS-DOS.

- IBM's OS/2 provides emulation for programs originally written to run under Microsoft Windows.

- Most programming language compilers for Intel microprocessors support floating-point emulation by including library programs that emulate the optional math coprocessor. You can then write a single version of your source program and compile it to run either on machines that have a math coprocessor or on machines that don't.

encapsulation

Localization of knowledge within a single module or within a small family of closely related modules.

Encapsulation is highly desirable in modular programming and virtually essential in object-oriented programming (OOP). The following are three kinds of knowledge you're especially likely to want to encapsulate:

- The representation of data items, especially structured data such as tables and lists
- The algorithms for manipulating those data structures, such as a table search strategy
- The names (or very existence) of internal data items needed only by those algorithms

You can change many aspects of encapsulated knowledge without affecting any other portion of a program that uses it. Such clean separation of knowledge helps greatly in developing reusable modules.

See also *accessor function, module coupling,* and *private class member.*

encode

To translate from one representation to another, as in assigning a part code to a part description, or assigning a numeric code to represent a color. Sometimes the term is also used as a synonym for *encrypt.*

See also *discrete data item* and *editing program.*

encrypt

To convert data into ciphered form for security purposes.

end of file—EOF

A flag indicating the end of a sequential file.

When a program attempts to read a record from an input file already positioned at the end, the end-of-file indicator is turned on. By testing for this indicator, the program knows when to terminate processing of an input file.

In BASIC, the EOF function returns true after reading the last record, rather than after attempting to read another record following the last record. This differs from the end-of-file logic in most other languages. For an empty file, EOF returns true after the execution of the OPEN statement.

end user

Anyone who uses an application system or program.

The more general term *user* can also denote programmers or others who have occasion to interact with a software product. *End user* is useful in designating the people for whom an application system is intended.

enhanced graphics adapter

See *EGA*.

entity

A high-level composite data item viewed as the subject matter of an application system.

Entity is a subjective term. There are no definite rules for determining whether a given data item is or is not an entity. Most entities, however, satisfy the following guidelines:

- Entities can serve as a starting point for analyzing data about an organization or a problem area.

- Entities are not components of any higher-level data structure of interest to the application system.

- Entities describe real-world objects or other objects in the domain of the application.

Examples of entities include employee, product, customer, vendor, sales transaction, and credit card account.

See also *attribute* and *entity-relationship diagram*.

entity-relationship diagram—ERD

A graphical representation of entities and their relationships to one another. Entity-relationship diagrams are commonly used for analyzing the data requirements of an application system and designing logical databases.

A common form of ERD uses the following graphics conventions:

- Each entity is represented by a named box.

- A relationship between two entities is represented by a connecting line, labeled by a verb describing the relationship and an arrow showing the direction of that relationship.

- The degree (sometimes called the "cardinality") of each relationship is shown by special connectors at each end: one-to-one, one-to-many, and many-to-many.

The following simple diagram illustrates these conventions:

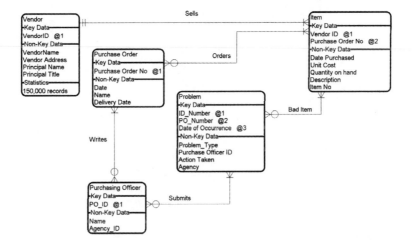

 CASE tools and various publications employ slightly different versions of ERDs. All ERDs need not look exactly the same or utilize the same symbols, as long as the basic concepts are maintained.

See also *entity.*

159

enum

A C keyword that declares discrete data items and gives integer constant names to each possible value.

enumeration

In the C programming language, the process of defining the possible values of a user-defined data type. The enum keyword is used both to start the data declaration and later to actually perform the variable declaration.

The following is an example of C programming code in which a data type for an automobile is defined and enumerated. Such a declaration might be used in a reservation system for a car rental agency.

```
enum cartype{
        subcompact
        compact
        standard
        full_size
        luxury
        van
        specialty}};
enum cartype rental;
```

Later in the program, any of the items in the enumeration (subcompact, compact, standard, full_size, luxury, van, or specialty) can be assigned to the rental variable.

Enumeration makes it easier to place logical limits on values assigned to a variable, and makes a program easier to maintain and understand.

environment

See *program environment* and *IDE.*

EOF

See *end of file.*

epilogue

In a high-level language, the code generated for execution as a procedure is exited. Depending on the programming language, tasks performed in the epilogue may include return of dynamically allocated random-access storage, and data type conversion (if needed) of returned values.

ERASE

A command in MS-DOS to delete a file or a group of files.

The ERASE command can have a drastic, unintended effect when the user makes an error, such as pressing the Enter key before typing a parameter. As a protection in some cases, the operating system asks for confirmation. In addition, MS-DOS now provides an UNDELETE command that can sometimes recover accidentally erased files, especially when the user notices the error immediately. Some organizations setting up desktop computers for naive end users remove or hide ERASE and other potentially damaging commands.

ERD

See *entity-relationship diagram.*

error handling

The set of messages and procedures used by a program when it encounters exception conditions that prevent normal execution. Such exceptions may be caused by any of the following:

- Erroneous input data. (See *diagnostic message* and *editing program.*)

- Equipment malfunctions, such as an unreadable file.

- Not-ready conditions, such as a printer out of paper.

- Program bugs or environment errors that prevent execution, such as a table overflow.

In interactive applications, the user can correct many kinds of errors immediately, for example, by reentering a value or by putting paper in the printer. A user-friendly program leads the user through these actions and then resumes normal processing.

For batch applications (or unrecoverable errors), a useful convention is to associate a severity level with each kind of error for which a program provides. These levels might include the following:

Severity	Action
Warning(1)	Issue a diagnostic message and continue
Serious(2)	Issue a diagnostic message, then continue unless the number of serious errors encountered exceeds a specified limit
Terminal(3) or fatal	Issue a diagnostic message and terminate the run

See also *condition code.*

errorlevel

See *condition code.*

error message

See *diagnostic message.*

escape sequence

A special kind of command interpreted by a terminal or console device and used to control the keyboard and screen. Such commands are called "escape sequences" because they begin with the escape (ESC) control byte.

See also *ANSI.SYS.*

Ethernet

A networking hardware standard (also known as the IEEE 803.2 standard) developed by Xerox, Digital, and Intel.

Ethernet is the most-used personal computer networking standard, and is supported by Novell, Microsoft, and Banyan. It uses a collision detection protocol to transmit information up and down a local area network (LAN), from node to node.

An Ethernet network consists of an Ethernet interface, such as an Ethernet card, and an Ethernet network connection. Currently, Ethernet comes in several cabling options or connection types, including 10BASE2, which is the "thinnet" (coax) version, and 10BASET, the RJ45 ("twisted pair") version. 10BASET requires a concentrator, and is characterized by enhanced performance.

event-driven

See *event-oriented programming*.

event-oriented programming

A programming style in which the sequence of actions is controlled not by the program itself but by external, often user-initiated, events, such as pressing a key, pushing a button, or turning a dial (or simulating such operations by clicking a mouse).

Event-oriented (or event-driven) programming is suited to those applications that enable the user to select from a variety of choices to accomplish desired results. The style is less suited to situations in which a fixed set of actions must be accomplished for each input transaction, with limited user responses.

Event-oriented programming under a graphical user interface (GUI) is generally considered much more difficult and complex than conventional procedural programming. The program must be prepared to respond to a variety of external events in unpredictable sequences and combinations.

That complexity is increased even further by the need to respond to events triggered by other programs (see *DDE* and *OLE*). Fortunately, object-oriented programming (OOP) can make event-driven programming somewhat easier, especially with vendor-supplied class libraries or higher-level tools that are already prepared to support commonly occurring kinds of events.

Excel

A Microsoft spreadsheet processor for Windows and Macintosh platforms.

Excel was the earliest spreadsheet processor to support a graphical user interface (GUI) as an integral aspect of its design rather than an afterthought.

See also *Lotus 1-2-3* and *Quattro Pro.*

exception

An event during program execution that prevents continuation of the normal flow of instructions.

Some exceptions arise naturally in the normal course of execution, and should be anticipated by the programmer (see *exception handler*). Examples of such exceptions include the following:

- An arithmetic error, such as overflow or division by zero

- An illegal value for an input data item, such as an attempt to convert a string containing alphabetic characters to a numeric type

- Encountering the end of a sequential input file

Other exceptions may result from program bugs, and are usually fatal errors intercepted by the operating system. Examples of these exceptions include the following:

- An array subscript beyond the bounds of the array dimension

- A branch to an area of memory not containing program instructions

- A reference to a protected area of memory

See also *condition, interrupt,* and *trap.*

exception handler

A module or block of program code that is to be invoked whenever a corresponding type of exception occurs. Unless the exception is a fatal error, the exception handler normally takes appropriate corrective action, then returns control to the point at which the exception occurred, or the point just following the occurrence of the exception.

Among higher-level languages, Ada and PL/1 have the most complete facilities for implementing exception handlers. BASIC provides the catch-all ON ERROR and RESUME statements, which are awkward to use in large programs because they can't be nested. C provides no explicit exception-handler facilities, but supports exception handling through packages of library routines specific to certain platforms.

See also *exception*.

exclusive or

See *xor* and *Boolean operator*.

.EXE

In several widely used operating systems (including MS-DOS, VAX/VMS, and OS/2), a file name extension for a file containing an executable program.

To invoke the program from the command prompt, the user enters the file name (with or without the .EXE extension).

An .EXE file is the main output from a linking loader.

See also *.BAT, .COM,* and *.DLL*.

EXEC statement

A job control language (JCL) statement used in IBM mainframe operating systems to invoke a program.

Compared to other command languages, JCL is very "horizontal": Instead of having a separate verb for each application or utility program that might be invoked, it uses the following syntax:

```
//stepname EXEC PGM=progname, . . .(other parameters) . . .
```

Thus the appearance of an EXEC statement in the input stream or in a cataloged procedure always delimits the start of a job step.

executable file

See *.EXE*.

execution

The processing by a computer of the instructions in a program.

Execution of an application program begins when the operating system, after loading the program into memory, branches (turns control over) to the first instruction in the program. Execution ends when the program either returns control voluntarily to the operating system or is terminated involuntarily by the operating system, perhaps in response to a kill request from the user or the operator.

executive program

A program that controls the execution of other programs, especially the task-management portion of an operating system, or a transaction-processing monitor.

exit

See *hook*.

expanded memory specification

See *EMS*.

expert system

A program that solves a problem posed by a user or that interactively assists a user in solving a problem, by using a knowledge base to draw inferences.

The term derives from the assumption that such systems emulate the problem-solving behavior of a human expert in the field.

One of the most interesting areas of expert system application so far is medical: given a set of symptoms, such an expert system helps to diagnose the disease and prescribe appropriate treatment. Other fields that have successfully used expert systems include legal, defense, financial analysis, and computer problem diagnosis ("help desk"). These are areas in which past experience or "expertise" is crucial for making decisions or solving problems.

See also *chaining of rules, knowledge engineering, rule base,* and *VP-Expert.*

export

To produce a file in a form other than the one used internally by the program or software product.

Software products often provide an export capability to help the user create data for competing or complementary software products. For example, a word processor might provide an option to store a file in the format expected by a competing word processor, or a database management system (DBMS) might enable you to create spreadsheet files.

See also *conversion, file,* and *import.*

expression

A mathematical function constructed by combining terms, operators, and functions according to the syntax rules of a programming language.

For example, if x, y, and z are numeric variables, then the following are numeric expressions:

```
x
(x + 2) * y
1 / sqrt(x^2 + y^2)
```

and the following are Boolean expressions:

```
x = 0
(x > y/2  and (y > 0)) or (z = 0)
```

If LAST$ and FIRST$ are character string variables (in BASIC), then the following are character-string expressions:

```
LAST$ + ", " + FIRST$
LEFT$(FIRST$,INSTR(FIRST$ + " ", " ")) + " " + LAST$
```

167

Similarly, other kinds of expressions correspond to other data types or defined classes.

See also *Backus-Naur form, function, infix operator,* and *recursive definition.*

extended memory

Memory from 1M and up, supported by Intel 80286 computers and greater.

Extended memory can be used for RAM disks, memory drivers, and programs that utilize DOS extenders. A memory driver controls extended memory and converts it into expanded memory (EMS) through the XMS driver, HIMEM.SYS. Extended memory also is called "raw memory," because a driver does not control access to this area; such memory can be accessed without the use of a memory driver.

extended memory specification

See *XMS.*

extension, file

See *file name extension.*

extern keyword

A keyword used in programming languages to inform the compiler or assembler that it should not expect to resolve a variable or subroutine reference within the source file being processed. The symbol designated as external is resolved during a binding or linking step.

external sorting

The process of ordering records stored on auxiliary storage in the sequence of one or more key fields.

External sorting is required when the file to be sorted is too big to fit in memory. It is usually much slower than internal sorting but potentially unlimited in capacity. Algorithms for external sorting are entirely different from those used in internal sorting, relying on successive passes in which sequences are split and merged.

External sorting is a built-in operation in COBOL (through the SORT verb) and in many database management systems (DBMS). (Sometimes COBOL programmers mistakenly refer to SORT as an "internal sort," probably because the verb is invoked from within the program rather than as a separate job step.)

See also *internal sorting.*

factorial function

A function on a non-negative integer N, yielding the product of the integers from 1 through N (usually referred to as "N factorial," but sometimes also "factorial N"). Zero factorial is conventionally defined as 1, and the function is undefined for negative or fractional values. For example, 5 factorial is 1 * 2 * 3 * 4 * 5 = 120.

Traditional mathematical notation uses a special notation for factorial: an exclamation point following the argument, as in 3!, K!, and (n–r)!. In most programming languages, however, you must use standard function notation, as in FACTORIAL (3), FACTORIAL (K), and FACTORIAL (n–r). Few programming languages or spreadsheet processors provide factorial as a built-in function, so programmers who need the function may have to write it themselves.

Factorial is often used to illustrate recursive definition or recursive functions, because it's one of the simplest functions that you can define recursively. The formula is as follows:

$$0! = 1$$

$$n! = n * (n-1)!, \text{ for } n > 0$$

Obviously it would be horrendously inefficient to implement factorial as a recursive function, as in the following example:

```
IF   N = 0
THEN RETURN (1);
ELSE RETURN (N * FACTORIAL (N-1));
```

Therefore, no one does so in serious programming. Perhaps less obviously, it's also extremely wasteful to implement factorial as an iterative loop, as follows:

```
RESULT = 1;
DO  K = 1 TO N;
    RESULT = RESULT * K;
    END;
RETURN (RESULT);
```

Each time you invoked such a function, it would recompute the same previously computed intermediate results.

Because the values of factorial increase rapidly with N, overflow occurs for all values of N beyond a rather small number. The largest possible factorial, with standard floating point representation, is 53! in IBM 360 architecture and 170! in Intel 80×87 architecture. The largest values that can be represented exactly are much smaller, depending on the chosen precision. A practical implementation, therefore, is a table of the possible values of factorial. You can generate such a table once, then include the result in all programs that need it.

fan-in

The number of modules that directly invoke a given program module.

High fan-in indicates both a successful factoring of common functions and a useful generalization of a module's specification. When the different modules that use a given module belong to different application systems, the module is said to be reusable, and is usually distributed through a module library.

Overzealous insistence on a strict top-down design sequence can lead to a pure tree-structured program in which few modules, if any, have high fan-in. Modules that ultimately have high fan-in often are specified, designed, and developed from the bottom up.

A perceptive designer or chief programmer may recognize at the start that certain useful functions will be required, before knowing exactly where they will be invoked. This is especially likely for macro definitions, object-oriented class definitions, and general-purpose subroutines such as error handlers and input-output routines. After specifying (and perhaps actually developing) such low-level modules, the designer returns to a top-down strategy, steering the design where appropriate toward the use of the specified low-level modules.

See also *fan-out, modular programming,* and *structured design.*

fan-out

The number of modules that a given program module invokes directly.

High fan-out indicates that a module design has properly delegated details that might otherwise have made the module complicated, difficult to debug, and difficult to maintain.

 Unlike fan-in, it is possible for a module design to have too much fan-out. Breaking a well-defined function arbitrarily into lower-level modules can actually introduce more complexity in intermodule communication than is delegated to the subordinate modules. High fan-out must not be achieved at the cost of high module cohesion and good module coupling.

See also *fan-in, modular programming,* and *structured design.*

far call

In a system based on a segmented-memory model, a temporary transfer of execution to another address within a different memory segment. Such a call requires the use of both a segment and offset address register.

See also *call* and *near call.*

FAT

See *file allocation table.*

fatal error

An error so serious that execution cannot continue. Also called a *terminal error.*

In a well-designed, user-friendly application, errors in individual input transactions are never fatal. After issuing appropriate diagnostics messages and attempting to correct the error, the program can continue with the next transaction. On the other hand, a program may not be able to recover from an error in a user-specified run parameter or an error in the environment, such as insufficient space or an inability to find an expected input file.

See also *ABEND* and *crash.*

fatware

Software that consumes excessive resources (such as memory, resident disk space, and machine cycles) in relation to the functionality it provides.

Although this is a somewhat subjective term, depending on what one considers "excessive," it is generally acknowledged that the past decade has seen an enormous increase in the resource demands of software products. Although part of that increase is due to increased functionality, another part is due to sophisticated user interfaces and marginal features that some users feel they don't need. Among the software features that have contributed to this growth are the following:

- Online help facilities that duplicate or replace user manuals
- Powerful reporting and graphics capabilities for products whose principal function is something other than reporting or graphics
- Graphical user interfaces (GUI)
- Dynamic data exchange support (DDE and OLE)

Users who need such capabilities are willing to upgrade their machines so that they can run such software products. Users who don't need such capabilities, however, may resent being forced to invest in a larger machine, especially if the upgrade is necessary simply to use a new version of the same product to which they are accustomed.

The continuing decrease in hardware prices and the continuing competitive pressures on software vendors ensure that the trend will continue through the 1990s. Software products will require amounts of computer resources that would have been unthinkable a decade earlier.

field

An elementary data item within a record, form, or template.

Although the terms *field* and *elementary data item* are near synonyms, *field* is used only in the context of some larger data structure to which the item belongs, especially a structure used for external input or output.

figurative constant

A COBOL term for an absolute constant that has a built-in name, such as ZERO, SPACES, or HIGH-VALUE.

Other languages support similar built-in constants (such as null, true, and maxint) but rarely use this term.

FIFO—first-in, first-out

A sequencing strategy in which items are removed from a queue in the same order they were added.

FIFO is the simplest, and in many situations the fairest, approach to job-scheduling and other situations involving competing demands for the same resources. The term *FIFO* also describes a method of accounting for inventory, in which units of the same product are bought at different times at different costs.

See also *LIFO*.

file

A collection of records, especially one stored on an auxiliary storage medium.

Files are central to most computer applications, and take on a wide range of properties. For more specific information, see *archive file, database, direct access file, flat file, keyed file, master file, permanent file, sequential file,* and *temporary file*.

file (UNIX)

A UNIX command that tests files in a directory and determines the file composition. For example, to use this utility to test the entire contents of a directory, you would enter the following command:

```
$file *
```

This command might generate the following sample output:

```
XErrorDB:       ascii text
XKeysymDB:      ascii text
Xcolors:        ascii text
Xconfig:        ascii text
Xconnections:   English text
Xservers:       directory
app-defaults:   directory
config:         directory
easywindows:    directory
examples:       directory
file.txt:       empty
fonts:          directory
kill.txt:       ascii text
net:            directory
rgb.dir:        data
rgb.pag:        data
rgb.txt:        ascii text
system.mwmrc:   ascii text
twm:            directory
xdaemon:        iAPX 386 executable
xdm:            directory
xinit:          directory
xman.help:      English text
```

The utility enables UNIX users to discover the substance of a particular file without displaying or editing the file itself. This is especially useful in UNIX, because UNIX files usually do not maintain file name extensions (such as .EXE, .TXT, and .COM) as does MS-DOS.

file allocation table

A reserved area on floppy and hard disk storage devices, used by an operating system to maintain a record of how sectors of the storage media are being used.

All operating systems maintain space availability and file location records on storage media; the complexity of this table depends on device characteristics and whether the operating system supports the allocation of a file in noncontiguous segments.

See also *directory* and *HPFS*.

file conversion

See *conversion, file.*

file maintenance

The process of updating a database or master file. The process is handled by a portion of an application system, usually by processing user-supplied file maintenance transactions, which add, change, or delete information in the database or master file.

file transport protocol

See *FTP.*

file name

1. The name by which a file is known to an operating system. This name must conform to the rules for file naming in the particular operating system.

2. The name by which a file is referred to by a program. This name must conform to the rules for naming data items in the particular programming language.

In the simplest situations, such as a BASIC program under MS-DOS, the two file names are often identical. However, some programming languages (such as PL/1, COBOL, and Ada) enforce a distinction between the two kinds of file names for two reasons:

- To avoid or localize a program's dependency on a specific operating platform

- To allow a program in production to use a different physical file each time it is run

See *data set* for further explanation of this distinction and how the connection between the two names is made.

MS-DOS file names are made up of two parts separated by a period:

- A name of up to eight characters
- An optional extension of up to three characters, most often used to identify the kind of information in the file or the program that created it

Examples of such file names include RPT-1994.DOC, RPT-PROG.BAS, TESTGRP2.DTA, and DUMMY.

Other operating systems (including OS/2, UNIX, MVS, and VAX/VMS) allow longer file names. No industry standards exist for file naming, so you must learn the specific rules that apply to each operating platform.

See also *data set* and *file*.

file name extension

A three-character suffix at the end of a file name in MS-DOS, VAX/VMS, and some other operating systems, usually used to identify the type of information in the file.

Some commonly used file name extensions appear in this dictionary under names beginning with a period, such .*TXT*.

See also *file name*.

file retention

A cyclic saving of files for a specified time or a certain number of generations.

In an application system, it is customary to save master files and backup files until it is certain that they won't be needed either for recovering information or for auditing.

See also *generation data group*.

firmware

A program or instructions stored in a nonvolatile memory chip.

Firmware is usually in the form of a ROM (read-only memory), PROM (programmable ROM), EPROM (erasable PROM), or EEPROM (electronically erasable PROM). The main feature of firmware is that, unlike random-access memory (RAM) chips, firmware's memory data stays intact when you shut off the system's power. The computer's main operating instructions (BIOS) are stored in ROM as firmware.

The computer manufacturer creates the programs stored in ROM. The programmer can create PROM by using a special setup called a ROM burner, which burns or permanently stores instructions in PROM. EPROM and EEPROM are similar in that the programmer can program or erase both. However, ultraviolet light is used to erase EPROM, and electronic signals are used to erase EEPROM.

first-generation computer—1GL

A computer system manufactured in the early to mid-1950s, characterized by the following:

- Vacuum tube circuitry

- Magnetic tapes as the main auxiliary storage medium

- A succession of memory technologies: mercury delay lines (Univac I and IBM 701), followed by much more reliable magnetic drums (IBM 650), followed by much faster magnetic core (IBM 704, IBM 705, and Univac 1103A), with eventual memory sizes up to about 64K

- The first assemblers and compilers (FORTRAN I)

See also *generations, computers.*

fixed disk

A disk that is permanently mounted, often inside a desktop computer. Also called a hard disk to distinguish it from the floppy disks used in removable disk drives.

The management of one or more large fixed disks with hundreds of data and software files in dozens of subdirectories is a particularly challenging problem for a PC user. It is not uncommon for a naive user to get into difficulty regarding file backup, availability of sufficient free space, naming conflicts, or just the ability to find a desired file. The several hundred megabyte size typical of modern fixed disks demands some of the same strategies used in administering auxiliary storage on mainframe computers or network servers.

fixed-length records

See *variable (or varying) length records.*

fixed-length string

See *variable (or varying) length string.*

flag

1. A data item that marks the beginning or end of a series or *stream* of data items, and may also identify the type of data that follows or precedes it.

   Some data transmission protocols use flags that are unique bit patterns which cannot otherwise occur within the data. Because the bit patterns are unique, such flags enable the receiver to resynchronize with the sender after a transmission error occurs.

2. A data item that indicates the occurrence of an event. In multitasking programming (see also *coroutine*), such flags are often called *semaphores,* whereas in conventional programming they are sometimes called *switches.*

flat file

A file that has no explicit structure; that is, a file in which no record is subordinate to any other record.

A flat file can be either a sequential or a direct access file; if sequential, the file may be a keyed file.

See also *database, header record,* and *hierarchical data structure.*

flat memory model

A memory allocation, addressing, and usage paradigm in which available memory is viewed as a linear series of consecutive addresses. This model is typically used on non-Intel microprocessors, whereas those from Intel use the segmented-memory model.

See also *segmented-memory model.*

floating-point

A data type for representing very large and small numbers, in which part of a data unit is reserved for an exponent, and part for representing a mantissa. Enhanced machine instructions and coprocessors optimized for this data representation are available (sometimes at extra cost).

See also *coprocessor.*

floor function

A standard integer function that returns the largest integer not exceeding its argument. Same as *integer truncation.*

The following are examples of floor functions:

```
floor(3.2)   is 3
ceil(3.0)    is 3
ceil(-1.5)   is -2
```

See also *round* and *truncation.*

floppy disk

A unit of removable storage containing a magnetic disk of flexible material inside a protective jacket. When inserted into a disk drive, the disk spins inside the jacket while information is read, written, or erased by a read or write head.

Floppy disks are available in double-sided or single-sided versions. Formatting writes the operating system to tracks and sectors on the disk, enabling the disk to accept information.

flowchart

A graphic representation of the logic flow in a program module or an information system, using standard symbols.

Before the "structured revolution" of the early 1970s, flowcharts often constituted the principal documentation of a program, other than the source code listing. It was generally considered good practice for a programmer to prepare flowcharts at two times:

- Before writing the code, to clarify what was to be done. In some organizations, systems analysts prepared flowcharts (see *coder*). In a few organizations, programmers had to get their flowcharts approved before they were allowed to code and test a program.

- After testing the program, as a part of the documentation for future maintenance programming.

Flowcharts were always burdensome to maintain, however, and were not always updated when changes were applied to a program.

Most experts today agree that a well-structured program written in a high-level language with appropriate commentary requires little if any separate documentation, and rarely if ever a flowchart. Flowcharts are still occasionally useful, however, for describing high-level system flow (see *job step* and *processing cycle*) and as an alternative to a decision tree for describing nested conditions.

See also *HIPO* and *structure chart*.

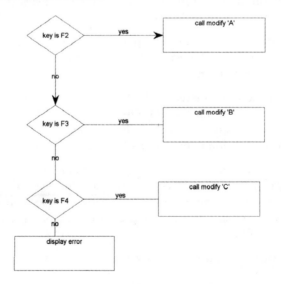

A flowchart.

flush

To empty buffers or queues intentionally, usually as part of file closing, program termination, or system shutdown.

See also *close (file)*.

folder

See *directory*.

for

A statement for implementing a common kind of loop, specifying these three elements:

- An initialization action, such as setting a loop-control variable to a starting value

- An action to be taken after each execution of the loop body, such as incrementing the same loop-control variable

- A condition that must be satisfied before execution of the loop stops, such as a terminal value for the loop-control variable

In those situations where it applies, the for statement is more powerful than do while or do until, because the for statement specifies all the preceding elements together in one place.

The statement originated as the FORTRAN DO statement, and corresponds to certain options for the COBOL PERFORM and the PL/1 DO statements. Ada, BASIC, C, and Pascal have chosen the verb "for," however, to empha-size the distinction between this loop construct and the others.

In C, the for statement is generalized further, allowing the three elements to be any expressions and not requiring any loop-control variable to tie them together. C's for statement is very flexible, but some programmers feel that the enforced discipline of a loop-control variable is less error-prone and more readable.

See also *do until, do while, iteration,* and *loop*.

format command

1. The MS-DOS and OS/2 command to initialize a disk.

2. To initialize a disk by invoking the format command.

Before any software can write data files on a blank disk, the disk must be prepared by recording control information showing the arrangements of tracks and sectors. In MS-DOS, using the FORMAT command is the standard way of doing so.

format statement

A list of specifications regarding the external format of corresponding data items embedded in a stream input-output (I/O) statement.

The use of format statements was originated by FORTRAN (the only language in which they are truly separate statements). PL/1 later provided, in a generalized form, FORTRAN-like "edit-directed stream I/O" capabilities of great power and flexibility. BASIC and C also provide facilities in which a stream I/O statement contains both the list of data items and the corresponding format specifications. This approach is far from universal, however: In COBOL and most report generators, the programmer specifies the data, the format, and the actual I/O action separately.

Since the passing of the age of punched cards and other offline input media, specification of external formats and layouts applies much more often to output (reports and screen displays) than to input. Most user-friendly programs either allow free-form input or construct their input through an interactive dialog with the user.

FORTH

A programming language developed by Charles Moore, initially to control telescopes.

The language is interpreted and highly extensible. It provides direct access to machine facilities in the interest of efficiency. Although FORTH has also been found useful in process-control applications and some business applications, it remains a "niche" language.

FORTRAN

The earliest procedural language to gain widespread acceptance.

IBM developed FORTRAN (for *for*mula *tran*slator) in 1957 for its first-generation 704 computer. The language was an experiment to demonstrate the following:

- That engineers and mathematicians unacquainted with machine language can successfully write useful programs

- That a compiler can generate code that is almost as efficient as equivalent code written in assembly language, at least for numeric computations.

FORTRAN succeeded far beyond expectations, and in a much improved form the language still thrives for straightforward "number crunching" jobs in which computing efficiency is the main consideration. Many newer languages, however, far surpass FORTRAN in power, flexibility, and maintainability—see *Ada, APL, BASIC, C, Modula-2, Pascal,* and *PL/1*.

fourth-generation language—4GL

See *generations, programming languages*.

fragmented disk

A disk containing one or more files that are stored as several noncontiguous areas on the disk.

This condition has a potentially serious impact on performance, but can be repaired easily with utility programs.

See also *defragment*.

frame

In communications, the block of data transmitted as a unit, including the start and stop bits (asynchronous) and SYN characters (binary synchronous communications).

freeware

Software that is available to the public, but of which the author retains ownership.

See also *public domain.*

friend function

In object-oriented programming (OOP), a function that has been given privileges to access all members of some class of which it is not itself a member. Compared to member functions (methods), friend functions can sometimes provide greater flexibility and improve performance.

FTP—file transfer protocol

A TCP/IP protocol used to gain access to other computers on a network, return file directory listings, and copy files from one remote computer to another at the user's request. In addition, this utility can translate ASCII and EBCDIC, as may be required to make the file compatible with the local operating system. This utility is usually associated with UNIX, but versions exist for most operating systems, including MS-DOS and OS/2.

full-duplex

See *duplex.*

fullword

A 32-bit word.

For older 16-bit computers, a *word* was defined as 16 bits. When 32-bit computers were introduced, the definition of a word as being 16 bits was retained for compatibility, and the 32-bit lengths were dubbed "fullwords."

See also *bit.*

function

1. In mathematics, a correspondence that assigns to each element of one set (the domain) a unique element of another (possibly the same) set (the range). A given element of the domain is called an argument, and the corresponding element of the range is the result or function value.

2. In programming, a module that implements a function, especially one for which the result can be used in an expression.

Languages that support user-defined functions with elementary data item results include Ada, ALGOL, C, FORTRAN, Pascal, and PL/1, as well as newer versions of BASIC and COBOL. Ada, C++, and Pascal also support composite data items and arrays as function values, with certain restrictions. The most general support for functions is found in LISP, where they are the central program construct. Most languages and spreadsheet processors also provide a repertoire of predefined (sometimes called "built-in") functions.

See also *function, function value, return, side effect,* and *void function.*

function key

A key on the keyboard (usually labeled F1, F2, F3, and so on) used to execute programming options, such as saving a file or switching spreadsheets.

The IBM PC/XT keyboard typically contains 10 function keys, and AT keyboards usually contain 12. The function keys on PC/XT keyboards are located on the left side of the keyboard, and across the top on AT keyboards. You also can combine function keys with the Alt and Ctrl keys, enabling additional functions to be performed with only a few function keys.

Many software products reserve the F1 key for requesting help, and provide keyboard templates (paper or plastic) to define the function keys "at-a-glance." In early desktop computer software, every product had its own specialized way of interpreting the function keys. However, the recent demand for more consistent user interfaces, especially in graphical user interface (GUI) systems, is now encouraging software vendors to avoid inventing their own function key schemes and to follow the prevailing practice.

function point

A unit of rough measurement of the complexity of a program or an application system, sometimes used in estimating the cost and time needed to develop software.

function value

The unique result of executing a function module, or the unique value returned by a function.

Side effects of a function are not usually categorized as function values. The term applies only to a result that can be used in an expression.

fundamental constant

A constant that defines some real-world parameter or some attribute of the environment.

The binding time of a fundamental constant is the point after which it becomes impractical to change the constant's value. Binding time is an important aspect of program design. The possibilities include the following:

- Coding-time binding (also called *hard coding*). The programmer codes the value inline wherever it is needed. Coding-time binding is considered extremely poor practice in all situations, and is avoided by experienced programmers.

- Compile-time binding. The value appears in a single occurrence in the source code. To change the value, you must change the line in the source code and recompile. Although an assignment statement can always accomplish compile-time binding, some languages provide special constructs for defining fundamental constants, such as the following:

Language	Construct
C	#define
C++	const
COBOL	VALUE clause
Pascal	const
PL/1	STATIC INITIAL or macro assignment

- Runtime binding. The program itself sets the value based on an input parameter or a computed value.

garbage collection

Searching an area of memory used for dynamically allocated data, to find data areas that are no longer in use and return them to the pool of free memory.

Garbage collection is unnecessary when the program releases storage it has finished using, either by an explicit action (invoking a "free" statement) or implicitly. With automatic allocation, such storage is always freed on exit from the block in which it was allocated.

In situations where a huge number of small areas of memory are allocated, however, the cost of explicitly freeing them may be prohibitive. This is typical in LISP, where dynamic data structures are constructed, manipulated, and abandoned at a high rate. In such cases, it may be more efficient simply to keep allocating new data areas until the free space is exhausted, then invoke a garbage collection routine to reclaim and coalesce all areas that are no longer pointed to by any active program or data structure.

generalization

The extension of functionality or the domain of a module or program so that it solves a wider class of problems than the specific one at hand.

Appropriate generalization is an essential part of reusability and often helps reduce programming costs significantly. Often a module can be generalized at very little cost in either development time or execution overhead. If such costs are significant, the designer or programmer must weigh the potential future usefulness of a more general module against the immediate requirements for the specific one.

For instance, a programmer might need to develop a programming module that prints information to a printer. Instead of making the module specific to a particular printer, generalizing the module may enable users to print to a wide variety of printers through the use of a printer definition file.

See also *fan-in* and *module cohesion*.

generation data group

A set of successive versions of a sequential file, managed according to rules governing the number of versions (generations) to be retained at any time.

Generation data groups were commonly used for master files in older batch processing applications. Today, they are used more for backup files and source code libraries. Many word processors, spreadsheet processors, and other desktop computer software products support specifically two generations: the current one and a single backup. For many kinds of sequential files, four or more generations are commonly retained as a backup in case of either damage or operational error.

In most second-generation environments, clerical personnel kept track manually of each generation data group. To eliminate the frequent costly errors resulting from that practice, some third-generation operating systems (such as the IBM MVS and VAX VMS) provide automated support for establishing and managing a generation data group. Whenever a job creates a new file in a given generation data group, the new file automatically becomes the current version, and the oldest version is deleted. For operating platforms that don't provide such support, programmers must design and implement their own schemes.

See also *.BAK*

generations, computers

The typical characteristics of commercially available computer systems during a given era.

The first three generations of computers were clearly differentiated both by hardware technology and by the state of the art in software and applications. Since the 1970s, however, both hardware and software technology have been evolving so rapidly and continuously that it is hard to draw lines that clearly differentiate one "generation" from another. Major trends of the 1980s and 1990s, such as desktop computers, networking, client-server architecture, and graphical user interfaces (GUIs), are much more significant than any arbitrary chronological boundaries.

Briefly, the first three generations of computers are as follows:

- The first generation (early to mid-1950s) is characterized by the use of vacuum tube circuitry, the use of magnetic tape as the main auxiliary storage medium, and the first assemblers and compilers.

- The second generation (late 1950s to early 1960s) is characterized by solid-state circuitry, the continuing use of magnetic tape but also disks as the main auxiliary storage medium, overlapped input-output (I/O) channels with asynchronous interrupt capability, magnetic core memory of up to more than 128K, the first operating systems, and powerful macro assemblers and compilers for new languages (including ALGOL, COBOL, LISP, and FORTRAN IV).

- The third generation (mid-1960s and the late 1970s) is characterized by integrated circuitry, the use of magnetic disks as the main auxiliary storage medium, magnetic core memory from 512K to several megabytes, more sophisticated operating systems, virtual storage supporting address spaces of up to 16M per user, and database management systems (DBMS) and more sophisticated programming languages (such as PL/1, APL, and Ada).

See also *first-generation computer, second-generation computer,* and *third-generation computer.*

generations, programming languages

A collection of programming languages exemplifying the state of the art in languages at a particular epoch.

Much confusion (and some deliberate distortion) surrounds the numbering of programming language generations. Unlike standard programming languages, most so-called "fourth-generation languages" are proprietary products developed, promoted, and owned by a single vendor.

Some writers associate the "first generation" with absolute machine code and the "second generation" with a symbolic version (assembly language) of machine code. For such writers, early languages like FORTRAN and COBOL belong to the "third generation," as do much more powerful procedural languages like Ada and PL/1. These writers use "fourth generation" as a synonym for "nonprocedural."

Other writers don't view machine code as a programming language at all.

They associate programming languages with the computer generations in use when they appeared or flourished. For such writers, FORTRAN and COBOL are "second-generation" languages, whereas languages designed to take advantage of the capabilities of third-generation computers are "third-generation languages." True "fourth-generation" languages await development and industry standardization.

generic class

In object-oriented programming (OOP), a class that contains functions (methods) and data required by other (derived) classes.

Generic classes can also be considered base classes, defining the basic properties such classes pass to objects. A generic class usually sits at the root of the class hierarchy. For example, a generic class of a "standard hotel room" might include a door, a bed, and a bathroom. A child class called "deluxe hotel room" can inherit the properties of the generic class "standard hotel room" and add things as required to define the new object, such as "whirlpool" or "king-size bed."

gigabyte

Literally, one billion (10^9) bytes, in American English usage.

Contrary to ordinary English usage, in programming a kilobyte has come to mean 1,024 (2^{12}) bytes when referring to random-access memory (RAM), mass storage space (such as hard disks), or storage media measured in powers of 2. Similarly, one gigabyte (1,024M) is 1,073,741,824 (2^{30} bytes).

The discrepancy caused by this exception is small, and not generally of practical concern in system design or implementation.

GIGO—garbage in, garbage out

An acronym for a common-sense phrase conveying the value of accurate input to a data processing system.

global module

A programming module that is available to all other modules in the system.

global variable

A data item that can be accessed by any module in a program.

In some cases, judicious use of global variables can simplify a program by reducing the number of parameters passed among modules. For example, an editing program typically must keep track of the number of errors encountered and the highest error-severity level encountered. By allowing any module in the program to update those global variables, you can avoid having to pass error code arguments through the entire hierarchy of modules.

On the other hand, using global variables indiscriminately can easily undermine the benefits of block structure and make programs hard to understand and maintain. Conveying the module input and output through explicit parameters and function values is considered better practice than using global variables and function side effects.

In block-structured languages such as Ada, Pascal, and PL/1, you can declare data items at any level in a hierarchy of nested blocks, which gives you full control over the scope of each data item. In non-block-structured languages such as COBOL and FORTRAN, the only choice is between local data that only one module can access, and global (or COMMON) data that all modules can potentially access. In many COBOL programs, a single DATA DIVISION shared by PERFORMED modules makes all data items global. Using C, you can declare variables at any level in a nested block structure; however, because you cannot nest function definitions, you cannot fully control the scope of data items.

See also *block structure*.

goto

A statement in most procedural languages to alter the sequential sequence of statement execution by transferring control to another designated statement.

The terms *branch, jump,* and *transfer* commonly denote the equivalent operation in assembly languages.

The target of a goto statement is a statement label or statement number.

goto-less programming

A coding style in procedural languages in which programmers avoid the use of goto statements.

Good programmers have long recognized that unrestricted branching can seriously undermine the readability of a program, and thereby greatly increase the cost of maintenance programming. In early programming languages such as FORTRAN and COBOL, goto statements were the main tool available for controlling flow logic, tempting programmers to develop so-called spaghetti code. Later languages such as C and PL/1 (although still providing an unrestricted goto statement) were designed with sufficient built-in constructs to render the use of goto statements unnecessary. The best programmers instinctively took advantage of those constructs, whereas other programmers kept on writing spaghetti code even in the newer languages.

A published comment by E. Dijkstra ("GOTO Statement Considered Harmful," *Communications of the ACM*, March, 1968) focused attention on the issue, and eventually led to the nearly universal acceptance of goto-less programming as the central component of structured coding. The popular older languages have now been updated to include the control structures necessary for goto-less programming.

See also *if-then-else construct, loop,* and *structured coding*.

GPF—general protection fault

A Microsoft Windows 3.1 critical system error generated when an application fails.

This error replaces the UAE (unrecoverable application error) of the earlier version (Microsoft Windows 3.0). Unlike UAE, which usually caused a crash of the whole operating system, most GPFs affect only the window or session in which the error occurred. Any concurrently running applications are normally unaffected by a GPF.

granularity

The changeability or degree of modularity of a system such as a graphical user interface (GUI). A system with a high degree of granularity can be altered to meet a certain exact need, but a system with a low degree of granularity cannot be customized as easily.

graph

An extremely general data structure that consists of the following:

- A set of nodes containing data (of an arbitrary type)
- A set of edges connecting designated pairs of nodes

Edges may have an associated length or cost, and may be either bidirectional or unidirectional; a graph whose edges are unidirectional is called a *directed graph*.

Graphs are useful for presenting large quantities of information and quickly diagnosing a variety of problems that typically can be solved through searching or pattern matching. Graphs are often used in applications such as natural language processing, data routing, and game playing.

Graphs can help to determine whether a path exists or to find a minimum cost path through a graph. A path exists from nodes V_1 to V_2 if either of the following is true:

- An edge connects V_1 to V_2
- Another node, V_x, exists, so that there is a path from V_1 to V_x and a path from V_x to V_2

In addition to the algorithms used to present data graphically, considerable attention has been given to efficient ways of representing graphs in a computer, but no single representation is best for all types of problems. For further information, see a textbook on algorithm theory.

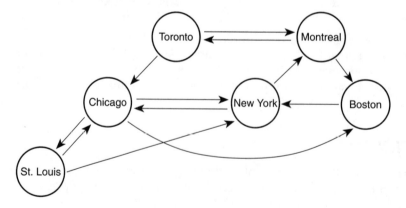

A directed graph (without costs).

	Boston	Chicago	Montreal	New York	St. Louis	Toronto
Boston	0	0	0	1	0	0
Chicago	1	0	0	1	1	0
Montreal	1	0	0	0	0	1
New York	0	1	1	0	0	0
St. Louis	0	1	0	1	0	0
Toronto	0	1	1	0	0	0

Representation of the same graph as an adjacency matrix.

See also *dynamic data structure, edge, list, recursive definition, recursive function,* and *tree.*

graphical user interface

See *GUI.*

graphics monitor

An output device with a screen suited for displaying graphic data rather than just text.

See also *VGA* and *video.*

graphics primitives

In computer graphics, a simple drawing element that cannot be decomposed into other drawing elements. More complex constructions can be built from combinations of graphics primitives.

GRAPHICS.COM

A terminate-and-stay-resident (TSR) program that enables DOS to use Print Screen (Shift+Print Screen) to print a graphics image on the printer.

For example, if a program can display a bar graph on the monitor, and GRAPHICS.COM is loaded into memory, the user need only use Print Screen to send the graph to the printer. The GRAPHICS.COM program supports CGA, EGA, and VGA graphics standards.

grep—global regular expression and print

A UNIX pattern-matching program used to search the contents of text files and print any line that matches a certain pattern. Versions for MS-DOS are also available.

For example:

```
grep client *.c
```

searches all files with the file name extension .c, for the word client. Wherever the word is found, grep displays the line in which it appears.

group item

In COBOL, a data structure or composite data item.

The manipulation of group data items is subject to several restrictions and nonintuitive results, especially where the components are stored in COMPUTATIONAL (rather than DISPLAY) form.

groupware

Any productivity tool designed to facilitate communication among multiple online users, especially to help users work together on common projects. Lotus Notes is an example of groupware.

See also *e-mail*.

GUI—graphical user interface

An approach to communication between online users and software, characterized by the following:

- The use of pictorial icons to represent the following:

    System objects, such as files, programs, peripheral devices, and windows.

196

Menu objects, such as commands and options

Entities or data items used in a particular software product or application system

- The use of a pointing device, such as a mouse, with which the user can do the following:

Select an object (see *click*)

Initiate a process or open a window (see *double-click*)

Move an object (see *drag and drop* and *cut and paste*)

- A view of the screen as if it were a desktop, a control panel, or both.

Although any such user interface is a GUI, the term has now come to connote a particular kind of highly standardized GUI derived largely from innovations developed in the 1970s by Xerox PARC and commercialized in the 1980s by Apple Computer with its Macintosh system. This kind of GUI is characterized also by the following:

- Multiprogrammed operation, with active processes communicating with the user through windows that occupy rectangular areas of the screen

- A highly standard arrangement of the main menu at the top of a window

- A repertoire of standard pictorial objects that have the same effect in all contexts, such as borders, boxes, buttons, pulldown menus, scroll bars, status lines, and toolbars

- Standard protocols for exchanging data among multiple applications (see *clipboard, DDE,* and *OLE*).

Other operating systems that support most of the preceding features include IBM's OS/2, Microsoft's Windows (an MS-DOS add-on), Windows NT, and the Open Software Foundation's Motif (a UNIX add-on).

The advantage of a GUI compared with a menu-driven or command-based user interface is the ease with which some users, especially those lacking computer skills, can master everyday computer tasks. Proponents claim that the various icons and metaphors are so intuitive that users need little formal training or recourse to manuals.

On the other hand, a GUI has these disadvantages:

- Considerable overhead in computer resources, including memory, disk space, machine cycles, and video, thus requiring the use of more expensive computers to accomplish what a less sophisticated interface could with fewer resources.

- Greatly increased programming complexity in both system software and application software, thus increasing the time and cost necessary to develop reliable and efficient software products or inhouse application systems.

So far, the marketplace has judged the benefits to be worth the costs, and a major trend toward GUIs is underway. In particular, Microsoft's Windows ranks among the all-time best-selling software products, and vendors of most leading productivity tools, compilers, and application software now offer Windows versions.

The acronym "GUI" is commonly pronounced as "gooey."

GUIDE

A user group for large-scale IBM computer systems.

GUIDE was founded shortly after SHARE by a group of organizations that had ordered the new 705 computer, a first-generation computer especially suited to business data processing. Since then, GUIDE has adopted each successor IBM mainframe as qualifying an organization for membership.

With the announcement of the System/360 as the successor to both series of second generation mainframe computers, SHARE and GUIDE had little reason to remain separate. In 1968 the boards of both user groups approved merger, but the memberships later rejected it, and the two organizations remained separate. Today they have very similar missions, but rather different personalities. GUIDE has overtaken SHARE in membership and exerts a major influence on IBM.

See also *SHARE.*

hacker

A technically proficient person who enjoys experimenting and exploring details of software, hardware, and systems, often without any systematic plan or predetermined goal.

The term has become closely associated with malicious activities, such as intrusion into dial-up services, unauthorized access to files, distribution of virus software, and various kinds of pranks. It is now considered pejorative in most contexts, and should not be applied to technically oriented professionals.

See also *techie*.

half-duplex

A communications channel that can transmit data in either direction, but only in one way at a time.

See also *duplex*.

halftone image

A photograph or other image having continuous shades of gray, from lightest to darkest.

Halftone images are created through a crossline or contact screen that converts the image to dots of various sizes. Although halftone images have played little role in traditional data processing, they are increasingly being used in desktop publishing and other applications that generate graphic output.

Hamming code

A data transmission code that is highly self-correcting.

Devised by R. W. Hamming, this scheme uses seven bits to represent each group of four bits. The extra three bits are used in combination to detect, and in many cases to correct, transmission errors.

handshaking

Synchronizing information passed between two devices to coordinate communication.

Handshaking applies mainly to serial communication. You can accomplish handshaking by manipulating hardware signals (changing voltages present on serial interface pins) or by exchanging special flow control characters.

hard-code

To embed knowledge in a program, especially the value of a constant.

In most situations, hard-coding is considered poor practice because it makes programs hard to understand and to change.

hard disk

Same as *fixed disk*. This term was coined to distinguish this medium from floppy disks.

hashing

A method of encoding data, used by indexing algorithms, to determine the relationship of individual data elements. A hashing algorithm is used to determine a hash index, which is an initial estimate of where a data item will fit within an index table.

head crash

See *disk crash*.

header file

In C programming, a source code file containing function declarations ("headers") and related data, referenced by the keyword #include at the beginning of the module that is using the file. (By extension, some C programmers call all #include files "header files.")

To use any of the standard C library modules, the programmer must first #include header files (such as stdio.h and string.h) for the appropriate groups of library modules.

header record

In a sequential file, a record containing information common to a group of "detail" records that immediately follow.

By using header records to factor out common data, the file designer can minimize the space required for a file and simulate a two-level hierarchical structure in a flat file. In a true hierarchical structure, the detail records would be subordinate to (children of) the header record.

heap

A binary tree in which the largest value is stored at the root node, and the value stored at each node is less than the value stored at its parent node.

heap sort

An efficient algorithm for internal sorting, in which the items to be sorted are maintained in a heap structure.

Like merge sort and quicksort, this algorithm sorts N items by using the theoretical minimum $N \log N$ comparisons, and is usually implemented by recursion. Heap sort also has the advantage of sorting in place (that is, swaps are made within the array or files containing the original information), so that it consumes much less space for a large N. However, a disadvantage of the sort is that programming the algorithm is more complicated. You can find details in most textbooks on algorithm theory.

help

Online instructions to assist users in using a program.

These instructions come in a variety of forms, including screens of information that users can scroll, menus that provide the user with help options, or small popup windows.

In many programs, you can invoke help by pressing the F1 function key or by choosing the **Help** option from a pulldown menu. MS-DOS lets you invoke help from the command prompt by typing **help** followed by the name of a command for which you want information. For example, if you want to access help on using the XCOPY command, you would enter the following:

HELP XCOPY

Hercules Graphics Adapter—HGA

A video display created by Hercules Computer Technology, Inc., widely used on Intel desktop computers.

This standard provides monochrome text and graphics capabilities with a resolution of 720 by 348 pixels. Created to meet the need for graphics in the first generation IBM PCs, HGA is still used as the standard for monochrome graphics.

hertz—Hz

A measure of frequency for a periodic event, in cycles per second. The term is usually used with standard prefixes, as in megahertz (MHz).

hex

See *hexadecimal*.

hexadecimal

The numbering system using 16 as its base, conventionally using the marks 0, 1, 2, ... 9, a (or A), b, ..., and f to represent its digits.

Hexadecimal is used as a compact, easily read, external representation of the contents of memory devices. Hexadecimal is particularly convenient in byte-oriented machines, because two hexadecimal digits can be used as a shorthand for eight bits without waste (each group of 4 left and right bits can represent 16 values).

Hexadecimal values that do not use the marks a through f can be confused with decimal representations, so various notations are used to make the base explicit; for example, 46H denotes $4 \times 16^1 + 6 \times 16^0 = 70$ decimal.

Hexadecimal is usually abbreviated as *hex*.

See also *octal*.

HGA

See *Hercules Graphics Adapter*.

hierarchical data structure

1. A composite data item, usually one with more than two levels.

2. A dynamic data structure in which each node has at most one parent node; a tree.

Most database management systems (DBMS) of the 1960s and 1970s were based almost entirely on hierarchical data structures, implemented by pointers within the records.

See also *relational database*.

hierarchy of operators

See *order of operators*.

HIMEM.SYS

An extended memory (XMS) device driver provided with MS-DOS and Microsoft Windows.

For example, a portion of CONFIG.SYS may look like this:

```
device = himem.sys
device = emm386.exe
device = smartdrv.sys
```

If you use another memory manager, such as 386 to the Max or QEMM 386, you don't need HIMEM.SYS.

HIPO—hierarchy plus input-process-output

A methodology for documenting program design, promoted in the 1970s by IBM as a component of structured programming.

A HIPO package for a complete program consists of two kinds of diagrams (both usually in landscape orientation):

- A structure chart showing the relationships, usually hierarchical, among the component modules. (In IBM literature, this document was usually called a "VTOC" for "visual table of contents." This kind of VTOC is unrelated to a VTOC in the usual sense of a disk directory.)

- A set of "input process output" (IPO) diagrams, one for each module shown on the structure chart. Each IPO diagram consisted of three panels:

  A list of the module inputs in the left panel.

  A list of the module outputs in the right panel.

  A description of the processing logic in the center panel, often in structured English, but alternatively as a flowchart or any other appropriate technique. Arrows between individual logic steps and the items listed in the adjacent panels showed exactly how the input was to be used and how each of the outputs was to be produced.

HLLAPI—high-level language application program interface

An IBM programming interface standard that enables personal computer programs to communicate with mainframe applications. Most 3270 emulation programs come complete with a HLLAPI interface.

Hollerith code

A scheme devised in the 1890s by Hermann Hollerith for representing numbers by holes in a punched card, and later extended to include alphabetic characters and punctuation.

Although punched cards are rarely used today, one popular character-encoding scheme, *EBCDIC*, is derived from Hollerith code. In the documentation of older *application systems*, you sometimes encounter the term *Hollerith* as a synonym for *character* or *alphanumeric*.

hook

An interface point provided by the developer of an operating system or productivity tool, usually intended for sophisticated programmers to exchange information with it, or influence its behavior.

Programming added at a hook sometimes becomes part of the larger software product, and may operate with the supervisory status of the host program. Such programs are often written in assembly language.

In older platforms (such as MVS) and programming languages (such as COBOL), hooks were called "exits."

hot key

A key or set of keys that invokes a program when pressed.

Hot keys are usually associated with a terminate-and-stay-resident (TSR) program that is activated any time the user presses a particular key combination.

See also *TSR*.

HPFS—high-performance file system

A file system first introduced with OS/2 and also used by network servers, Macintosh computers, and some UNIX operating systems.

It can handle very large disk volumes and file names up to 254 characters. Also, HPFS enables a user to execute a program simply by referencing a data file associated with that program.

HyperCard

A software product, available for the Apple Macintosh computer, for developing information systems based on the hypertext paradigm.

Developed by Bill Atkinson, HyperCard is distributed by Apple bundled with Macintosh computer hardware. Its low price as well as its power and flexibility have made it a popular tool among Macintosh programmers and nonprogramming users.

A HyperCard database is viewed as a stack of cards, each of which may contain text, graphics, and even sound, as well as active control elements such as buttons that the user can use to navigate through links to other cards in the stack.

In the HyperCard literature, programming is called "authoring."

hyperlink

In a hypertext system, a link established between a word or phrase and a related issue or further explanation of that word or phrase.

hypertext

A paradigm for implementing a database consisting of text, graphics, and links to other parts of the database. Such techniques enable the user to navigate through the links depending on his or her interests.

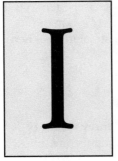

ICCP—Institute for Certification of Computer Professionals

An organization that conducts examinations to measure professional knowledge and awards certificates to those who pass.

The original CDP (Certificate in Data Processing) was launched in the early 1960s by DPMA. Later, with the joint sponsorship of ACM and other professional societies, the certification program was transferred to the ICCP, which was specifically chartered for that purpose. The certificates awarded include the following:

CDP   Certificate in Data Processing (for managers and systems analysts)

CCP   Certified Computer Programmer (with various subspecialties)

Enthusiasts hoped these certificates would attain a stature comparable to the CPA for accountants. Others worried that they might lead to premature legislated requirements for licensing of programmers and other professionals, and questioned whether the examinations test what is relevant and important. Most critics concede that the examination content has improved over the years.

After more than a quarter century, the program is flourishing, and some employers recognize certification as an indication of competence and individual initiative. However, few if any employers, government contracts, or professional activities require a certificate as a mandatory qualification.

icon

A small, pictorial representation of an object such as a program, a file, or a device. Graphical user interface (GUI) systems display icons on the user's screen to represent objects.

Advocates of GUIs claim that, on a crowded screen, the user can more easily spot colorful icons than names. However, others complain that icons take up too much room on the screen and require an unnatural two-dimensional space on which to represent one-dimensional lists of items. User-friendly interfaces tend to use icons to represent objects that the user can manipulate (see *drag and drop)*, and use text to present simple lists of items when the user needs only to choose items.

IDE—integrated development environment

An interface used by programmers that provides a user-friendly means of checking syntax and editing, compiling, and testing a program; sometimes called a "workbench."

IDE—integrated drive electronics

A fixed disk drive technology that provides a built-in controller.

Connected to the IDE controller by a 40-pin connector, this drive provides advanced features, such as look-ahead caching, to enhance the performance of the drive. The IDE drives are cost-effective and come in a wide variety of sizes, such as 100M, 120M, 240M, 360M, and 1.2 gigabytes.

IDENTIFICATION DIVISION

Introductory source code in a COBOL program that assigns a name to the program or subprogram and describes the purpose and usage of the program.

Older versions of COBOL enforced a rigidly structured IDENTIFICATION DIVISION with special entries for documenting such things as the programmer's name, the operating platform, and the date the program was originally written. These entries were seen as irrelevant and hard to maintain, and current practice relies more on free-form commentary, often guided by an organization's standards.

See also *comment.*

IEEE Computer Society—Institute of Electrical and Electronic Engineers Computer Society

A suborganization of IEEE that holds meetings and technical conferences on computer-related topics.

IEEE floating-point standard

A standard set of specifications that outline how an extensive group of mathematical operations are to be implemented in a computer system. This IEEE 754 standard covers operations with 32-, 64-, and 80-bit operand sizes.

if statement

An executable statement in a procedural language for testing whether some condition is satisfied.

In older programming languages (including early FORTRAN and COBOL) as well as most assembly languages, the if statement took various forms, many requiring the use of companion goto statements or branch instructions. Consequently, programs containing much decision logic were usually characterized by extensive spaghetti code.

In modern programming languages, the more disciplined if-then-else construct avoids these shortcomings in two ways:

- By allowing arbitrary sequences of statements along each branch

- By ensuring that the flow from the two branches comes back together at a common exit point

See also *goto-less programming, if-then-else construct, if-then-else statement,* and *structured coding.*

if-then-else construct

A flow-control construct that takes different actions depending on whether some condition is satisfied. It is represented graphically by the flowchart.

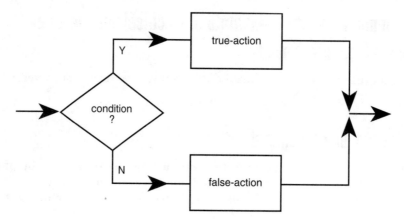

The if-then-else construct.

if-then-else statement

An executable statement in most procedural languages directly implementing an if-then-else construct. The most general form, illustrated here in pseudocode notation, is

```
IF   Boolean expression
THEN true action;
ELSE false action;
```

or if the *false action* statement is empty, just

```
IF   Boolean expression
THEN true action;
```

where the actions can be a simple executable statement or a sequence of statements (including further if-then-else statements). Some sort of bracket pair or terminator is usually required to make the scope of the THEN and ELSE clauses unambiguous.

immediate addressing

A mode of addressing in machine language in which the actual data value is embedded in a part of the instruction that operates on it.

See also *indirect addressing*.

implementation dependency

Programming that exploits knowledge of the hardware or system software beyond the published interfaces to the programming languages, productivity tools, and operating system.

Implementation dependency can greatly complicate attempts to port software to another platform. Even worse, it can be an obstacle to upward compatibility with future versions of the same operating system, compiler, or other hardware or software.

Many implementation dependencies are unnecessary for the proper functioning of the software. Nevertheless, software developers, especially vendors of competing products, sometimes exploit them for these reasons:

- To make programs run faster than they would if they used only legal facilities of the programming language or tool being used

- To circumvent the limitations of an inappropriately chosen programming language

- To fool an operating system or productivity tool into doing something it wasn't designed to do

The impact of implementation dependencies can be minimized by localizing them in a small number of modules that can be rewritten for other operating environments.

See also *encapsulation* and *version dependency*.

implicit declaration

The use of an identifier in a program that has not appeared in an explicit declaration. Languages that permit implicit declaration determine the attributes of such data items according to either the context in which they are used or the form of the identifier.

FORTRAN introduced implicit declaration with the convention that an identifier beginning with the letters I through N denotes an integer variable and all others denote floating-point variables. BASIC adopted a convention whereby a special-character suffix determines the data type. Ada, C, COBOL, and Pascal do not permit implicit declaration.

Although sometimes convenient, implicit declaration is now widely viewed as a dangerous practice, because a simple misspelling may go undetected and result in two distinct variables where the programmer intended only one.

211

implode

1. To apply any data compression to a file.

2. To apply a specific compression technique (see *ZIP file*).

3. To form a high-level data structure out of its substructures.

import

To read a file that was created by some other program in a form different from the format and structure normally used in the importing program.

Most word processors, spreadsheet processors, and database management systems (DBMS) now support importing of files that were written by competing products. Vendors can then more easily sell their software to current users of competing products.

Many products also support the importing of files created by completely different types of software. For example, you may be able to import a spreadsheet file into your database management system or even into a word processor.

See also *export*.

IMS—information management system

The dominant hierarchical database management system (DBMS) for IBM mainframe computers.

As organizations increasingly are adopting the simpler relational database model and moving to client-server platforms, the use of IMS is diminishing. Components of IMS also include IMS/DC, a teleprocessing monitor competitive with CICS, and DL/I (data language one), an interface language.

include file

See *header file*.

include library

See *source code library*.

incremental development

Development of an application system or software product without explicit specifications, by providing successive versions to the users, who then, based on actual experience with the system, request specific changes and enhancements for the next version.

This approach, although unnamed, was the most common way of developing software in the 1950s and early 1960s. Incremental development may be appropriate for small applications in which the users are unsure of exactly what they need. For major projects, however, the absence of an overall vision is likely to lead to dead ends and considerable rework.

See also *SDLC* and *prototype*.

index register

A high-speed register used to store the relative position of an item in an array or set of contiguous memory addresses.

Intel computers like the 80386 have two index registers: the SI (source index) and DI (destination index). Although you can use both as general-purpose registers and for memory access, they also are used by specialized string instructions and are coupled to specific segment registers, such as the following:

Index	Segment	Assembler String Instructions
SI	DS	MovSb, MovSw, LodSb, LodSw
DI	ES	MovSb, MovSw, StoSb, StoSw, ScaSb, ScaSw

indicator

A Boolean data item. The term is often used as a synonym for *switch* or *flag,* as in "end-of-file indicator" or "error indicator."

indirect addressing

A mode of addressing in machine language in which an instruction specifies the address of a cell that contains not the actual data value to be operated on but the address of that value.

See also *dereference* and *immediate addressing.*

infect

To move a computer virus to a computer in which it hides in the file system or memory, waiting for a chance to move to another computer over a network, through modem communications, or through disk transport.

After a computer is infected, the computer virus can reside on the computer system without incident, or it may erase data or cause other problems. Computer viruses are programs written by hackers, either with malicious intent or just for fun. In recent years, the computer virus problem has become serious.

See also *disinfect.*

inference engine

The control mechanism of an *expert system.*

An inference engine is a general-purpose program, independent of any specific knowledge base. It manages the interaction with the user and the strategy for inferring conclusions.

See also *chaining of rules* and *rule base.*

inference rule

An element of an expert system's rule base, which often is specified using the following syntax:

IF *condition* THEN *assertion*

where both the condition and the assertion may contain one or more variables that can be instantiated to specific values.

Although the preceding syntax closely resembles that of an if statement, its effect is quite different. In this syntax, the assertion following THEN is not an action to be performed but rather another condition to be set true for possible testing by another inference rule; for example, IF X has feathers, THEN X is a bird.

When the condition portion is true, the rule is said to "fire."

See also *expert system, inference engine,* and *rule base.*

infinite loop

A loop that specifies no termination condition (or specifies a termination condition that will never be true).

Many infinite loops are program bugs, the result of errors in specifying a loop exit. However, an infinite loop can also be a legitimate way of implementing never-ending processes, such as polling for events.

In either case, a program containing an infinite loop must eventually be forcibly terminated from an external source, such as a timer interrupt, job cancellation by the operator, or shutdown of the computer.

See also *bug* and *termination*.

infix operator

A binary operator written between its two operands, the usual operator notation in mathematics and most programming languages.

See also *binary operator, order of operators,* and *Polish notation*.

information

The result of processing data; usually the output of an application system.

Although the terms *data* and *information* are sometimes used as synonyms, careful writers make a distinction between them. Information is used for some purpose by the end users of a system. Data is merely collected (or entered) from some source.

inheritance

In object-oriented programming (OOP), the availability to a derived class of members (data and methods) of the base class.

inhouse

Belonging to one's own organization. This term can describe the following:

- A full-time employee, as in an inhouse networking expert
- Software developed and used within the organization, as in an inhouse project management system

- A problem solution or other abstraction developed and used internally, as in an inhouse life-cycle methodology or an inhouse professional training program.

Large data processing organizations formerly preferred inhouse solutions for almost everything, either because they believed their requirements were unique or because they trusted their own competence more than others'. The semi-facetious pejorative "NIH" (not invented here) characterized a nearly automatic dismissal of software or methodology arising from outside sources.

That picture has changed due to the continuing proliferation of specialties, the smaller size of typical organizations, the availability of well-regarded packaged application software, and growing budget pressures. Today, most organizations resort to inhouse solutions only when no suitable existing solution can be found.

initialization

Statements in a program concerned with initializing something.

It was once common practice to begin program execution by invoking a module to initialize everything that needed to be initialized. Such a catch-all initialization module, however, demonstrates poor module cohesion (because it groups logically unrelated actions) and poor localization (because a statement that initializes something may be far from the statements that later manipulate the same thing). Many bugs were traced to a programmer forgetting to make corresponding changes in initialization routines and other parts of the program.

Today, most experts agree that initialization is best done at a point immediately preceding (in time) and close to (in the source code) the related processing.

initialize

To set to an initial value or state. Examples of initialization include the following:

- Setting a counter or accumulator to 0 before entering a loop

- Turning off a switch or Boolean variable

- Opening a file

- Filling a character string with blanks

inline code

See *inline function*.

inline function

A function or module implemented by a sequence of instructions that are executed in the normal flow rather than by a calling sequence linkage. Inline functions were once called "open subroutines," but that term is rarely used today.

Because it avoids the overhead of subroutine linkage, an inline function executes faster than an equivalent, separately defined function. Unless it is very small, however, it can consume much more space, because a separate copy of the function is generated for each reference in the program. Therefore, inline functions are most useful as very small functions, such as the accessor functions and overloaded operators used in object-oriented programming (OOP).

Programmers often want to take advantage of the speed of an inline function without actually having to repeat the source code throughout the program. In some languages (such as C and PL/1), the programmer can do so either by defining a macro or by having the compiler generate inline code for a separately defined function.

inner product

See *dot product*.

input

See *module input* and *system input*.

INPUT

A BASIC instruction that gets one or more data items from an input stream.

input focus

In an operating system with multiple active windows, the process (or window) that currently is logically connected to the user's keyboard and therefore will receive any keystrokes.

217

input-output—I/O or I-O

The transfer of data between main memory and a peripheral device (such as auxiliary storage, a printer, or a keyboard).

Input-output operations under program control fall into three major categories:

- Formatted or stream I/O, usually involving an end user interface, with conversion of all data items to (output) or from (input) character string form. See also *editing program, report,* and *sequential file.*

- Unformatted or record-oriented I/O, involving a database or other files not seen directly by end users. See also *direct access file, ISAM, keyed file, master file, sequential file,* and *temporary file.*

- Graphic I/O (mostly but not exclusively output) involving a video screen, a plotter, or other two-dimensional display or scanning device.

See also *auxiliary storage, keyboard,* and *printer.*

input transaction

A set of related data items that:

- Are entered into an application system together

- Cause that system to take some specific action corresponding to the transaction type

In a typical business application system, common transaction types include the following:

- Inquiry transactions, to retrieve information from a database

- File maintenance transactions, to update a database

- Accounting transactions, to record a real-world event.

In a batch processing system, input transactions are usually collected in one or more sequential files, which are first processed by an editing program. In an online system, transactions are usually built up interactively as a result of some combination of the user performing the following actions:

- Responding to prompts

- Selecting menu options

- Entering data into forms or dialog boxes

instantiate

To create an object or data item in memory and make it addressable.

See also *allocate* and *bind*.

Institute for Certification of Computer Professionals

See *ICCP*.

Institute of Electrical and Electronic Engineers Computer Society

See *IEEE Computer Society*.

instruction

The unit of machine language code executed by a computer, usually consisting of the following:

- An operation code instructing the computer what to do, such as add, compare, branch, or store

- One or more operands: either actual data values, or addresses of memory cells containing the data

In assembly language programming, most of the statements are symbolic forms of instructions.

See also *command, immediate addressing,* and *statement*.

instruction counter

A register that contains the location of the next instruction to be executed.

In the Intel family of microprocessors, the instruction counter is the IP or instruction pointer register. The IP is coupled with CS or the code segment to give the full address of the next instruction.

In the IBM System/370 mainframe computer, the instruction counter is part of the program status word (PSW) to facilitate rapid switching between tasks.

int86

A C function that causes an MS-DOS interrupt.

The following code fragment uses the function to get the current disk transfer address (DTA):

```
Reg.h.ah = 0x2f;
int86 (0x21, &Reg, &Reg, &SReg);    /* Invoke MS-DOS (21) to */
CDtaSeg = SReg.es;                  /* retrieve DTA          */
CDtaOff = Reg.x.bx;
```

See also *interrupt*.

integer

A whole number, either positive or negative. As implemented in programming languages, integers are usually defined as numbers within a certain range. This range is defined by the number of bytes allocated in memory to represent the integers.

integer data type

A data type that can assume one of an implementation-defined subset of the whole numbers. In mathematics, the integers are a countable infinity, but machine design enables a system's instruction repertoire to handle only a finite subset of this range.

Machine architectures and programming language features may expand the set of integer data types to include long, short, and byte integers and allow signed and unsigned integers. Avoid exploiting the full range of these possibilities, because such exploitation reduces the portability of code.

integrated drive electronics

See *IDE*.

integration test

Testing of a complete program.

Integration testing is the second stage of testing new or modified software. Because all component modules will already have been unit-tested individually, any bugs to be discovered are likely to be in the interfaces between modules rather than in the modules themselves.

When testing is being done top-down, integration testing is just the end of unit testing, when the final bottom-level modules are added to the program being developed. On the other hand, when testing is done bottom-up, many component modules are executing together for the first time. Therefore, integration testing as a separately planned activity normally takes longer when testing is done bottom-up.

See also *module coupling* and *system test.*

Intel CPU

A microprocessor chip manufactured by (or under license to) Intel Corporation.

The Intel line has dominated the market in desktop computers since the 1970s. The widely used Intel central processing units (CPUs) include the following:

CPU Model	Year Available	Width of Data Path (bits)	Typical Clock Speed (MHz)	Comments
8080	1975	8	3	See also *Zilog CPU*
8086	1978	16	10	
8088	1979	8	4.77	The first IBM PC; a slower 8086
80286	1982	16	12	IBM PC AT; protected mode
80386	1985	32	25	Full 32-bit memory address
80486	1989	32	50	Built-in cache
Pentium	1993	32	100	Originally called "80586"

Starting with the 8088, computers using these CPUs have been popularly called "IBM PCs" or, for those computers not manufactured by IBM, "IBM clones." That terminology is fading in the 1990s, as Intel is seen as the main source of hardware innovation.

Starting with the 80286, many writers, including Intel itself, have optionally dropped the "80" prefix, referring, for example, to a "386 computer."

For the 386 and 486, the suffix "SX" denotes a somewhat less expensive CPU that lacks some feature or runs slower than the corresponding standard model. The suffix "DX" denotes the standard model in contexts where a writer wants to exclude the SX version.

The generic term 80×86 denotes any of the machines 286, 386, 486, or Pentium.

interactive program

A program that requires dialog between the user and the computer. Software that prompts the user for input is interactive.

See also *batch processing, input transaction,* and *interface.*

interface

A set of conventions and procedures that define the communication between the following:

- A program and the user; for example, the screen the user sees and interacts with to control the actions of the program.

- One program and another; for example, the set of functions an application program can call to control a graphical user interface (GUI).

- Software and hardware; for example, a device driver that handles interaction with a printer or a disk drive.

See also *GUI, module coupling,* and *user-friendliness.*

interlaced video

A method of projecting an image to a video screen, by displaying odd lines, then even lines, in a scan pattern.

A scan pattern image is created by many lines, each containing a horizontal portion of the picture. Interlaced video projects the image on the screen in two passes or scans, first by displaying the odd lines, then the even lines. This process is done very quickly. Through the scan pattern's *persistence,* or the length of time the phosphor on the screen holds the glow of the image, the human eye can perceive the image.

Interlaced video produces a lower quality display than non-interlaced video. Television signals and most low-cost video monitors for computers use the interlaced technique. However, high-end super VGA and above systems use non-interlaced video.

See also *display adapter, non-interlaced video, monitor, and video.*

internal sorting

The process of ordering elements of an array in the sequence of their values or of the values of key fields within each element.

Considerable attention has been given to analyzing sorting algorithms to minimize the number of comparisons and the number of exchanges. Although the difference in efficiency among sorting algorithms is trivial for small arrays, it becomes highly significant for large ones.

If an array has N elements, execution of a naive bubble sort requires N^2 comparisons. The theoretical minimum of $N \log_2 N$ comparisons is attained by several well-known algorithms, including heap sort and merge sort. Thus, for N = 30,000, bubble sorting would require a prohibitive 900,000,000 comparisons, whereas merge sorting would require only 450,000.

See also *bubble sort, merge sort, quicksort,* and *Shell sort.*

interpolate

Given a table of corresponding arguments and values of a function, to compute (or estimate) the function value corresponding to an argument that lies between two entries in the table.

interpreter

A program that executes another (target) program by loading that program into memory, then repeating the following three steps until the target program terminates:

1. Fetching the next statement in the target program

2. Decoding (parsing and classifying) the statement

3. Producing the effect of executing the statement

Interpreting is more flexible than compiling, because the programmer can more easily interact with the program in source code form while it is executing. Many implementations of LISP and BASIC are interpreters. On the other hand, interpreting is usually extremely inefficient. It is suitable, therefore, for one-time programs and for development of complicated algorithms, but not for most operational software that will be used many times.

See also *compiler.*

interrupt

A break in the sequential execution of instructions by the central processing unit (CPU), caused by any of the following:

- Some external event, such as the completion of an input-output (I/O) operation, the expiration of a timer interval, or a mouse click or keyboard action by the user

- An exception condition in executing an instruction, such as an attempt to divide by zero

- Execution of a supervisor call interrupt by an application program

The first type is called an asynchronous interrupt, because it can occur at any time, unrelated to what the CPU is doing. The other two are called synchronous interrupts because they occur as a result of the CPU instruction being executed.

The terms *trap* and *interrupt* are often used interchangeably. Writers who make a distinction between them usually reserve *interrupt* for the asynchronous type and use *trap* or *supervisor call* for the synchronous type.

When an interrupt occurs, the hardware transfers control to a fixed memory address. This instruction at that address is usually part of the operating system, which then determines what action to take.

intersection

A binary operation on two sets, yielding the set of all elements that belong to both sets. Formally:

x is an element of A ∩ B

if and only if x

is an element of A

or

x is an element of B.

See also *union*.

invoke

To initiate execution.

Invoke is a more general term than *call*, which often refers specifically to the *call* verb in a programming language. The term *invoke* can also refer to actions initiated by a program or by a user. For example:

- A graphical user interface (GUI) user can invoke a process by double-clicking on its associated icon.

- A spreadsheet processor user can invoke a keystroke macro by pressing the associated Alt-*x* key.

- A C function can invoke a lower-level function.

- A LISP function can invoke itself recursively.

- A batch file can invoke an MS-DOS command.

See also *call*.

I/O (or I-O)

See *input-output*.

IPL—initial program load

The procedure initiated when the computer is turned on.

ROM (read-only memory) chips control the IPL procedure, which is executed automatically when you start the computer. During the IPL procedure, the computer may undergo a series of system checks (such as memory, monitor, disk, and processor) before loading the operating system into memory and passing control to the operating system.

This term is standard with most minicomputers or mainframe computers. The synonym *bootstrap* (or informally "boot") more commonly refers to desktop computers.

irrational number

A quantity that cannot be represented exactly as the ratio of two integers.

An example of an irrational number is the square root of two. There are no two integers M and N such that $M^2/N^2 = 2$.

See also *rational number* and *real number*.

ISAM—indexed sequential access method

1. A file organization in which records are ordered by unique primary keys and can be retrieved either in the sequence of those keys or by a key value.

2. The IBM mainframe software (now obsolete) to create, maintain, and manipulate ISAM files. (Also other implementations intended to be compatible with IBMs.) ISAM was replaced by VSAM.

In business applications, ISAM was the most common vehicle for implementing master files before the widespread use of database management systems (DBMS).

Although the term is now obsolete in both senses, it is still used informally, especially among mainframe programmers, to describe indexed files or the software that manages them.

See also *B-tree* and *VSAM*.

ISPF—interactive system productivity facility

An IBM mainframe software program used to control interactive user interfaces on 3270-type terminals for application development.

ISPF also provides job management facilities for controlling the execution of batch jobs, and file editing facilities for editing source code and other text files. Mainframe software developers use ISPF extensively, despite an interface that is somewhat clumsy by modern standards.

See also *IDE (integrated development environment)*.

iteration

Repeated execution of a sequence of instructions.

The term *iteration* is a near synonym of *loop*. In addition, it connotes the computing of successively closer approximations to a problem solution, such as occurs when summing the terms of a convergent series.

JAD—joint application design

A methodology promoted by IBM for accelerated application system development, especially for the systems analysis phases.

As in more traditional approaches (see *SDLC*), JAD forms project teams whose members include both end users and systems analysts. Unlike traditional approaches, however, JAD encourages full-time participation by everyone, even the user representatives, until they produce the actual system or a prototype of the system. A "facilitator" keeps the team focused on its goals, secures additional resources when needed, and keeps thorough records.

For many kinds of application systems, JAD can indeed compress the time between the start of a project and the availability of usable software. On the other hand, it can also lead to hasty, ill-considered choices that complicate future maintenance programming, especially if the system is large and affects multiple user groups.

Some projects use this approach only for the early phases. After they develop the complete set of users' requirements, they switch to a traditional project-team approach for the remaining phases.

JCL—job control language

The command language for IBM mainframe operating systems.

JCL was widely criticized for its rigid, error-prone syntax, but praised for its power in automating the operation batch processing jobs in production status. Incompatibilities between versions of JCL for IBM's two operating systems, OS/370 (MVS) and DOS, can greatly complicate attempts to port applications between those two mainframe operating systems.

See also *command language.*

job

The unit of computer work submitted (requested, initiated, and launched) by a user. A job may consist of a single program or a series of programs.

See also *batch processing, job step, production status,* and *scheduler.*

job control language

See *JCL*.

job step

A sequential subdivision of a job, often initiated by a command in a cataloged procedure (batch file). Each step of a job must finish before the next one starts.

Job steps are particularly common in batch processing, in which a sequence of operations such as the following is to be performed:

1. Edit the input data (see *editing program*).

2. Update the database (see *file maintenance*).

3. Print reports (see *report* and *report generator*).

Job steps also appear in rudimentary form in more interactive processes, as in the following example:

1. Edit a source program (see *editor*).

2. Compile the program (see *compiler*).

3. Link-edit the program (see *linking loader*).

4. Execute (run) the program.

join

In a database, a relationship specified between two or more tables, resulting in the creation of either a composite table or a unique view of the data in the original tables.

A join is a relation (R) formed by the composition of two other relations (S and T) based on common values in one designated column each of S and T. (For binary relations, a join is simply the composite relation in which x R z if there exists a y such that x S y and y T z.)

Joins are used frequently in relational database systems and associated query languages to link the rows in one table with those in another table based on common values in a particular column. The common value (in the previous example, y) is usually considered part of the corresponding join rows. A join may be logically viewed as a file, whether the database management system (DBMS) physically creates a file or simply constructs each row as needed.

joint application design

See *JAD.*

Jolt Cola

A soft drink with greater caffeine and sugar levels than most competing products.

Programmers working "all-nighters" to meet deadlines are said to favor it to maintain wakefulness. *Computer Language* magazine and Jolt Cola co-sponsor an annual programmer's product competition.

Julian date

A five-digit representation of a date in the form *YYDDD,* where *YY* are the last two digits of the year, and *DDD* are the day number (with leading zeros) within the year. For example, the Julian representation of December 25, 1995, is 95359.

The origin of this misleading term is uncertain. Although Julian should refer to the Julian calendar, which was abandoned by most countries in the 16th century, that calendar has nothing to do with this date format.

jump

A synonym for *branch* that some computer vendors prefer.

justify

To align data within a field.

Typically, data is left-justified within a field, but it may also be right-justified, if the language allows it. For instance, assume that a data field is defined as allowing up to 10 characters, and the actual data only requires 6. If the data is left-justified, then the first character of the data field is also the first character of the actual data; the four character positions at the end of the field are either set to nul (no value) or to spaces. If the data is right-justified, then the four character positions at the beginning of the data field will have the nul or space fillers.

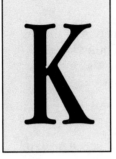

Kermit

A data transfer protocol widely used in academic systems and larger mainframes. It is implemented as a 7-bit system, even though it can be used to transfer files that contain 8-bit information.

Kermit was developed at Columbia University and named after the Muppet character (a lanky green frog) of the same name.

kernel

The portion of an operating system that manages central processing unit (CPU) and input-output (I-O) activity.

The kernel is in memory at all times. Among the functions it provides are the following:

- Memory management
- Interrupt handling
- Device interfaces
- Task scheduling

See also *device driver* and *paged memory.*

keyboard

The initial and primary input device for almost all computing equipment.

There are many variations of terminal and microcomputer keyboards, but all have at least the standard typewriter characters. Computer keyboards add special function keys, cursor-movement keys, and terminal control keys. Virtually all keyboards used for programming or general applications have the standard "qwertyuiop" arrangement for letters, numbers, and most special characters, but the placement of function, cursor-movement, and terminal control keys varies considerably.

keyed file

An indexed file in which the information is ordered according to the contents of a particular field within each data record. This field is called the *key,* because it determines the order of the records.

231

keystroke macro

1. An association between a designated key (or combination of simultaneously pressed keys) on a keyboard and a series of other keys. Whenever the user presses the designated key, the software responds as if he or she had typed the associated series of keystrokes.

2. More generally, a program triggered when the user presses a particular key or combination of keys.

Strictly speaking, the second type of keystroke macro is not a true macro, but simply a procedural program. However, in popular spreadsheet processors, word processors, and other general-purpose software, the term macro is used for such programming because their proprietary programming languages evolved from earlier versions that mainly supported true keystroke macros (that is, those described in the first definition). In such code, the programmer can often intersperse symbolic representations of keystrokes with procedural program statements. Whatever such facilities are called, they provide considerable power and flexibility beyond the basic functions provided by those products.

Most software products that support the true keystroke macros described in the first definition provide a recording mode, in which the software tracks the user's actions in defining a model for a macro. Many users who lack programming skills can define useful and powerful macros in this way.

keyword parameter

A parameter identified by a fixed keyword.

For example, if a module is declared with a parameter list (P, Q, R), and invoked with the arguments (Q=fctn(x - y), P=errsw), then the value of fctn(x - y) will be bound to the parameter Q, and a specified default value will be bound to the parameter R.

When a keyword parameter is a Boolean data item (logical, switch, or option), the corresponding argument is customarily specified without any accompanying value. When the parameter is any other kind of data item, the argument is followed by a delimiter—such as an equal sign or a colon—and the value.

In the MS-DOS command language, an argument corresponding to a keyword parameter is introduced by a slash (/) followed by a one-character parameter name. A colon (:) is then used as the delimiter. Some widely used compilers and utility programs use a minus sign (–) to introduce an argument corresponding to a keyword parameter.

Some languages support both positional parameters and keyword parameters in the same invocation. In such cases, all the positional parameters customarily precede the first keyword parameter. For example, in the MS-DOS command

```
FORMAT  B:   /V   /F:360
```

B: is an argument to be used as the first (and only) positional parameter, V is a Boolean keyword parameter, and F is a numeric keyword parameter. The order of the keyword parameters may be interchanged, but B: must precede both of them.

Keyword parameters are suited to situations in which the number of possible parameters is so large that a positional parameter list would be unwieldy and error-prone, and in which many of the parameters have default values. They are also useful as a way of avoiding errors with shorter parameter lists in which the parameters have no natural or obvious order. Many programming languages, however, don't support keyword parameters.

See also *positional parameter*.

kill

The UNIX utility that sends a signal 15 (terminate) to a process.

The process number of the process to be terminated is passed as an argument of the kill command. You can determine the process number by using the UNIX ps (process status) command.

kilobyte

Literally, one thousand bytes, usually abbreviated as *K*.

Contrary to generally accepted usage, in programming a kilobyte has come to mean 1,024 bytes when referencing random-access memory (RAM) or mass storage space (such as hard disks). Thus a 640K machine actually has 655,360 bytes. The ambiguity resulting from the use of the same prefix to represent both 1,000 and 1,024, while regrettable, is seldom serious, as the difference is relatively small.

The RAM addressing limits and cache, page, and segment sizes of modern machines are almost always given as a power of two, because data paths on the motherboard and within chips are parallel sets of lines carrying binary signals.

See also *gigabyte* and *megabyte*.

kludge

A messy, inelegant, and cumbersome solution to a problem.

As you might expect, kludges are seldom reliable. A kludge is often the result of a hasty, incremental approach to solving a problem.

knowledge base

A collection of information describing some area of experience. In an expert system, the knowledge base consists of a rule base of inferences plus a database of facts.

See also *database* and *inference rule*.

knowledge engineering

The methods and disciplines used in specifying, designing, and building expert systems.

A knowledge engineer is simply a systems analyst who specializes in expert systems. A particularly challenging part of knowledge engineering is knowledge acquisition, the process of discerning and codifying knowledge from human experts.

Korn shell

A UNIX shell that replaces the Bourne shell.

The Korn shell can act like the Bourne shell, processing commands in the same manner. However, this shell is larger than the Bourne shell and provides many enhancements, including additional shell programming operators, string-handling functions, command editing, and command history. Command editing enables the user to use standard vi or emacs commands to make changes to a command. Command history enables the user to recall previously used UNIX commands, and thus avoid having to repeatedly retype commands.

See also *Bourne shell*.

label

See *data set label, statement label,* and *volume label.*

label (spreadsheet)

Character-string or text data in a spreadsheet.

This rather misleading term is used in manuals and training materials supporting popular spreadsheet processors, largely for historical reasons. Such spreadsheets were first used almost entirely for numeric calculation. Text data could be placed in cells mainly to identify or "label" columns, rows, or other adjacent cells. With modern spreadsheet processors that support a full range of text-handling facilities, however, it is usually more clear to use the terms "text" or "character" to denote nonnumeric data items.

LAN—local area network

A network of computers that uses direct cable connections rather than telecommunications. LAN configurations are limited by the distance that signals can be sent over the physical media (the wires) linking the nodes on the network.

laser printer

An output device that uses a laser to paint dots of light onto an electrophotographic drum or belt.

After the laser transfers the image to the drum, toner is applied to the drum or belt, then paper moves through the printer, similar to a copier.

Laser printers usually are more expensive than, but preferable to, dot-matrix and daisy-wheel printers. Laser printers can print more pages per minute, at resolution of 300 to 600 DPI (dots-per-inch). Printouts typically are crisp and clean, and visually superior to those generated with other printing methods.

Hewlett-Packard introduced a PC-oriented version of their laser printer in 1984, and in recent years the HP Laserjet has set the standard for laser printing; however, many other manufacturers produce laser printers. Most laser printers use normal copier paper, although some use tractor-fed computer paper.

latency

On a rotating storage medium such as a disk, the time between completion of a seek that positions the read-write head at the desired track and the start of data transmission. Latency is sometimes called "rotational delay."

lazy evaluation

A strategy for minimizing computation by dynamically determining which parts of a function will actually affect the result, then evaluating only those parts. For example, if a particular branch of a tree determines the result of the whole tree, then evaluating the other branches is unnecessary.

Lazy evaluation is important in artificial intelligence and other applications that involve deep search strategies or traversal of large data structures. LISP programming commonly uses a sophisticated way of implementing lazy evaluation in which the result of evaluating one function may include a list or agenda of further functions to be evaluated.

lead programmer

A role within a software development project team. The lead programmer is responsible for technical issues affecting the whole project rather than just one program or module, such as high-level program structure, programming standards, library management, and reusable modules.

See also *chief programmer* and *designer*.

level, programming language

A rough measure of the ratio of source code to equivalent machine code.

The meaning of this imprecise term can vary, depending on the speaker's point of view. It is more useful in comparing two or more languages than in characterizing any single language.

Starting from the lowest level and working up, the following levels are generally recognized:

- Machine language consists of the absolute bit patterns that a computer executes, or is a relocatable object module containing equivalent bit patterns. Since the 1950s, no one has actually written any significant amount of original code in machine language.

- Assembly language is a symbolic representation of machine language.

- Higher-level languages include most procedural languages and some problem-oriented languages. A statement in a higher-level language can generate up to several hundred machine language instructions.

- Very-high-level languages (VHLs) include most of the newer nonprocedural languages, application generators, and some problem-oriented languages. A statement in a VHL can be equivalent to up to a dozen statements in a higher-level language.

These levels are, of course, very rough and oversimplified. Languages that include a powerful macro processor, including most modern assembly languages, give the programmer the opportunity to raise the level of the language by defining higher-level constructs. In the hands of a skilled programmer, a macro assembler can have power equivalent to FORTRAN or C for certain kinds of applications. Furthermore, the most powerful of the higher-level languages may well outperform some VHLs.

See also *generations, programming languages.*

level number

A notation for specifying static hierarchical data structures, and the standard way of specifying such structures in COBOL, PL/1, and some proprietary software.

Slightly oversimplified, the notation works like this:

- A level number precedes each data name declaration.

- A level 1 item is independent (subordinate to no other data item).

- An increasing level number is like a left parenthesis—that is, the item on that line is subordinate to the preceding item.

- A decreasing level number is like a right parenthesis—it returns to the level of the last item that had the same level number.

For example, examine the following Pascal structure:

```
var employee_record   : record
    identifier         : packed array[1..11] of char;
    name               : packed array[1..30] of char;
    date_of_birth      : date;
    spouse             : record
```

237

```
        name              : packed array[1..30] of char;
        date_of_birth     : date;
    date_hired            : date;
    current_position      : record
        date_effective : date;
        title             : packed array[1..48] of char;
        salary            : money
end;
```

This Pascal structure is equivalent (assuming appropriate Pascal type definitions) to the following COBOL structure:

```
1     EMPLOYEE-RECORD.
      5     IDENTIFIER              PIC 999-99-9999.
      5     NAME                    PIC X(30).
      5     DATE-OF-BIRTH           PIC S9(7) COMP.
      5     SPOUSE.
            10    NAME              PIC X(30).
            10    DATE-OF-BIRTH     PIC S9(7) COMP.
      5     DATE-HIRED              PIC S9(7) COMP.
      5     CURRENT-POSITION.
            10    DATE-EFFECTIVE    PIC S9(7) COMP.
            10    TITLE             PIC X(48).
            10    SALARY            PIC S9(9) COMP.
```

Note that you get the identical structure by using level 2 instead of 5 and level 3 instead of 10. Skipping level numbers is an old COBOL tradition, to facilitate later changes. However, with today's powerful editors, the tradition no longer serves any real purpose.

lexical analysis

A method of analyzing (parsing) a text string in which a lexicon (dictionary) is searched for possible matches. The dictionary contains words and phrases to be matched, along with symbolic or token representations of those words and phrases into which the original text is to be parsed.

See also *parse*.

library

A group of related files.

In most platforms all the files in a given library reside in the same directory and have a common file name extension.

See also *object module library*, *PDS,* and *source code library*.

life cycle

See *SDLC*.

LIFO—last-in, first-out

Sequencing strategy in which items are removed from a stack in the reverse order from the order in which they were added; that is, the newest are added first.

LIFO sequencing arises in handling nested structures, such as in parsing parenthesized expressions or searching trees. The need for a program to manipulate LIFO sequencing can sometimes be avoided though the use of recursive functions.

During execution of a program containing a hierarchy of subroutines, a LIFO stack is often used for temporary storage of parameters an local environment data.

See also *FIFO*.

LIM—Lotus/Intel/Microsoft

A standard memory configuration agreed to and supported by these three influential vendors.

This specification provides MS-DOS software developers with the instructions needed to create EMS memory boards and EMS drivers, and explains how an MS-DOS application program can use EMS. LIM is an open standard, so other companies needn't pay royalties to use the specification.

line printer

An output device, usually connected to a mainframe or minicomputer, that prints one line at a time, commonly on 11-inch by 17-inch "greenbar" paper.

Line printers are very fast and often provide excellent print quality, but they lack the capability of laser printers to print graphics images and different fonts.

link

See *linking loader.*

LINK.EXE

Microsoft's linking loader for MS-DOS.

Many compilers provide their own linking loaders that support special features of a particular language. Those linking loaders may have slightly different names (TLINK.EXE, for example) but their use and functionality are similar to that of LINK.EXE.

Linkage Editor

A sophisticated linking loader used in IBM mainframe operating systems.

linked list

A data structure whose elements are logically connected by a pointer to the next element.

Each element in the list comprises a pointer and the application data. List elements may be in random-access or disk memory, and are typically not contiguous. A fixed-length list head containing the list name and a pointer to its first element (and often, its last) is usually implemented as an element of an array containing all the lists the program is using.

linked list, double

A variation of the linked list data structure in which each list element contains two pointers, one to the next element in the list, and the other to the previous element.

The additional pointer enables the programmer to search the list in a forward or backward direction, at the cost of additional overhead in maintaining the pointer structure.

linker

See *linking loader.*

linking loader

A system software component that builds an executable complete program from component object modules.

The object modules generated by compilers or assemblers often contain unresolved references. Suppose that module A contains a call to module B, which was compiled separately. The compiler, while compiling A, has no way of knowing the eventual address of B. It can only insert the symbolic name B into the appropriate place in object module A. Similarly, while compiling B, the compiler has no way of knowing the identities of the other modules that may call B. It can only insert the symbolic name B as the entry point to the module. When the linking loader encounters these modules in its input, it replaces those symbolic references with the real (relocatable) addresses.

Many linking loaders provide other functions, including the following:

- Automatically searching object module libraries for any external references that were not found in the main input. This feature is essential for collecting the standard runtime support modules a compiler knows about, because the programmer is usually unaware of their identities.

- Arranging modules in overlay structures to conserve memory at runtime. The use of this feature has greatly diminished because of the falling cost of memory and the growing availability of virtual memory.

Especially in MS-DOS, linking loaders have proliferated as software vendors compete by including their own versions with their compiler products. Although these linking loaders all support a common, mutually compatible standard, each has its own special extensions and features designed to work with a particular compiler, debugger, or other proprietary product.

lint

1. A program that checks C programs for erroneous, nonstandard, or simply wasteful usage.

2. An abbreviation for *long integer*.

LISP

A functional programming language originated in the 1950s by John McCarthy and still used widely, especially in the United States, for artificial intelligence applications.

In its orignal form, LISP (for "list processing") was a small and elegant applicative language. In its long history, LISP has been extended in many ways, and is now a very large language, having procedural aspects as well.

The fundamental data structure in LISP is the list, a sequence of elements. Because elements can be of different types, including other lists, you can build up data structures of any complexity from this one structure.

The fundamental program unit in LISP is the function, defined by the defun primitive. When LISP recognizes the first element of a list as the name of a defined function, it evaluates the result of applying that function to the remaining elements of that list.

Because lists are constructed and evaluated dynamically during execution, LISP is suited to processes that require heavy recursion, searching, and backtracking. In the hands of a clever programmer, LISP can often express, with surprising conciseness, processes that at first seem immensely complex. Efficient execution is usually a secondary consideration.

Among the numerous dialects of LISP, Common LISP has become dominant.

See also *CLOS* and *PROLOG*.

list

The most general dynamic data structure, a sequence of items.

A list is much like a vector except that the items may be of different types. Thus, you can construct any data structure, such as a tree or a graph, out of lists of lists, and so on. For example, suppose you want to set up a classification scheme, and you have just one model list with only two members:

```
(type, list-of-subtypes)
```

You can then build the following taxonomy:

```
    (vehicle, (vehicle-type1, vehicle-type2, . . . ))
=   (vehicle, ((car, (mid-size, compact, sports, limo, jeep)),
            (truck, (semi, pickup)), bus, motorcycle ))
```

List structures are often well-suited to highly recursive processes, playing a prominent role in pattern recognition, natural language understanding, robotics, and other branches of artificial intelligence.

See also *LISP, queue,* and *stack.*

list box

In graphical user interface (GUI), a small window that presents to the user a list of mutually exclusive alternatives, such as a list of fonts.

When such a list is too long to fit in the window, the user can scroll it by using a scroll bar or the cursor keys.

A list box.

See also *combo box* and *dialog box.*

listing, program

A printed display of the source code of a module (or collection of related modules) with additional related information to help readers understand the code. A program listing is usually produced by a compiler or assembler, but can also be generated by an editor or some other software development tool.

Because the readability of a program has a strong impact on its maintainability, many compilers and assemblers provide facilities for controlling page breaks, indentation, headings, vertical spacing, and other aspects affecting the appearance of the source code on the listing.

Supplementary information generated by the compiler typically includes the following:

- Error and warning messages

- Nesting level indications

- Generated code from macro expansions or library include files

- A list of data names, with their type and other attributes

- A list of references to data names from program statements

See also *pretty print.*

literal

A constant named by its value.

For example, a reference to 8 in source code really means "an integer data item having the constant value 8." A reference to "Hello!" really means "a six-byte data item containing the ASCII codes for 'Hello!'"

A compiler or assembler will normally consolidate multiple references to the same literal, storing the value in a single storage location that the program cannot modify directly.

little endian

Representation of a 16-bit integer with the less significant byte first. This representation is a legacy of early eight-bit microcomputers and is still used, for compatibility, in Intel 80x86 and a few other architectures.

In contrast, the conventional integer representation is called "big endian." These terms originated in Swift's *Gulliver's Travels,* in a debate over which end of an egg should be eaten first.

load module

An executable program; the output of a linking loader.

This term is standard in IBM mainframe environments, but not widely used elsewhere.

local area network

See *LAN.*

local variable

A data item known within a block, but inaccessible to code outside the block.

Restricting knowledge of and access to data items eliminates many opportunities to introduce errors, and thus facilitates debugging and promotes operational reliability. Most modern programming languages now support some form of block structure, encouraging the use of local variables. BASIC and COBOL originally lacked such a facility, however, and in most programs written in those languages, all variables are global.

locate-mode I/O

An option in which records are processed in the buffers used for input-output (I/O) operations. Instead of allocating space for such records, the program sets a pointer to the appropriate position within the active buffer.

COBOL, PL/1, and some input-output library routines for other languages give the programmer a choice between operating directly on records in the buffers (locate mode) or moving records between working storage known to the program and hidden buffers (transmit mode). Locate mode, by avoiding the need to move the whole record, offers greater efficiency. However, it also presents more opportunities for error, especially with variable-length records and record blocking.

log file

A file containing a record of computer activity.

Log files are used by different kinds of programs for a variety of purposes, as in the following examples:

- An operating system may record the times that users on a multiuser system log on and off and the system resources they use. Such a usage log can later be used for billing, for capacity planning, or for security audits.

- An application system may record input transactions. Such a transaction log can later be used for auditing.

- A database management system (DBMS) may record changes to a database. If the database is later damaged, those changes can then be re-applied to an earlier backup copy.

logical database

A specification that identifies the data items to be stored in a database and shows the relationships among those data items.

A logical database is independent of any physical database implementation. It *doesn't* specify or imply any of the following:

- The use of any specific database management system (DBMS)

- The number, names, or structure of any files

- Any pointers or other control data used to represent relationships in a computer

- The internal data representation of the component data items

There is no standard method of specifying a logical database. Many systems analysts use entity-relationship diagrams (ERDs) to specify a logical database graphically. Others prefer to prepare a normalized relational model.

A logical database specification is useful for providing the following:

- An understandable description of permanently stored data in a proposed new application system, so that the prospective users can review it for completeness and correctness.

- A starting point for designing one or more physical databases.

- A reference for other components of a specification of a new application system. See *data-flow diagram* and *structured analysts*.

logical record

A data structure stored on an auxiliary storage medium and treated by programs as a single record.

On the auxiliary storage medium, data is grouped into contiguous physical records. When a logical record corresponds to the physical record or block, the records are considered to be "unblocked." For efficiency, however, multiple logical records can be stored in a single physical record (see *record blocking*) and a single logical record may span multiple physical records.

In the context of programming, the terms *logical record* and *physical record* are often dropped in favor of simply *record* and *block*.

See also *block*.

long integer

An integer data type with extended length.

In standard C, the signed long integer type handles integers from $-2,147,483,647$ through $2,147,483,647$ (2^{31}). For other compilers, the maximum values for long integers are implementation-dependent.

loop

A flow construct in which a sequence of statements (the loop body) is executed repeatedly; also called *iteration*.

Loops are among the most fundamental constructs in procedural programming languages, and occur in almost all nontrivial programs. They are supported by explicit loop-control constructs in all procedural languages:

- In the most general form, the loop body is executed repeatedly until a governing condition is changed by some event in the loop body. See *do until* and *do while*.

- In more specialized forms, the loop body is executed a definite number of times, often with associated incrementing of a counter (loop-control variable). See *for*.

See also *infinite loop*.

loss of control

A program bug whose symptom is a failure of a module to execute its expected sequence of statements leading to normal termination.

A loss of control can be difficult to diagnose, because the output statements that could display the status of variables and reveal the cause of the problem may never be executed. In the worst case, the program may destroy vital control blocks or pointers.

Programmers should look for the following common causes of loss of control:

- Mismatched arguments and parameters between separately compiled modules

- An error in assigning a value to a pointer (or in assembly language, a base register)

See also *breakpoint, debugger,* and *infinite loop.*

Lotus 1-2-3

Lotus Development Corporation's spreadsheet processor, available in versions for most operating platforms. 1-2-3 is one of the first such products to integrate graphics and sophisticated presentation tools with BASIC spreadsheet capabilities.

At one time Lotus 1-2-3 so dominated the market for desktop computer spreadsheets that some people began using the term *Lotus* generically to refer to spreadsheet processors or spreadsheet language. Careful writers, however, distinguish between references to this specific family of products and references to spreadsheets in general.

See also *Excel* and *Quattro Pro.*

Lotus Notes

Lotus Development Corporation's groupware product for network platforms.

lower CASE

CASE (computer-assisted software engineering) tools or techniques used in the second half of the life cycle, which consists of automated design and code generation.

See also *upper CASE.*

lowercase

The small, noncapitalized alphabetic letters *a* through *z.*

See also *ASCII, EBCDIC,* and *uppercase.*

LRU—least recently used

A common paging strategy in which, when memory is full and a page fault occurs, the operating system chooses to remove from real memory the virtual memory page that was least recently accessed.

This strategy is based on the assumption that if a page hasn't been referred to for a long time, it is comparatively unlikely to be referred to very soon. However, certain patterns of memory access, such as the repeated sequential search of a huge array, might make LRU perform poorly. Sophisticated paging algorithms may combine LRU with other strategies.

Economical implementation of LRU requires special hardware to keep track of references to pages, either in a stack or with a time stamp. Without such special hardware, a FIFO paging algorithm may be an acceptable compromise.

See also *dirty bit.*

ls

A UNIX utility used to list the files in a directory.

From the shell prompt, the user enters **ls** to display all the files in the current directory. Wild cards can be passed to ls, as in as `*.txt` or `syste*`, to filter the file names to be displayed.

See also *dir.*

lvalue

A data item that has an address or can be referenced by a pointer. The term is an abbreviation of "left-side value," because it can appear on the left side of an assignment statement.

Understanding the distinction between lvalues and other data items is especially important for C programmers, because the C language relies heavily on side effects within expressions. Because neither constants nor most kinds of expressions can be updated or have values stored within them, they may not appear in any context that implies that they are lvalues.

m4

A macro processing language for UNIX that converts input into source code for a particular programming language (such as C). The language is a source code preprocessor.

machine language

The instruction codes that control a computer.

Machine code is the result of an assembly or compile task, perhaps augmented by a link operation. For some systems, working at this level of detail is called "programming in actuals." Sometimes you can use a low-level program editor to make minor program modifications in machine language; however, doing so is seldom a good idea.

macro

A named source code structure that expands into other source code structures, substituting source code parameters.

Macros were introduced in assembly languages used on second-generation computers to accomplish the following:

- Subordinate detail and provide a higher level of expression
- Standardize commonly used programming techniques
- Localize dependencies on data formats or machine characteristics

Here's a rather oversimplified example, assuming a machine architecture that provides the following instructions:

```
LOAD   R,X  (Puts contents of memory cell X in register R)
ADD    R,X  (Adds contents of memory cell X to register R)
STORE  R,X  (Stores contents of register R in memory cell X)
```

The programmer could define a macro to increment a variable by 1:

```
INCR MACRO  X
     LOAD   AC,X
     ADD    AC,=1
     STORE  AC,X
     END
```

then use the following code to increment the counter LINE_NO:

```
INCR    LINE_NO
```

In addition to their use with assembly languages, macros have been provided for some higher-level languages, most fully in LISP and PL/1, and to a limited degree in C. In addition to the previously listed goals, the macros of higher-level languages enable the programmer to achieve the following:

- Extend the language to support an application area

- Extend the language to support the environment, such as a graphical user interface (GUI) platform

- Improve program readability by concealing unattractive characteristics of the base language

- Improve program reliability and facilitate debugging by localizing error-prone characteristics of the base language

Here's an example of a C macro defining a function that returns the smaller of its two arguments:

```
#define MIN(X,Y) ((X) < (Y) ? (X) : (Y))
```

Whenever the program refers to MIN(*expr1*,*expr2*), the macro preprocessor will then substitute *expr1* for X and *expr2* for Y in the expanded source code, simply treating *expr1* and *expr2* as strings of text. Although this substitution mechanism allows MIN to work for any data type for which the less-than operator (<) is defined, it also can lead to results unforeseen by the programmer who defined the macro. In the preceding example:

- The extra parentheses enclosing each occurrence of the parameters X and Y are needed to enable expressions to be substituted for those parameters, as in the following use of MIN:

  ```
  fee = MIN(hours * rate * discount_factor, contract_limit)
  ```

- The parentheses enclosing the whole expression are needed to enable an occurrence of MIN to be an argument of an operator, as in the following statement:

  ```
  fee = MIN(hours * rate, contract_limit) * discount_factor;
  ```

- Neither the inner nor the outer parentheses protect against unintended results from side effects in a repeated C expression:

  ```
  x = 1;
  z = MIN(x++,2)      // x is now 3!
  ```

macro, keystroke

See *keystroke macro*.

macro assembler

An assembler that includes a macro processor.

This term has become redundant, because almost all modern assemblers are macro assemblers.

See also *assembler* and *macro*.

mainframe computer

A large computer capable of providing processing services to thousands of users through thousands of terminals, connecting users directly or through a network. (The term *mainframe* refers to the main cabinet that held the central processing unit when the computer was first introduced.)

Mainframes can have hundreds of gigabytes of disk space and hundreds of megabytes of memory.

Mainframe computers have been around since the 1950s and are still used in many large organizations. IBM has been the dominant mainframe vendor. The use of the mainframe in recent years, however, has decreased as more applications move to the less-expensive workstations or PCs.

See also *third-generation computer,* and *generations, computers*.

main module

The module that initially gets control when a complete program is invoked.

Some programming languages identify the main module by a reserved name (main in C). Other languages identify the module by a clause in the declaration (OPTIONS(MAIN) in PL/1), by the absence of any subroutine declaration (in FORTRAN and COBOL), or by being the first module in the input stream (in certain proprietary languages).

See also *complete program*.

main program

See *main module.*

maintainability

See *maintenance programming.*

maintenance programming

The programming activities that support existing application systems, including the following:

- Diagnosing and repairing bugs that arise in production operation

- Adding new features and enhancements

- Updating tables and other data hard-coded into the source code

Maintenance programming demands different skills and temperament than development programming. Although some organizations separate the two functions organizationally, most assign development of new applications and maintenance of existing ones to the same programming staff.

During the life span of an application system, the cost of maintenance often far exceeds the initial cost of development. The quality of the original design, coding, and documentation strongly influences the ongoing cost of maintenance and the ease with which the maintenance programmers can respond to requests from users of the system. The payback for applying structured techniques, well-chosen programming standards, and appropriate programming languages is realized mainly in future maintenance.

make

A programming utility, originally implemented on UNIX systems, that assists in managing the program modification and maintenance process, by creating a shell program used to re-create the application system.

mask

In programming, a pattern of bits used to select which bits in a byte are to be tested or which machine interrupts are to be disabled. Interrupts that this method cannot control are said to be non-maskable, hence the term non-maskable interrupt (NMI).

master file

A permanent file containing descriptive and status information about some entity. Examples of such files include the following:

- A personnel master file for a payroll or human resources system

- An inventory master file for a warehouse inventory control system

- A general ledger file for an accounting system

A master file serves the same role as a database, and in some contexts the two terms are used interchangeably. However, the terms have different connotations:

- *Master file* is the older term, having originated before computers were widely used in business applications. It therefore conveys a somewhat old-fashioned flavor.

- A database is not limited to one file, but can contain a family of related files describing different entities in an organization.

- A master file usually belongs to a single application system, whereas a database may be shared by two or more systems.

- A database is likely to have more structure than a master file; many master files are implemented as flat files. To create and manipulate a database usually requires database management system (DBMS) software, whereas a master file can usually be created and manipulated by the lower-level input-output facilities provided by an operating system.

Master files are a central focus of traditional business applications. Processing transactions to update master files (file maintenance) and deriving reports from them (report generation) comprise a major part of the functionality of many application systems.

matching

Finding a structure by searching for a known pattern, usually by examining corresponding elements of two data structures. A sophisticated matching strategy may require substitution of values for variables in one or both structures, in which case it is called *unification*.

See also *backtracking* and *search*.

math coprocessor

A circuit board that can be added to Intel computers to support hardware floating-point operations.

Many desktop computer uses, such as word processing, do very little numerical calculation, and therefore gain little from a math coprocessor. On the other hand, many spreadsheet models and computational programs run much faster when a math coprocessor is available.

Floating-point is now a standard feature of the newest Intel (80486DX and Pentium) computers, which therefore do not need a math coprocessor.

See also *emulation*.

maximum supported configuration

A standard specifying limits on the resources an application program can use.

To avoid costly surprises when new applications are installed in production, organizations publish in their programming standards manual the amount of each resource available to application programs. New applications that require more than the standard maximum configuration must obtain advance approval to deviate from that standard. Organizations that support multiple operating platforms specify a maximum supported configuration for each platform.

Observing such a standard is especially important for applications that will run on either of the following:

- Large mainframe or network platforms, in which one application's disproportionate resource demands could seriously affect each user's throughput, response time, and operational reliability.

- Large numbers of desktop computers, either networked or stand-alone, for which a larger than expected new application could require simultaneous upgrades.

A maximum supported configuration standard for a given operating platform usually consists of the following:

- The amount of memory (or address space) available, in kilobytes

- The amount of disk space for permanent files and databases

- The amount of disk space for scratch or work files

- The number of tape drives available

- The volume of printing that can be handled per run or per hour

- Any limitations on invocation of operating system services

- Rules for using shared resources, such as the user's screen in a graphical user interface (GUI) environment.

See also *minimum required configuration.*

MDI—Multiple Document Interface

A Microsoft Windows concept that minimizes or maximizes multiple windows as a group rather than one window at a time.

megabyte

Literally, one million (10^6) bytes, usually abbreviated as M.

Contrary to generally accepted usage, in programming a kilobyte has come to mean 1,024 bytes when referencing random access memory (RAM) or mass storage space (such as hard disks). Thus 1M (1,024 kilobytes) is 1,048,576 (2^{20}) bytes. The ambiguity resulting from the use of the same prefix to represent both 1,000,000 and 1,048,576, although regrettable, is seldom serious, because the difference is relatively small.

See also *gigabyte* and *kilobyte.*

257

member function

In object-oriented programming (OOP), a function defined as a member of a class. Member functions are also called *methods.*

A member function can be a private class member (see *encapsulation*) or a public class member. An object that is an instance of the same class as a member function may receive a message instructing it to execute the member function. Consider, for example, a member function of class A that clears the screen when executed. An object that is an instance of class A might receive a message to execute the member function, in which case the object would clear the screen.

member object

In object-oriented programming (OOP), an object that is a member of a class.

See also *object-oriented programming.*

memory

Any medium that can store and retrieve data, most often specifically the high-speed internal random access memory (RAM) storage used for instructions and data.

RAM is volatile; when the computer is shut off or restarted, the contents of memory are lost. You must save to disk any information loaded into memory (such as a spreadsheet) before shutting off the computer's power, or the information will be lost.

After programs are loaded from disk into RAM, they are executed in the computer's memory. When data moves into memory, it replaces the previous contents of that portion of memory.

Memory also can be read-only memory (ROM), in which data is preloaded and cannot be changed as with RAM. ROM contains the PC's lowest-level operating system, the BIOS (Basic Input Output System). ROM "remembers" its data after the power is turned off.

All types of memory are accessed by address. Each address is simply an electronic representation of a unique number which, in turn, can represent text, characters, numbers, images, or instructions for the computer.

memory model

An option, especially on Intel computers, that specifies how a program addresses memory.

Memory model options in compilers provide information for program code and data addresses. Some computers support a flat address space with a single memory model, whereas others use a segmented address space to support multiple memory models.

Intel memory models are designated tiny, small, compact, medium, large, and huge, as explained in the separate entries that follow. If you do not choose the right memory model, your program might not work properly.

memory model (compact)

A memory-efficient memory model used by compilers.

For the Intel 8086 processor, this memory model enables only one 64K segment for program code, and multiple segments up to 1M for data.

memory model (huge)

A memory model that allows both code and data for the Intel 8086 processor to occupy more than one 64K segment.

The combined total for code and data must be less than 1M.

memory model (medium)

A memory model for the Intel 8086 processor that allows only one 64K segment for data, and multiple segments up to 1M for program code.

memory model (small)

A memory-efficient memory model for the Intel 8086 processor that allows one 64K segment for code and one 64K segment for data.

memory model (tiny)

A memory model for the Intel 8086 family of processors that allows both code and data no more than one 64K segment. In MS-DOS, a .COM extension on an executable program file indicates that the program uses the tiny model.

memory-resident program

A program that remains in memory, even when it is not executing.

Programs that respond to frequently occurring events are appropriately made memory-resident. They include many modules of the operating system's kernel, most device drivers, and hot key handlers.

See also *.DLL* and *TSR*.

menu

A list of user options or selections displayed on a screen.

When a menu is displayed, the user chooses an alternative by moving the cursor keys, clicking the mouse button, or typing an appropriate key.

See also *list box, menu,* and *pulldown menu*.

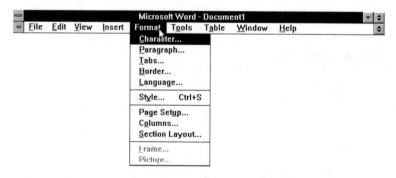

A pulldown menu.

menu-driven

An input mode in which the computer presents a series of menus from which the user makes a selection, sometimes augmented by occasional variable information such as a file name.

Menu-driven input is well suited to applications that have a natural hierarchy of options or transactions.

See also *event-oriented programming*.

merge

To combine two or more sorted files, arrays, or lists, into a single sorted file, array, or list. The inputs all have the same structure, and are in sequence by the same key field.

Here's BASIC code to merge two text files:

```
OPEN  IN_FILE1$ FOR INPUT  AS #INF1% : LINE INPUT #INF1%,
 RCD1$
OPEN  IN_FILE2$ FOR INPUT  AS #INF2% : LINE INPUT #INF2%,
 RCD2$
OPEN  OUT_FILE$ FOR OUTPUT AS #OUTF%
INF.END% = 0

WHILE INF.END% = 0
   IF   MID$(RCD1$,KEYPOS%,KEYLEN%) <
    MID$(RCD2$,KEYPOS%,KEYLEN%)
   THEN PRINT #OUTF%, RCD1$ : LINE INPUT #INF1%, RCD1$
   ELSE PRINT #OUTF%, RCD2$ : LINE INPUT #INF2%, RCD2$

   IF   EOF(INF1%)
   THEN PRINT #OUTF%, RCD2$  INF.END% = INF2%
   IF   EOF(INF2%)
   THEN PRINT #OUTF%, RCD1$  INF.END% = INF1%
WEND

WHILE NOT EOF(INF.END%)
   LINE_INPUT #INF.END%, RCD$
   PRINT      #OUTF%,     RCD$
WEND
```

See also *collate*.

merge sort

An elegant and efficient algorithm for internal sorting.

Like quicksort, this algorithm exploits recursion, using a divide-and-conquer strategy. To sort the N items stored in S[j] through S[j+N-1], this strategy consists of the following steps:

1. If N = 1, do nothing; if N = 2, compare the two items, and swap them if necessary.

2. Recursively invoke merge sort twice:

   First, to sort the first half of the original array, S[j] through S[j+N/2-1].

   Second, to sort the second half of the original array, S[j+N/2] through S[j+N-1].

3. Merge the two sorted subarrays produced by step 2 into a single array.

The trivial cases in step 1 stop the recursion. Assuming integer truncation on division, when N is odd, the lower half sort will process floor(N/2) items and the upper half sort will process ceiling(N/2) items.

The number of comparisons is proportional to N log N, the theoretical optimum for internal sorting. Because of the high overhead of recursion, however, other methods may run faster on small arrays.

See also *quicksort* and *Shell sort*.

message

See *diagnostic message*.

method

See *member function*.

methodology

Any integrated set of methods for some aspect of software development. A particular methodology may specify standards, conventions, guidelines, techniques, and procedures. It may or may not include (or be supported by) software tools, such as CASE. Common kinds of methodology include:

- System development life cycle (SDLC) methodologies, defining the phases of a project and the tangible results or "deliverables" to be produced in each phase

- Systems analysis methodologies, such as specialized versions of structured analysis

- Program design methodologies, such as top-down stepwise refinement

- Alternatives to the traditional life-cycle, such as joint application development (JAD)

Large organizations may develop some of their own methodologies internally, documenting them in a standards manual. Vendors sell proprietary methodologies, which may include extensive documentation, software tools, and training assistance. Many methodologies are described in published books; organizations can draw from them and customize them for their special needs.

Methodologies are often named after their creators or promoters—for example, the Yourdon/DeMarco Structured Design Method is a variant of structured design that Edward Yourdon and Tom DeMarco published.

See also *paradigm*.

microchip

A small square of silicon and other materials that holds circuits (such as transistors and resistors). Also called an integrated circuit.

A chip is classified by the number of elements it contains.

microcomputer

See *personal computer*.

microprocessor

A processing unit that resides on a single small chip.

In addition to the central processing units (CPUs) in desktop computers, microcomputers are used in household appliances, printers, automobiles, and other electronic devices that require intelligence.

See also *CPU*.

migrate

1. To move from an expensive (online, fast-access) auxiliary storage medium to a less-expensive (usually offline, slower access) medium, usually as a result of some automatically triggered procedure.

2. To switch from the use of an old or obsolete version of a product or platform to a different or new version of a product or platform.

In both senses, *migrate* is always intransitive. That is, data sets or files may migrate to archive storage, or users may migrate to a new release of a word processor, but it is a misusage to speak of users migrating their files, programmers migrating applications, or a vendor migrating its customers.

Migrate often connotes multiple individual actions over an extended or indefinite time period. Avoid using the term as a synonym for either *convert* or *move*.

See also *archive file, auxiliary storage, conversion,* and *stage.*

minicomputer

A central processing unit (CPU) suited to running a small number of multiple-user application systems.

Minicomputers constitute a middle ground between large mainframe computers and single-user desktop (or workstation) computers. Originally, any small, general-purpose computer was considered a minicomputer. However, because of the rapid decrease in the price of hardware and the accompanying increase in computer power at all levels, the size ranges now overlap and it is more useful to categorize computers according to their use than according to their size or computing power.

Vendors seeking a marketing niche sometimes call minicomputers "departmental computers." Examples of widely used minicomputers include the VAX systems (DEC), the AS/400 series (IBM), and products from Data General, Hewlett Packard, and Tandem.

See also *distributed processing.*

minimum required configuration

A specification of the resources needed to run a given program or software product.

A minimum configuration specification usually consists of the following:

- The operating platform (processor and operating system)
- The amount of memory (or address space) required, in kilobytes
- The amount of resident disk space occupied by permanent files, programs, and databases
- The amount of temporary disk space used for scratch files
- Identification of any dedicated devices used

Vendors commonly specify a minimum configuration in the following instances:

- On the outside of the package containing a software product sold in retail stores
- In descriptive software product literature, especially if soliciting orders
- In a contract for custom software development

See also *maximum supported configuration.*

mini-spec

Documentation of the rules controlling the transformation of data moving in and out of an associated primitive process.

Tom DeMarco coined this somewhat misleading term in his version of structured analysis. A mini-spec is not a small version of a module specification, but simply an elaboration of an algorithm, logic specification, or policy statement for some process on a data-flow diagram (DFD).

For every process on a DFD, the systems analyst should do one of the following:

- Expand the process in a lower-level DFD; see *decomposition*
- Prepare a logic specification (or "mini-spec"); see *HIPO* and *structured English*
- Confirm that the process is obvious; that anyone reading the DFD would immediately understand exactly how the process is performed

MIPS—million instructions per second

The commonly used unit of measure for the internal speed of a computer.

Computers are rated using this standard, although the measurement alone may not be sufficient to provide an accurate comparision of the performance of widely different types of computers. High-performance personal computers can operate between 20 to 50 MIPS, and this speed is increasing with each new development in the technology.

mixed-language programming

Developing a single complete program in which different component modules are coded in different languages.

Programmers sometimes need to use more than one programming language in a program, for the following reasons:

- A particular part of the program demands capabilities for which the principal language being used is less suited than some other language. Examples of such special capabilities include graphical user interface (GUI) handling, heavy numeric computation, file manipulation, sophisticated pattern matching, and low-level hardware access.

- An existing reusable module provides a needed function, but is written in a different language than that being used for the rest of the program.

- The principal language has intolerable overhead for some critical function in which high performance is required. (This applies mainly to justifying the use of assembly language.)

Unfortunately, combining modules written in different languages is not always easy or even possible. The obstacles to invoking a module written in one language from a module written in another language (even if both languages support subroutine calls and function invocation) include the following:

- Different calling sequence conventions

- Lack of support in one language for data types or data representations used in the other language

- Conflicting assumptions by each language's runtime support modules about how to process interrupts or exceptions

Of course, it is always possible to code either of the modules in assembly language, as long as the assembly language programmer knows and observes the implementation conventions of the higher-level language. These conventions are usually well-documented in the compiler vendor's manuals.

To combine modules written in two higher-level languages, the programmer usually must rely on interface capabilities specifically implemented in one or both compilers. For example, many C compilers provide an option to use the Pascal calling sequence conventions when invoking a particular module. Even then, of course, the programmer must be aware of restrictions and limitations on data types and the runtime environment.

mixed-mode expression

An expression containing terms of two or more different data types, most commonly integer (or fixed-point) and real (floating-point).

For example, if X and Y are real variables, J is an integer variable, and numeric constants containing no decimal point are considered integer, the following are mixed expressions:

```
X + J

K * (Y + X)

X * (Y + 1)

J + (1.5 * K)
```

A mixed-mode expression was considered a syntax error in FORTRAN and other strongly typed languages. Compilers for today's more permissive languages generate the appropriate code to convert terms to compatible forms wherever it is meaningful to do so. Strongly typed languages, however, usually provide explicit conversion functions to accomplish the same results.

See also *casting* and *coercion*.

mixed-unit representation

The use of two or more units to specify the value of a numeric data item.

Examples of data commonly represented in mixed units include the following:

Dates	<year,month,day> (or any permutation) or <year day-number>
Time of day	<hours,minutes,seconds>
Weight	<pounds,ounces>
Length	<feet,inches>

In each of these examples, the larger unit is not an exact power of 10 multiple of the smaller unit. Therefore, ordinary arithmetic does not generate the required carries from the low-order units to the next higher-order unit. (Representing money as dollars and cents is not an example of mixed-unit representation.)

Mixed-unit representations are appropriate as external representations to cater to the traditions and experience of the end users of an application system. Because of the complexity and inefficiency of using such data in computations, however, they are almost never appropriate as internal representations in programs or permanent files.

See also *data representation* and *date representation.*

mod

A common name for the modulo (or remainder-after-division or residue) integer function, which is supported as a built-in function by many programming languages and spreadsheet processors.

In BASIC and Pascal, mod is an infix operator; for example, if the year is 1995, then the value of

```
year mod 4
```

is 3.

PL/1 and most spreadsheet languages use ordinary function notation, as in MOD(YEAR,4) or @MOD(YEAR,4). However, the following languages don't use mod, but a special syntax to accomplish the same result:

C	year % 4
APL	4 ¦ year
COBOL	DIVIDE YEAR BY 4 GIVING Q REMAINDER YEAR-MOD-4.

Some languages require both arguments to be positive integers, and others provide detailed rules for the result of negative or fractional arguments.

A common programming problem is to correct for 1-origin numbering; for example, to compute the day of the week so that Monday is represented as 1 and Sunday as 7, you would simply code the following:

```
((days + 6) mod 7) + 1
```

or

```
MOD(days+6,7)+1
```

or more generally

```
((M+N-1) mod N) + 1
```

See also *infix operator*.

modem

A device that converts a digital signal to analog for transmission (usually over the public switched network), then back to digital form after reception. A modem is required at each end of the link. The term is a contraction of *m*odulator/*dem*odulator.

Modula-2

A programming language designed by Niklaus Wirth, derived from his earlier Pascal language.

Modula-2 overcomes certain limitations of Pascal that inhibited modular programming and reusable code. Specifically, Modula-2 provides the following:

- Incorporation of mechanisms for rigorous enforcement of encap-sulation
- Support of separate compilation of independent modules

In addition, some implementations support execution of concurrent coroutines.

Modula-2 often is compared to Ada, with which it shares many features and underlying concepts. Ada is more powerful and has a wider scope, but Modula-2 is less expensive to implement, an important consideration on small computers.

269

modular programming

An approach to program organization with the following characteristics:

- Every attribute or parameter of the program appears in only one place.

- Each section of code (or "module") performs one well-defined function at a consistent level of detail (see *module cohesion*).

- Modules communicate with one another only through explicitly defined interfaces (see *module coupling*).

- Each module is limited to an amount of source code that can easily be read and understood (see *readability*).

In contrast to a monolithic program, a program that satisfies these criteria to a high degree is likely to be not only easy to develop, but also, over its lifespan, economical to maintain and reliable to operate.

Note that a program which contains a large number of subroutines is not necessarily modular. If many subroutines contain embedded knowledge of the same constants, the same data structures, or the same environmental parameters, then the organization of that program would in fact be extremely unmodular, and the benefits of modular organization would not be realized.

See also *encapsulation, reusable module,* and *structured design.*

module

A sequence of program code that is named, packaged, and kept track of as a unit.

Although closed subroutines and functions are the most common kinds of modules, modules are by no means limited to code packaged in that form. A module also can be any of the following:

- A macro definition or package of related macro definitions

- A definition of a data structure, record, or control block

- A collection of named constants

- An object-oriented class definition, with encapsulated local data and functions

- A sequence of inline statements

- A table
- A package of related instances of some combination of the preceding options

See also *modular programming* and *reusable module.*

module cohesion

A qualitative measure of the degree to which a module performs a well-defined function at a single level of detail.

Modules that have poor cohesion greatly add to the cost and difficulty of program maintenance. Some writers on structured design prefer the term "module strength."

The following are examples of modules that have poor cohesion (or low strength) because they don't perform a single well-defined function:

- A payroll system subroutine to compute net pay and print a paycheck
- An "initialization" module to open all files and set all counters to zero
- A data structure grouping all switches used in a large program

The following are examples of modules that also have poor cohesion because they perform their well-defined function at a mixture of detail levels:

- A payroll system "deductions" subroutine that computes federal withholding tax using formulas and table lookup, but invokes subroutines to compute all the other deductions
- A module that prints a report from a sequential file, and contains all the logic for reading the input records, for pagination, and for line-by-line formatting.

See also *encapsulation, modular programming,* and *module coupling.*

module coupling

A qualitative measure of mutual dependency between two modules.

The less a module knows about its environment, including the module that called it, the easier that module is to maintain. A module invoked through a standard calling sequence with explicitly passed parameters is said to have "low (good) coupling." Conversely, a module with the following characteristics is considered to have "high (bad) coupling":

- Reference to its arguments by name in a shared DATA DIVISION (COBOL), COMMON (FORTRAN), or external (PL/1, C, Pascal) area of memory.

- Knowledge about the relationship of one of its argument data items to some structure that contains it—a file, an input transaction, or a report—that is itself irrelevant to the module's purpose.

module input

A data item whose value is set in the calling module and used in the called module.

Module inputs include both of the following:

- Explicit parameters. See *calling sequence* and *module coupling*.

- Global variables.

See also *DATA DIVISION* and *system output*.

module output

A data item whose value is set in the called module and later used in the calling module.

Module output includes any of the following:

- A function value

- Explicit module parameters

- Global variables

See also *module input* and *side effect*.

modulo

See *mod*.

modulus

See *mod*.

monitor program

1. Software that collects data about the execution of another program, usually by intercepting control when significant events occur.

    A performance monitor, for example, collects data about the whole workload running under an operating system. Such data can be used to analyze capacity and identify bottlenecks in the configuration.

2. An obsolete term for the kernel of an operating system.

monitor, video

An output device for computers that provides a display screen, available in color or monochrome.

The clarity of a monitor is based on the pixel concentration, bandwidth, dot pitch, and refresh rate. The video adapter in the computer sends signals to the monitor through a cable connected between the two. Monitors can be analog (VGA, SVGA, or XGA), digital, or transistor-to-transistor logic (TTL) (monochrome, CGA, or EGA).

See also *display adapter.*

monochrome monitor

A computer display that uses one foreground color and one background color.

Standard colors are amber, green, black, and white. Some users find monochrome monitors clearer than color monitors. Monochrome monitors are less expensive than color monitors of comparable quality.

Motif

A graphical user interface (GUI) created by the Open Software Foundation (OSF) to operate with the X Window interface.

Motif, which consists of a development library and an interface manager, provides support for enhanced graphical user interface (GUI) applications.

Motorola CPU

Any of a number of CPUs manufactured by the Motorola Corporation. Motorola CPUs, such as the 68000, 68020, 68030, and 68040, are used in computers manufactured by Apple Computer, such as the Macintosh and Quadra series.

mouse

A computer input device used for pointing and drawing with computer programs. When the device is moved on a flat surface, a cursor or pointer makes corresponding moves across the screen.

You can use a mouse to select a block of text, draw a line, select a menu option, and so forth. Some graphics-oriented programs require a mouse for easy operation. A mouse connected to the serial port of a computer is called a *serial mouse.* A mouse connected by a special PC card is called a *bus mouse.*

See also *click, double-click, drag and drop,* and *GUI.*

mouse button

On a mouse, the key or switch that enables you to control software. Pressing a mouse button results in a mouse click.

mouse event

An interrupt signal received from a mouse, generated either by a movement or by a button click.

Software must react appropriately to all mouse events. When the user moves the mouse over a surface, for example, the mouse mechanism sends mouse events to the software, which must then move the cursor across the screen in a direction corresponding to the mouse movement.

MS-DOS—Microsoft disk operating system

The most widely used operating system for desktop computers that use an Intel CPU (8088 and its successors).

Developed by Microsoft under contract to IBM, DOS appeared first as PC DOS for the IBM Personal Computer and later as MS-DOS for other compatible machines. MS-DOS was based loosely on Digital Research's CP/M, an operating system for earlier personal computers. MS-DOS has been greatly enhanced since its first release, but its basic structure and command prompt interface are largely unchanged.

By the standards of the 1990s, some people consider MS-DOS rather clumsy and inflexible. As a stopgap, higher-level system software running under MS-DOS, such as Microsoft's Windows and Quarterdeck's DesqView, provide such sophisticated capabilities as multitasking and graphical user interfaces (GUI) while hiding the less attractive aspects of DOS from the user.

multiple document interface

See *MDI*.

multiple virtual storage

See *MVS*.

multiprocessing

Using two or more processors in one computer, or two computers sharing a common memory.

You can increase the processing power of lower-speed processors by combining them into one multiprocessing computer. A multiprocessing computer also can perform as a *fault-tolerant* computer; that is, if one processor fails, the other takes over. Multiprocessing computers require operating systems that are designed to utilize the additional processors.

multitasking

The capability of an operating system to run two or more programs in the same computer at the same time. Operating systems that provide multitasking to personal computers include UNIX, Microsoft Windows, and OS/2. In a multitasking operating system, the user can move from application to application while the applications continue processing. Generally, multitasking operating systems require larger portions of memory and processing power than single-tasking operating systems such as MS-DOS.

multithreaded

A programming style that allows the concurrent processing of different portions of the same program. Under an operating system that supports multithreading, a program can be broken down into individual tasks that can be processed at the same time. This allows for faster overall throughput and possibly better response to external events.

For instance, if you use threads in writing a spreadsheet program, you could have one thread monitor the keyboard, another perform background recalculations, another monitor activities in related spreadsheets on the network, and still another update the display.

MVS—multiple virtual storage

The largest and longest surviving version of the IBM mainframe operating system that began with OS/360.

OS/360's original high-end option, MVT (multiprogramming with a variable number of tasks), supported multiprogramming within the limits of the 360's physical memory addressing scheme. With the introduction of virtual memory technology on the successor 370 series, MVT evolved into VS/2, later renamed SVS (single virtual storage). SVS managed virtual memory as a single address space of 2^{24} bytes (16M) to be allocated among the jobs executing concurrently. That is, each job was bound to a specific range of virtual addresses while executing.

To provide greater flexibility and to enable programs access to larger address spaces, IBM introduced MVS in 1974, which managed virtual memory as a set of independent address spaces, each one of which could be up to 16M. That is, all jobs occupied the same range of virtual addresses. A later version, MVS/XA (extended architecture), expanded addressability to 2^{31} bytes (2 gigabytes).

Although OS/MVS is one of the most powerful and flexible operating systems for large-scale computer configurations, it is often criticized for its cumbersome user interfaces and high overhead.

See also *JCL* and *TSO*.

nanosecond

One-billionth of a second.

near call

In a system based on a segmented-memory model, a temporary transfer of execution to another address within the same memory segment. Such a call requires only the use of an offset address register, and can be executed more quickly than a far call.

See also *call* and *far call*.

nested loop

A loop contained within another loop.

The following BASIC code shows a nested loop:

```
FOR Y = 1 TO 25            'rows 1 - 25
  FOR X = 0 to 79 STEP 5   'every 5th column from 1-80
    LOCATE X,Y             'place cursor
    PRINT "*";             'print a star
  NEXT X                   'get next column
NEXT Y                     'get next row
```

network configuration

Loosely, the summary description of the major influences on network performance, functionality, and stability. These influences include the following:

- Node and server hardware (with capacities)

- Network infrastructure including routers, hub, bridges, and so on

- The number of print servers

- Application descriptions

neural network

An artificial intelligence modeling technique based on a system of interconnected units (neurons), in which the following are true:

- Each unit acts as a function to transform one or more numeric input signals into a numeric output signal.

- Input signals are either external (user-supplied inputs to the model) or outputs of other units in the network.

- Output signals are either external (the result of the model) or fed to other units in the network.

- Each connection between a pair of units is (a) multiplied by a positive or negative weight, (b) added to a biasing factor, or (c) both.

- Several layers of units may be between the external inputs and the external outputs.

For some applications, neural networks can learn to recognize patterns or to model a complicated function without any specification of an explicit formula or algorithm. An initial neural network configuration is put through a training phase in which the connection weights adjust themselves through a feedback process. The following is a very simplified view of the training phase:

1. Sets of inputs for known cases are presented to the network.

2. When the network provides the right output, the current connection weights are strengthened.

3. When the network gives the wrong output, the connection weights are weakened in some proportion to the difference between the desired result and the one that was produced.

This process is repeated for a number of training cases, perhaps thousands of times, until the network becomes stable and produces the expected results for all or most training cases. The network is then ready to process real input data.

There's no guarantee that an arbitrary network applied to an arbitrary class of problems will ever become stable. The study of neural networks deals with a variety of specific techniques for configuring and training networks and classifying types of problems for which these techniques yield useful results.

Some researchers believe neural networks model the way animal brains work. So far, however, artificial neural networks, whether built from hardware or simulated by software, have been limited to a few thousand units, a tiny fraction of the billions in a human brain. Although artificial neurons individually operate much faster than those in the brain, animal and human intelligence is believed to arise from the extremely high degree of parallel activity among the interconnected neurons.

nibble

Part of a byte, specifically the left or right four bits.

For machines that support packed decimal data formats, using the terms "left nibble" or "right nibble" is sometimes useful.

NMI—non-maskable interrupt

See *mask*.

nondisclosure agreement

A formal contract in which one party agrees to provide confidential or proprietary information to a second party, who in turn agrees not to disclose that information to any third party. Under a nondisclosure agreement:

- Software or hardware vendors can provide advance information on (or actual copies of) unreleased products to potential users (see *beta version*) of the product, and to developers of textbooks, courses, ancillary software, or other related products.

- User organizations in competitive businesses can use the services of outside consultants, contract programmers, or other specialists.

non-interlaced video

The method by which an image is projected onto a video screen. The image is created by many lines, each containing a horizontal portion of the picture. Non-interlaced video projects the image in one pass or scan on the screen, displaying the lines one after the other, from top to bottom.

"Flickers" that occur during normal interlaced scan operations are reduced, making non-interlaced video superior to interlaced video.

See also *interlaced video.*

nonprocedural language

A programming language that relies on a mechanism other than the specification of a sequence of steps to be performed. Nonprocedural languages include the following:

- Functional (or applicative) languages, in which the programmer defines a hierarchy of functions and then applies the top-level function to a set of inputs to produce a result. Example: LISP.

- Report generator languages and database languages, in which the programmer specifies the content and layout of the desired outputs. Example: RPG.

- Logic languages, in which the programmer defines a set of predicates to be evaluated according to the rules of formal symbolic logic. Example: PROLOG.

- Spreadsheet languages, in which the programmer prepares a model of the problem based on a two-dimensional array of data and functions. Example: VisiCalc and its modern successors.

- Pure object-oriented languages in which all executable code is encapsulated in class definitions. Example: Smalltalk.

Many popular nonprocedural languages are proprietary, being controlled by a single vendor or a small group of vendors. They are often promoted as "fourth-generation" tools, so as to give the impression that they are more advanced and powerful than any procedural language.

See also *generation (programming languages), level (programming language), paradigm,* and *procedural language.*

normal form

See *normalization.*

normalization

The process of decomposing a data structure (or a complete logical database) into a set of simple relations.

The following are advantages of normalizing a database:

- To simplify both the stored data and the programs that manipulate it.

- To avoid certain anomalies that otherwise arise when a database is updated. For example, when all the orders placed by a given customer are deleted, should the master record for that customer be deleted also?

Normalization relies on a set of rules that describe the dependencies among data items. These normalization rules were first published by Edgar Codd, who is considered the founder of the relational database model.

See also *attribute, decomposition,* and *relational database.*

normalized floating-point number

A floating-point number in which the most significant bit is in the leftmost position of the mantissa.

not

A unary logical operator that negates the value of the variable it operates on: if A is TRUE, not A is FALSE. The not operator is often used to construct logical expressions for controlling program execution or for developing database selection criteria.

NT—New Technology

See *Windows NT.*

n-tuple

An ordered sequence of items. The term is a generalization of *couple, triple,* and so on; sometimes just the general term "tuple" is used, other times a specific number of items is referred to, as in 5-tuple, 6-tuple, and so on.

An n-tuple is similar to a vector (or one-dimensional array), except that the elements of a vector are usually expected to be all of the same type. No such restriction applies to an n-tuple.

N-tuples can denote the rows of a multiple-column table or a relational database. In writing, an n-tuple is usually shown as a bracketed list with comma separators, as in the following example:

```
<Nixon, 1969, 1974, California>
```

nul (or null) device

An artificial device, provided by an operating system, that ignores any output sent to it; also called a "dummy file."

Some systems also allow a nul device as an empty input file, treated as having reached its end-of-file. A nul device is useful during testing and parallel running to save time and materials.

null character

A byte consisting of all 0 bits.

See also *ASCIIZ character string*.

null pointer

The constant value of a pointer that currently doesn't point to any actual data item.

Programming languages provide a null value for pointers, for the following reasons:

- To detect errors, such as when a program attempts to refer to data that hasn't been allocated, that has already been freed, or that lies beyond the end of a data structure.

- To enable a program to test for such a value, either to determine whether a data item is currently allocated or to recognize the end of a data structure such as a linked list. In C, the null pointer is simply the numeric value 0, so that such tests need not refer to NULL in statements such as the following:

```
while (p) . . .

if   (!p) . . .
```

null string

In languages that support character string operations, a zero-length or empty string. In BASIC, you can create a null string by coding the following:

```
A$ = " "
```

Note that a null string is not the same as the null character used in C as a string terminator.

numeric data item

A data item on which it is meaningful to perform some arithmetic operation $(+, -, *, \text{or} /)$.

Some data items commonly represented by numeric digits (such as U.S. Postal ZIP codes) do not satisfy this definition, and therefore are not true numeric data items.

Most numeric data items have these attributes:

- A unit of measure

- A range (maximum and minimum possible values)

- Precision (the smallest fraction of the unit or measure to be kept track of); for example, if the unit of measure of elapsed time is the second, the precision might be chosen as 1 (whole seconds) or 1/1000 (milliseconds).

See also *data item definition, data representation, discrete data type,* and *numeric data type.*

numeric data type

Any of the forms of numeric information supported by a computer architecture, together with the operations that can be performed on them.

Programming languages and database management systems (DBMS) typically support most, if not all, of the available numeric data formats. Where files are shared among programs written in different languages, the representations chosen for numeric items may have to cater to the weakest of those languages.

The following table shows how a variable X might be declared in each language:

	BASIC	C	COBOL	PASCAL	PL/1
Small integers (counters, array dimensions, string lengths, etc.)	X%	short x;	1 X PIC S9(4) COMP.	x: integer (+ range)	FIXED BIN(15)
Integers (quantities, exact measurements)	X&	int x;	1 X PIC S9(8) COMP.	x: integer (+ range)	FIXED BIN(31)
Packed decimal for exact fractional money, percentges, etc. to 2 decimal places	(none)	(none)	1 X PIC S9(7)V99 COMP-3	(none)	FIXED BIN(9,2)
Floating point (single)	X!	float x;	1 X COMP-1.	x: real	FLOAT(6)
Floating point (double)	X#	double x;	1 X COMP-2.	(none)	FLOAT(16)
Boolean (switches, flags)	(none)	(none)	(none)	x: boolean	BIT(1)

Internal data representations vary with machine architectures, so you can't expect to read records containing, for example, VAX floating-point numbers on a Macintosh without some intervening conversion step.

numeric function

A function returning a numeric result.

object

In object-oriented programming (OOP) and object-oriented analysis and design, an instance of a class defined by an OOP language such as C++. An object may be an abstract concept, such as a user action, or a real concept, such as a car.

An object encapsulates data defined by the class, and provides functions and facilities to assess data contained within the object. Objects are usually runtime, and are created when an object constructor is used to invoke a program. The class is the "blueprint" used to create the object. When an object is no longer needed, the object destructor can be invoked to erase it from memory. The OOP language provides the constructor and destructor functions.

Once created, the object can communicate with other objects by sending and receiving messages. Messages are electronic instructions that pass from one object to another. These messages—which are sent to objects from other objects, or from non-object-oriented procedures—provide the receiver objects with instructions on how to behave.

See also *class, constructor, destructor, diagnostic message, encapsulation,* and *object-oriented programming.*

object code

Compiler-produced code that is the intermediate form between source code and an executable program.

Object code contains the machine instructions for the executable program, but has unresolved data and function call addresses. The linking process resolves the data and function call addresses, which completes the process of making the finished executable program.

See also *.EXE* and *linking loader.*

object linking and embedding

See *OLE.*

object module library

A group of object modules that can be linked into an executable program by a linking loader.

A special object module library accompanies almost all compilers. It contains language support modules of which the programmer may be unaware, but that are referred to by the generated object code.

object-oriented analysis—OOA

The application of class hierarchies with inheritance to systems analysis.

In OOA, classes play more or less the same role as entities or data flows in structured analysis. By exploiting inheritance, however, the systems analyst may be able to simplify the specification and also to package parts of a system specification for possible later reuse in other application systems.

OOA is not yet a mature discipline. Several OOA methodologies are competing for acceptance. They include Yourdon/Coad and Booch, named after the authors of the first OOA textbooks, Grady Booch, Edward Yourdon, and Peter Coad.

See also *object-oriented programming* and *structured analysis.*

object-oriented programming—OOP

A programming concept in which a program consists of interacting groups of objects (that is, collections of data and methods, or internal function calls) that are defined within the program.

This type of programming enables developers to create a class that defines the object as an instance of a class.

Object-oriented programming supports the concepts of encapsulation, inheritance, and polymorphism. The Simula language and SmallTalk are considered the first object-oriented programming languages, although C++ is the most popular object-oriented programming language currently used.

See also *encapsulation, inheritance, member function, object,* and *polymorphism.*

octal

The numbering system using 8 as its base, conventionally using the marks 0, 1, 2, and ... 7 to represent its digits. It is most often used as a compact, easily read, external representation of the contents of memory devices. Recent machine designs favor word lengths in multiples of four bits, so hexadecimal (base 16) representation is more heavily used than octal.

Although octal values can be confused with decimal representations, each octal digit has a value based on a power of 8, not 10, depending on its position in the number. Therefore, 24 octal is $2 \times 8^1 + 4 \times 8^0 = 20$ decimal.

od—octal dump

A UNIX utility that displays the contents of any file, normally in octal but optionally in hexadecimal, ASCII, or decimal.

See also *dump, file.*

offline device

A tape drive, disk drive, printer, terminal, or other device that is not currently connected to, or communicating with, a computer or a network.

See also *online device.*

offline process

An action or procedure performed manually or on equipment other than a computer.

Offline data entry, for example, may be done on machines that transcribe data from a keyboard to some machine-readable medium for later computer processing.

offset

1. The value added to a base register or segment register to denote an address in memory.

On the Intel 8086, the 16-bit offset occupies two bytes that are easy to manipulate in the registers. The 8086 processors manage addresses internally as 16-bit values, then use segmented addressing to achieve 1M of addressability.

See also *segment*.

2. More generally, a value added to some starting address, such as the address of an array, to designate the location of a data item.

OLE—object linking and embedding

A Microsoft Windows facility that enables a user to link two objects maintained by two different programs, such as a word processing document and a spreadsheet.

OLE is a sophisticated, active form of dynamic data exchange (DDE) in which a reference to an embedded object can automatically trigger the invocation of the program that maintains that object. Although OLE can provide elegant and highly automated linkages, it requires complex programming in both programs.

one-shot program

A program written not with the intention of being used in regular operation, but simply to obtain a single set of results.

Sometimes a program originally intended for one-shot use turns out to be more useful than expected, and is then made available to a user community. This phenomenon poses a dilemma for the programmer. If a program is truly a one-shot, the programmer needn't be concerned with following the organization's programming standards, preparing full documentation, or submitting the work to walkthrough or quality assurance review. However, if that program then becomes part of a permanent application system, it must retroactively be brought up to the level of quality expected of a permanent program. Under pressures of time, this work is often postponed, leading to the release of substandard software.

online device

A tape drive, disk drive, printer, terminal, or other device that is currently connected to and accessible by a computer or network.

See also *offline device*.

OOA

See *object-oriented analysis*.

opcode

See *operation code*.

open, file

An operation to connect a physical file (data set) to a program and prepare for subsequent input-output (I/O) operations.

Most procedural programming languages provide an explicit open statement and require its execution before the program can write data to or read data from that file. FORTRAN and PL/1 permit implicit file opening when a program attempts an input-output operation on an unopened file, but it is considered poor practice to take advantage of that feature except in one-shot programs and test drivers.

The options of an open statement, in combination with information from the job control language (JCL) or command language of the operating system, identify and define the file and specify the kind of operations to be performed.

For an existing (permanent file) input data set, modern operating systems require little information beyond the name of the file. Any required information about such characteristics as its location, size, and record blocking can be obtained from the data set label and from any relevant catalog, VTOC, or directory.

For a new output data set, additional information is required. Depending on the operating system and programming language, such information may include the following:

- Estimated or maximum size of the file
- Retention period or expiration date
- Record size and blocking factor

Programmers disagree about the best placement of open and close statements in a modular program. In general, the same module that opens a file should also close it, but that may or may not be the same module that performs the actual input-output operations on it. A low-level module that encounters an end of file on a sequential input file can immediately issue the close, because no further operations on that file would be meaningful. On the other hand, allowing a low-level module to close an output file could be presumptuous, because a higher-level module might need to append something, such as a report summary page, to the same file. Such choices are especially difficult in COBOL, which imposes severe restrictions on file access by subroutines.

See also *close (file)*.

Open Software Foundation

See *OSF*.

operand

1. A data item input to an operator. Although the term is nearly synonymous with argument, *operand* is rarely used to denote input to a function other than a unary or binary operator.

   See also *argument* and *parameter*.

2. A data item operated on by a command-language command or an assembly language instruction. For example, the following MS-DOS command has four operands:

   ```
   XCOPY  MEMOS  E:  /S /E
   ```

operating platform conversion

See *conversion, operating platform*.

operating system

A set of software and standards for managing the hardware resources in a computer system and for providing standard interfaces between other programs (jobs) and both the hardware and human users.

In addition to the services provided by the operating system kernel, a typical operating system for a multiple-user configuration does the following:

- Controls access by users to the system

- Enforces security and privacy of files

- Schedules batch jobs

- Allocates resources to jobs, including memory, disk space, and devices

- Controls peripheral SPOOL functions, especially printing

In the past, the hardware vendor provided almost all operating systems. Today, however, multiple operating systems from different vendors often compete for customers who use a given type of computer hardware.

The following operating systems have had special importance and lasting influence on the way computers are used:

Year	Machine	Name and Developer	Distinguishing Features, Influence, or Innovations
1960	IBM 7090	SOS (SHARE/IBM)	Device independence. Interrupt handling. Modular organization.
1966	System/360	OS/360 (IBM)	Multiprogramming support. Wide range of configuration sizes.
1974	DEC PDP-7	UNIX (AT&T)	Replaceable shell. Portable across a wide range of hardware architectures.
1979	8080, Z80	CP/M (Digital Research)	Simple, single-user operation. Support for personal computers. Precursor of MS-DOS, the most widely used operating system ever.
1981	Xerox Star	(Xerox PARC)	Graphical user interface (GUI). Precursor of highly successful Apple Macintosh line.

Earlier terms *monitor* and *executive system* have now been supplanted by *operating system.* The term *control program* is still used, but usually refers more narrowly to the operating system's kernel.

operation code

A numeric value in a machine instruction, telling the computer which operation to perform (such as add or branch); also called "opcode."

In an assembly language, each operation code is expressed by a mnemonic abbreviation, usually between one and five letters. Most of these mnemonic codes represent an English verb that describes the operation. The following are examples for an Intel computer:

Assembly Language Mnemonic	Machine Language Opcode
ADD	B8h
MOV	05h

operator precedence

See *order of operators.*

optimize

1. To improve the performance or efficiency of a program, especially through sophisticated techniques applied by a compiler.

2. To adjust or tune a hardware configuration or software options in order to improve performance.

Note that neither definition is consistent with the normal English meaning. Almost any improvement is called "optimization," even if it falls far short of the theoretical optimal level.

optimizer

A program development tool used to improve the speed or reduce the size of an executable program.

Typically, optimizers are considered part of the language compiler. They perform their function by analyzing the source code and determining which set of program instructions or code blocks can be used to best implement the necessary functions.

If you are developing on a segmented-memory model system, a classic (although trivial) example of optimization is to analyze the destination of a call or jump, then generate either a short (near) or long (far) call or jump as necessary. In instances in which a short call is used rather than a long one, the code is optimized, and thus runs faster and takes less memory than otherwise.

option

1. An action made available to the user through a menu selection.

2. A Boolean data item (switch) that is used to determine whether the program is to perform some action.

   The user of a program often sets options by using input parameters reserved for that purpose. In MS-DOS commands, an option is usually set by a parameter of the form /x, where x identifies the option, as follows:

   ```
   DIR    a:  /P

   FORMAT  b:  /V
   ```

or

1. A binary logical operator that is assigned the value true only if either or both of its operands are true.

2. One of the class of logical machine instructions that apply the or operation bit-by-bit to two bits, bytes, or words, producing a result of the same type.

ORACLE

A relational database developed and marketed by ORACLE Corporation. One of the key advantages of ORACLE is that it can be implemented across a variety of hardware platforms, from large computers to microcomputers.

order of operators

The language-defined sequence in which arithmetic and logical operations are performed in complex expressions; also called *operator precedence*.

Almost all languages follow the traditional order of evaluation familiar in algebra: Quantities in parentheses are evaluated first, then exponentiation, then multiplication and division, and finally addition and subtraction. When using an unfamiliar language, particularly an operator-rich language, you should review the order of evaluation for some of the less common operators.

OS/2

An operating system for the Intel (IBM-compatible) series of desktop computers (80386 and above). OS/2 features a graphical user interface (GUI), multithreading, dynamic data exchange (DDE), and a diverse repertoire of highly integrated services including LAN operation, communications, and a relational database manager.

OS/2 was originally planned jointly by IBM and Microsoft as a proposed standard for the 32-bit processor architecture. It was expected to provide much greater power and flexibility than MS-DOS, as well as easier and more efficient operation than Windows. When Microsoft later elected to pursue an independent direction (see *Windows NT*), OS/2 became known as IBM's entry in a hotly contested operating system market.

output

See *module output* and *system output*.

OSF—The Open Software Foundation

A nonprofit organization formed to promote nonproprietary computing environments, especially on UNIX or UNIX-like operating platforms.

The organization's members include several computer companies. OSF has created such software standards as the OSF Motif graphical user interface (GUI) and development system, and OS/1, an operating system based on UNIX. Additionally, OSF solicits innovations from the industry, and publishes agreed-on technical standards for its members.

See also *Motif*.

output device

Any peripheral component capable of displaying information for people.

Examples of output devices include printers, video displays, and plotters. Auxiliary storage devices, such as disk and tape, are not considered output devices, even though they receive data from the computer.

overflow

1. A exception that occurs when a result of a computation is larger than the register available for it.

2. Any attempt to exceed some fixed storage capacity, such as the capacity of a table, a stack, a disk, or a file.

overhead

Use of computer resources (central processing unit cycles, input-output operations, memory, disk space, and so on) for activity that does not directly contribute to producing results for the user.

Overhead often results from generalization in system software. Extremely flexible software often must spend considerable computing power to determine what to do and to provide for rarely encountered demands. The following are several technologies that are often associated with high overhead:

- The relational database model
- Graphical user interfaces (GUIs)
- Multiprogramming
- Interpreters
- Very-high-level (VHL) languages

Programmers, managers, and users often must determine whether the flexibility of a high-overhead facility justifies the cost of the additional hardware resources it requires.

overlay

1. To structure a complete program so that it can execute in an address space smaller than its total size.

In a hierarchical module structure, modules on different branches of the tree are never simultaneously active, and therefore can share the same area of memory. An overlay manager keeps track of which parts of the program have been loaded into memory. When the program attempts to invoke a module that is not in memory, the overlay manager intercepts the call and loads the required part of the program.

2. A part of an overlaid program that is loaded as a unit.

The programmer can create a structure of planned overlays through control statements to a linking loader (or a compiler that supports its own overlay management scheme). Because of the growing availability of virtual memory support and the falling cost of real memory, overlay structures are used less often than they used to be.

See also *fatware*.

3. A data structure that shares the same area of memory as another data structure.

See also *union*.

4. A transparent template used to show constant information superimposed on a keyboard, screen, or other surface, indicating the positions of fields, the functions of special keys, and so on.

overloading

Using the same name for more than one function or operator. The compiler is then expected to choose the appropriate one based on the context in which the name appears.

Overloading is a central feature in object-oriented programming (OOP).

See also *polymorphism*.

override

To specify a value or an action different from the default.

pack

1. To convert data (usually in ASCII or EBCDIC) from its external form to one suitable for packed decimal arithmetic.

2. To store multiple small data items together in a single word or other unit of storage.

packed decimal

In some hardware architectures and programming languages, a data type that participates in variable-length exact decimal arithmetic. One half-byte is given up to a sign; all other bytes store two decimal digits.

See also *nibble.*

pad

To add blank or null characters to the end of a record.

Padding makes different logical record types the same length when variable-length record processing is not used. Also, pad characters are added to the last block in a blocked sequential file if the number of records is not an integer multiple of the block size.

See also *align* and *justify.*

PAD—packet assembler/disassembler

A device that receives packets of data in a standard format and distributes them among multiple serial ports. The PAD at the transmitting site does the opposite.

PAD devices are usually microcomputers dedicated to this task.

paged memory

A portion of total system memory divided into pages, then moved to and from disk as required by the program.

Paged memory is brought into memory as memory becomes available, depending on the execution scheme of the program. Pages not brought into memory are kept on disk until they are necessary.

See also *paged memory* and *virtual memory*.

page fault

An exception that occurs when a program refers to an address in virtual memory that is not currently resident in real memory.

A page fault is not an error. The operating system responds by moving the required page into memory from disk and updating the virtual memory status information.

pagination

The division of a report or other printed document into a sequence of pages.

In paginating, a program, a report generator, or a spreadsheet processor is usually concerned with the following:

- Determining when to start each new page (page break), either because the current page is full or because some control break is reached

- Printing a heading at the top of each page, either constant or with variable information corresponding to one or more data items in the body of the page

- Printing a subheading below each heading, possibly containing column headings for tabular data

- Printing a footing at the bottom of each page

- Inserting sequential page numbers into either the heading or the footing

Pagination can be complicated, especially in procedural programming languages that don't explicitly support it (such as BASIC, C, Pascal, and versions of COBOL that lack the report generator feature). Consequently, many organizations now prefer to implement such reports by using higher-level report generators.

paging

See *paged memory*.

palette

In video displays and adapters, the set of colors from which the current set of displayable colors is taken. For example, the VGA standard enables you to choose, from a set of 262,144 colors, up to 256 that you can display at the same time.

paradigm

A comprehensive model or framework for looking at a system or a process.

Although marketing people and overzealous advocates of new techniques sometimes misapply the term *paradigm* to relatively minor improvements in approach, it should be reserved for major differences in methodology. The following qualify as true paradigms:

- Traditional procedural programming

- Object-oriented programming (OOP)

- Client-server architecture

- Normalized relational database design

Paradox

Borland's relational database management system (DBMS) for MS-DOS, Windows, and network platforms, derived from an original version by Ansa Software Corp. Paradox also includes a proprietary procedural programming language, a query processor, and a report generator with graphics capabilities.

Borland's acquisition of its leading competitor, Ashton-Tate (former vendor of dBASE) brought two leading, but mutually incompatible, DBMS products together in one vendor's offerings. Borland appears to be committed to continued support of the two user communities, moving new versions of both products gradually toward each other.

paragraph

In COBOL, a named sequence of sentences, especially in the PROCEDURE DIVISION.

A paragraph name serves the function of a statement label. It is the only way of identifying a point in the program that is the target of a GOTO or a PERFORM. In addition, COBOL recognizes a paragraph as a kind of parameter-less subroutine, with an implied return preceding the next paragraph name. For this reason, COBOL programmers often refer to paragraphs as "procedures."

parallel port

An input-output (I/O) connector used to attach a printer (or other device) to a computer.

A PC uses a DB-25 connector to provide this connection. Data is transferred through a parallel port in 8-bit-wide pieces, enabling a complete character to be sent in one move. Serial devices, in contrast, pass only one bit at a time, requiring eight moves for one character. Parallel ports also can be used to connect portable network adapters to the computer, so that the parallel ports can transmit data to a network.

Intel computers name the parallel ports LPT1, LPT2, and LPT3.

parallel processing

Performing one or more computer operation(s) simultaneously, enabling a computer to perform many tasks simultaneously. A parallel-processing computer, for example, can processes a database application, statistics application, and normal operating system functions simultaneously.

Multiprocessing also is considered a form of parallel processing. In this case, one or more processes (or several computers linked together) can share a processing load across the processors. The execution of a database application, for example, can be shared among several processors, each processing portions of the cycles required by the application.

parallel test

An extended acceptance test in which a new system and the old system it is to replace are both in operation.

Parallel testing may offer protection against a premature commitment to an unreliable system. However, parallel testing may be impractical in either of the following situations:

- The user organization cannot afford the personnel, computers, floor space, or other resources needed for extended dual operation.

- The new system produces output that differs from that of the old one. A new inventory control system, for example, might implement a more sophisticated forecasting and replenishment strategy. If the users were still acting on the basis of output from the old system, the new system's inventory database would soon deviate sharply from the actual inventory in the warehouse.

parameter

1. In a program module, a data name that represents an input to the module, or an output from the module. When the module is invoked, the parameters become bound to actual data items (arguments).

   Such parameters are not limited to subroutine and function modules. Macros, commands, cataloged procedures (or batch files), and even manual procedures also can have parameters.

   Parameters are usually specified in a list as part of a module's definition.

   See also *keyword parameter* and *positional parameter*.

2. Any fundamental constant whose value affects the behavior of a program.

   Programs in which such parameters are easy to change are said to be highly "parameterized."

   See also *fundamental* and *constant hard-code*.

parity

An extra bit appended to a byte, a word, or a record, representing the number of 1-bits modulo 2 (or the exclusive or of the bits). Parity bits are used to detect errors in data transmission, input-output (I/O) operations, or internal machine operations.

Depending on the device or transmission protocol, a convention may call either for even parity or odd parity. With odd parity, the parity bit is the complement of the 1-bit count modulo 2. For example, for a single byte, odd parity would generate a ninth bit as follows:

Byte Configuration	Parity Bit	Decimal Value
1 0 0 0 0 0 0 0	0	128
1 1 0 0 0 0 0 0	1	192
0 0 0 1 0 1 1 1	0	23
0 0 1 0 0 0 1 0	1	34

Although you can manipulate parity bits in software, most computers, modems, and input-output (I/O) devices both generate and check parity through hardware circuitry. Whenever the hardware detects a parity error, it causes an interrupt or turns on an indicator.

parse

To decompose an expression and categorize its components.

The term can apply to natural languages such as English, to programming languages, and to any other structured input data. For example, a compiler usually begins by parsing the source code.

See also *decomposition* and *syntax*.

partition table

An area of a fixed disk that defines how the disk is separated into separately addressable portions.

You can create or modify a partition table in MS-DOS with the FDISK command. You then refer to the resulting partitions as if they were separate disk drives, such as C, D, and E.

Partitioning a disk in this way may be necessary for either of two reasons:

1. To allow two or more operating systems that use incompatible disk formats to share a single fixed disk.

2. To circumvent software limitations on the maximum size of a disk. Early versions of MS-DOS, for example, could not address disks larger than 32M, so when the first fixed disks larger than that limit appeared, users had to partition them into 32M (or smaller) pseudo-disk drives.

.PAS

The file name extension of a file containing Pascal source code.

Pascal

A programming language designed by Niklaus Wirth, named in honor of the 17th century French mathematician/philosopher/theologian Blaise Pascal.

Although Pascal is used for both business and scientific applications, its greatest success is as a teaching language. Pascal supports the structured coding, block structure, and data structures needed to convey programming, data representation, and algorithm concepts. Some of the following shortcomings, however, make it less attractive for large programs:

• Independent modules cannot be compiled separately.

• Procedures must be specified in a strict bottom-up sequence.

• The syntax is somewhat error-prone.

The newer languages Ada and Modula-2 are derived from Pascal, and overcome many of its deficiencies. In addition, some vendors have extended standard Pascal to include modern object-oriented facilities and separate compilations.

passing by reference

In a calling sequence, the representation of an argument to a subroutine or function by its address in memory. This representation is also called *passing by name* or *passing by address*.

Passing by reference is the most general way of communicating a parameter to a lower-level module. It allows the module being invoked not only to retrieve the parameter's value, but also to change it.

Note that passing by reference is meaningful only when an argument is a variable. If the argument is an expression or a constant, passing by reference makes no sense.

See also *passing by value* and *side effect.*

passing by value

In a calling sequence, the representation of an argument to a subroutine or function by its current value.

See also *passing by reference.*

Passing by value has two potential advantages over passing by reference:

- For arguments that fit in a word (such as most scalar numeric data items), the value can be passed in a register for greater efficiency.

- The module being invoked cannot alter the value of the corresponding argument, which eliminates the possibility of error-prone side effects.

Most programming languages specify definite rules that determine when an argument is to be passed by value or by reference. Some programming languages enable the programmer to override these rules and to specify how a given parameter is to be passed; this facility is useful either to provide for a planned side effect, or in mixed-language programming to cater to assumptions made by a different compiler.

paste

See *cut and paste.*

patch

A temporary change to a program, usually to correct a bug, applied in a crude or undocumented manner.

In urgent situations, a software vendor may send a patch directly to the software owner or make it available for downloading from bulletin board services (BBSs). Patches are considered a risky last resort in correcting problems with software.

path

The disk drive address and list of directory nodes leading from the root directory to the directory containing a specific file.

For example, in the path

B:\CUSTOMER\EUROPE-W\FRANCE\PTT\PROPOSAL.DOC

everything up to PROPOSAL.DOC defines the path from the root directory to that file.

Older MS-DOS manuals also use the term *path* (or *pathname*) to designate the fully qualified file name; that is, in the preceding example, the path would also include the file name PROPOSAL.DOC.

PC DOS

A version of the MS-DOS operating system distributed by IBM. PC DOS is nearly identical to the version distributed by Microsoft.

See also *MS-DOS*.

.PCX

The file name extension of a widely used raster graphics file format created by Zsoft Corporation.

This file format, which is used by many graphics editors, provides a means of exchanging images between one graphics program and another.

See also *raster*.

PDS—partitioned data set

A file organization that groups a collection of similar, usually small, sequential files in a single data set.

Normally, the PDS is used to implement a library, by grouping source modules, include modules, object modules, executable (load) modules, cataloged procedures, and so on. For this reason, PDSs are also commonly called "libraries."

305

Partitioned data sets are supported by IBM mainframe operating systems. In MS-DOS and other platforms, the equivalent function is provided by the combination of a directory and a specific file name extension.

Pentium

See *Intel CPU.*

PERFORM

A hybrid COBOL verb used for both loop control and invocation of parameterless subroutines.

Two simple cases are easy to understand:

- The pair PERFORM (with no target paragraph) and END-PERFORM play the same loop control role in COBOL as for, do while, and do until play in other procedural languages.

- PERFORM with a target paragraph name but no END-PERFORM transfers control to that paragraph. When control reaches the end of the target paragraph, it returns to the statement following the PERFORM.

The following example demonstrates both uses of PERFORM:

```
PERFORM VARYING TRANSACTION-COUNTER BY 1
                UNTIL NO-MORE-TRANSACTIONS;
    PERFORM GET-TRANSACTION;
    PERFORM EDIT-TRANSACTION;
    IF  LEGAL-TRANSACTION
        THEN  PERFORM PROCESS-TRANSACTION;
        ELSE  PERFORM REJECT-TRANSACTION;
    END-IF;
END-PERFORM;
```

 The use of PERFORM for subroutine invocation in the preceding example demonstrates a practice that is common, but frowned on by experienced programmers who observe the spirit of structured design. Because NO-MORE-TRANSACTIONS, LEGAL-TRANSACTION, and the whole transaction record (unnamed here) are implicitly shared among multiple routines, this example has very poor module coupling. Such programmers prefer to use the CALL verb with explicit parameters.

In addition to these two simple uses, the PERFORM verb permits other options and combinations of options, some of which can greatly complicate program structure and impede readability.

See also *calling sequence.*

performance

For a configuration of hardware and software, a quality that is measured by such dynamic characteristics as response time, turnaround time, frequency of failure (by type), and frequency and duration of unavailability (outage).

Performance encompasses both efficiency and reliability, but is a more general term. It can be applied to the full range of hardware and software, including the following:

- A mainframe or network configuration supporting multiple applications
- An application system supporting multiple users
- A program
- A single module within a program

peripheral device

Any hardware device connected to a central processing unit (CPU) or main memory.

Although some writers limit the term *peripheral* to input devices and output devices, most use the term more broadly to refer also to auxiliary storage devices, including disk drives of all types.

Be careful not to confuse *peripheral* with *external.* A peripheral device can be installed either in the same cabinet with the CPU or in a separate external box; in most cases the software can't tell the difference.

permanent file

A file that continues to exist after the job or process that created it finishes executing, and that can be used later in other jobs.

Permanent files include the following:

- Master files
- Databases
- Archive files

See also *temporary file.*

personal computer

A computer utilizing only one microprocessor or central processing unit (CPU). Also called a *microcomputer* or *desktop computer.*

Once considered an underpowered class of computer, personal computers are becoming as fast as or faster than the mainframes and minicomputers of a few years ago, at a greatly reduced cost. The most common family of personal computer utilizes 8088/8086, 80286, 80386, or 80486 Intel processors, and can run large operating systems such as MS-DOS, UNIX, and OS/2.

Apple computers are considered personal computers; however, they are not considered PCs, because the abbreviation *PC* is commonly associated with IBM or IBM-compatible personal computers.

Some organizations prefer the term *desktop computer* to the older *personal computer,* to emphasize the role of such machines in the everyday business activities of their users.

See also *microchip* and *CPU.*

phased life cycle

See *SDLC.*

physical record

See *record blocking.*

PICTURE

A COBOL keyword that specifies the format of an elementary data item in a DATA DIVISION.

In COBOL, data declarations are representation-based rather than type-based. That is, the programmer describes what the data item looks like rather than what kind of thing it actually is. The data name is followed by the keyword PICTURE or PIC, which is followed by a string of characters defining the external format of the item.

See also *COMPUTATIONAL, data representation, data type, DISPLAY,* and *level number.*

pipe

A mechanism for directing the standard output from one process (a program, task, or command) to the standard input for another process. The user sees only the output from the second process.

Pipes are used extensively in UNIX. Some MS-DOS programs are designed to operate as the second process in a pipe. In both UNIX and MS-DOS, the command syntax uses a vertical bar to specify a pipe. For example, to see a listing of all files in the current directory whose names contain a hyphen, you would enter the following DOS command:

> **DIR ¦ FIND** " "—" "

See also *command prompt* and *redirection.*

pixel

The smallest addressable element on a display screen.

The term *pixel* and its less-used relative, *pel,* are derived from the term *picture element.* Resolution of video monitors and laser printers is often expressed in pixels—for example, a VGA monitor has a resolution of 640 × 480 (640 pixels horizontal and 480 vertical).

PKZIP

In the MS-DOS environment, a shareware program developed by PKWare, Inc., which implements dynamic file compression. PKZIP uses a Lempel-Ziv algorithm to compress data to the smallest number of bytes. The advantage of using such a program is that the smaller file sizes allows for quicker data transmission (and subsequent phone charges) and smaller disk-storage requirements.

PL/1—programming language 1

A programming language designed by a joint working group of SHARE, GUIDE, and IBM in the mid-1960s. PL/1 was intended to complement the introduction of third-generation computer systems such as IBM's System/360 by providing tools to exploit the capabilities of those computers.

PL/1 has an extremely broad scope, attempting to support whatever a programmer might want to do while developing almost any commercial, scientific, or real-time application. As a result, the language has generated vigorous controversy between programmers who welcomed its flexibility and those who considered it too big to do any one thing well.

PL/1 directly supports the following:

- Structured coding constructs
- Block structure
- Multitasking
- Interrupt handling
- Comprehensive input-output (I-O)
- All basic data types (but no definition of new types), arrays, and structures
- A powerful macro preprocessor

PL/1's use faded in the 1980s with the coming of desktop computers too small to support efficient implementation of such a large language. However, with the recent increase in the size of desktop computers and other programming languages, PL/1 has reappeared in OS/2 and UNIX implementations, and its future popularity is uncertain.

platform

The hardware and/or software used by a specific computer installation.

pointer

1. A data element whose value is a random access memory (RAM) address. Some programming languages (such as C, PL/1, and Pascal) support pointer data types, thereby facilitating manipulation of arbitrarily complex data structures.

2. A data element whose value is a location on a random access device: some combination of track, sector, offset, or relative position. Database management systems (DBMS) use such pointers to keep track of relationships among records and to improve the speed of access to records.

3. In graphics, a trackball, mouse, or other device that controls a graphics cursor.

pointing device

A device used to move the cursor on the screen from one position to another, such as a graphics tablet, a pen, or a mouse.

See also *cursor* and *mouse.*

Polish notation

A notation proposed by logician Jan Lukasiewicz to represent complex mathematical expressions without the use of parentheses. Compilers and interpreters often use Polish notation to represent formulas, so as to simplify analysis and minimize intermediate storage and execution time requirements.

In reverse (postfix) Polish notation, the expression

a * (b + c)

is written as

a b c + *

A prefix form exists, but is less useful for computational needs.

polling

A communications systems technique in which devices attached to a computer are interrogated sequentially to see whether they want to communicate.

polymorphism

An object-oriented programming (OOP) concept that enables an object to behave differently, depending on the object sending a receivable message.

Polymorphism is considered a key concept of object-oriented programming. An object created to pay employees, for example, could utilize the concept of polymorphism to react differently if the employee is exempt and thus not qualified to receive overtime, or if the employee is nonexempt and thus qualified to receive overtime. When a "Pay Employee" message is received, the receiving object checks the object that sent the message and pays the employee accordingly.

pop (stack operator)

An operation that removes the first item on a stack and returns it to the invoking routine. Pop and push are the primitive stack operations.

See also *push* and *stack*.

popup window

A small window, usually a menu or dialog box, that is invoked by a program and displayed on top of that program's main window, to prompt the user for a reply. After the user responds, the popup window disappears.

Programs often display a popup menu in response to a user-initiated action, such as a mouse click or a hot key. This is a common way for users to request a function under a graphical user interface (GUI).

port

1. To convert software to another operating platform.

   Derived from "portable," the term *port* is a near synonym of *convert*. However, *port* connotes a degree of compatibility of source code and data, allowing an easier and more economical effort than completely rewriting the software from scratch.

   See also *conversion* and *migrate*.

2. A connection between a computer and data transmission lines, usually through a modem.

port address

The device designation of a port.

On an Intel central processing unit (CPU), these designations are called COM1, COM2, and so on, each of which is associated with the address in memory of the corresponding interrupt handler. Communications software utilizes these fixed locations to gain access to the modem.

portrait orientation

The property of an output (hard copy or display) having its vertical dimension longer than its horizontal dimension. Portrait orientation is the converse of landscape orientation, in which output is displayed with a longer horizontal dimension.

Portrait orientation is standard for business letters and most publications and other documents. Landscape orientation is suited to many accounting reports and spreadsheets. Modern graphics printers and software products let the user or the software choose the orientation for a given output.

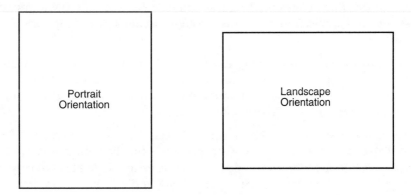

Portrait orientation versus landscape orientation.

positional parameter

A parameter identified by its position in a parameter list.

If a module is declared with a parameter list such as

```
(P, Q, R)
```

then invoked with arguments such as

```
(glop, fctn(x - y), errsw)
```

then the value of fctn(x - y) will be bound to the parameter Q, because both the value and the parameter appear in a corresponding position of the parameter list and the argument list.

Most programming languages support positional parameters. For another way of identifying parameters.

See *keyword parameter.*

POSIX—Portable Operating System Interface for UNIX

A standard that defines the language interface between the UNIX operating system and application programs through a minimal set of supported functions.

Compliance with this standard from the IEEE (Institute of Electrical and Electronic Engineers) makes programs easy to port between platforms. Use of the POSIX standard is not limited to UNIX; other operating environments are free to adopt POSIX, as Windows NT has done.

To validate a system's POSIX compliance, standard POSIX "test suites" are available. These tests are diagnostic programs that help an evaluator identify which POSIX functions are supported in the system being tested. Potential buyers of UNIX operating systems and UNIX applications use POSIX test suites to evaluate software.

PostScript

A proprietary programming language of Adobe Systems Inc. The language is useful for the following purposes:

- To describe printed pages containing text, geometric figures, and sampled images in almost any layout

- To direct the printing of such pages on a graphics printer

PostScript is supported by most full-featured word processors and by GUI-oriented operating systems on desktop computers and networks. In typical use, PostScript programs are not written by programmers, but rather are

- Generated by a word processor or other printing software

- Downloaded along with their data (text and graphics) to an attached printer

- Executed by a special-purpose microcomputer within the printer

By executing time-consuming formatting in the printer itself, PostScript relieves the main (usually desktop) computer of a significant processing load. The resulting gain in capacity, however, is sometimes offset by the overhead of WYSIWYG, in which the main computer must duplicate much of PostScript's formatting functions in order to maintain the screen display.

precedence of operators

See *order of operators.*

predicate

A function yielding a truth value (Boolean) result.

In symbolic logic, a predicate (also called a formula, in a more general sense than the common arithmetic formula) asserts something about one or more objects, such as that they have some property or that some relation exists among them. The following are some simple predicates:

Symbolic Predicate	Meaning
parent(X,Y)	X is the parent of Y
female(X)	X is female
M > N	M is greater than N

Logical manipulation of predicates is helpful in many areas of systems analysis and programming, such as in analyzing and simplifying combinations of decision rules. Predicates are central to logical programming languages like PROLOG, in which a program consists mainly of a sequence of predicates.

A PROLOG predicate with constant arguments is considered a *fact*—that is, part of the database of a program—as in the following examples:

```
female(Victoria).
```

```
parent(Victoria, Edward).
```

A predicate with variable arguments is considered a *rule*—that is, part of the rule base of the program. Rules imply that if the right side is true, then the left side also becomes true, as in the following example:

```
mother(X,Y) := female(X) AND parent(X,Y).
```

From just the last three example predicates, PROLOG can deduce answers to the following queries:

```
mother(Victoria,Edward).    Is Victoria the mother of Edward?
```

```
mother(X,Edward).           Who is the mother of Edward?
```

```
mother(Victoria,X).         Whose mother is Victoria?
```

To enhance readability, the preceding examples deviate somewhat from strict PROLOG syntax.

See also *binary relation*.

pretty print

Automatic formatting of a source code listing according to a set of language-specific rules aimed at enhancing program readability.

Some of the changes pretty print logic may make in source code are the following:

- To indent lines of code according to the nesting level of conditionals (if-then-else), loops, blocks, parentheses, data structure levels, or other bracketed constructs.

- To insert blank lines or page breaks before or after significant sections of code.

- To divide very long statements at suitable points for multiple-line display.

- To align corresponding elements of successive lines of code.

Pretty printing is often welcomed by maintenance programmers trying to understand someone else's program. However, it may annoy good programmers trying to lay out their own code. It is most valuable in programming languages in which very deep nesting levels are common; for example, pretty printing is useful with LISP because of its extensive use of parentheses for nesting.

print

1. To generate output to be printed on paper by a printer.

2. To generate output in printer format for a screen or a file.

PRINT (BASIC)

A stream input-output (I-O) statement in BASIC, used for output of a list of items to a screen, a printer, or a sequential file.

The corresponding input statement is INPUT.

PRINT (MS-DOS)

An MS-DOS command that copies an ASCII file (text file) to a printer.

PRINT is an exception to MS-DOS's otherwise single-tasking operation, in that it operates concurrently as a background process, that is, as a spooler.

printer

An output device that converts information to a printed page. Various types of printers are available, including dot matrix, laser, ink jet, daisywheel, chain, thermal, and drum-type.

printf

A stream input-output (I-O) function in C, used for output of a list of items to a screen, a printer, or (as fprintf) a sequential file.

The corresponding input function is scanf.

print preview

The display on the user's screen that displays on the user's screen a reduced-size image of a report or other printable output.

Non-WYSIWYG programs that offer sophisticated printing capabilities, such as word processors, spreadsheet processors, and query processors, often offer a print preview option in addition to regular printing options. By invoking print preview, the user can see what the output would look like if it were printed. Then if something isn't right, such as a page break, the user can correct it without wasting time or paper actually printing the output.

Because details usually appear too small to be readable, print preview is used mainly to examine the larger layout aspects of printed output, such as margins, columns, and the placement of headings, tables, and figures. At the cost of a few seconds of waiting, print preview serves much the same purpose as WYSIWYG with less cost in computer overhead.

private class member

A class member object that can be used only by that particular object, or can be accessed only by functions (methods) that belong to the same class. For example, in the following code sample, the code directly under the `private:` line and over the `public:` line is private to the class/object, and cannot be accessed by other objects:

```
class my_class {
private:
    init number;
    one_number(int value);
public:
    virtual void inc(void);
    int get(void);
};
```

See also *class, member function, member object, object,* and *public class member.*

problem-oriented language

A programming language designed to support a specific application area, and embodying knowledge of the terminology and practices of that area.

Early languages like FORTRAN and COBOL were once characterized as problem-oriented to distinguish them from computer-oriented assembly languages. Today, however, a problem-oriented language is expected to cater specifically to an application area (like accounting, publishing, or civil engineering).

procedural language

A programming language in which the programmer specifies the chronological sequence of steps to be performed.

The most widely used programming languages are procedural. They reflect both the way people naturally think about many kinds of problems and algorithms, and the way computers run. Even languages that are essentially nonprocedural (such as LISP, PROLOG, and spreadsheet languages) often provide procedural aspects or options.

Procedural languages span a wide range of levels, from machine-specific assembly languages to the highest-level standard languages such as APL, PL/1, and Ada, and beyond to various proprietary languages. Therefore, the fact that a language is procedural implies little about its power or productivity.

See also *nonprocedural language* and *generations, programming language*.

procedure

1. A subroutine or function.

2. The keyword introducing a subroutine or function in ALGOL-like languages, such as Ada, Pascal, and PL/1.

3. An algorithm or series of steps to be executed by human beings; called a "manual procedure" to distinguish this usage from the preceding ones.

Manual procedures, usually designed and written by a systems analyst, are fundamental components of typical application systems. Before the 1980s, many manual procedures involved the preparation of input transactions. With the trend toward more built-in tutorial and help capabilities, such user-interface procedures have now become less important. However, manual procedures are still essential for defining standard methods for system startup and logon, troubleshooting, and error diagnosis, and a wide variety of purely offline activities.

PROCEDURE DIVISION

The part of a COBOL program or subprogram that contains executable statements.

processing cycle

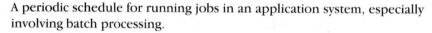

A periodic schedule for running jobs in an application system, especially involving batch processing.

Accounting systems and many other business applications are tied to regularly recurring processes. A major system may contain components run on some or all the following processing cycles:

- Non-stop online operation
- Daily online operation during specified hours
- Overnight daily batch cycle
- Weekly batch cycle
- Monthly batch cycle
- Quarterly batch cycle
- Annual batch cycle

Properly synchronizing different processing cycles in an application system is an important aspect of application system architecture. A monthly batch job may consolidate the results of either four or five weekly cycles, depending on which month it is. An overnight batch job may have to wait for online operation to shut down.

See also *batch processing* and *closing*.

production status

For an application system, the state of being operational.

When a system is in production status rather than development status, several formal disciplines must be in effect to ensure system integrity. These disciplines typically include the following:

- System operation can be initiated only by operational personnel authorized to do so.

- Access to the system is restricted to authorized users.

- Access to the master files or databases is restricted to the application system software in normal operation.

- Changes to the executable programs are prohibited.

In particular, the programmers who developed or who currently maintain the system should have no special access privileges. When they need to make changes, they use a separate "test" version of the software, and later submit the new version to production turnover procedures.

production turnover

The process whereby a developer or a development team delivers a completed application to the group that will be responsible for running the application; also called *installation*.

See also *production status*.

productivity tool

Software that end users can use independently of any application system. Categories of productivity tools include word processors and spreadsheet processors, as well as those database management systems (DBMS) that emphasize query processing and report generation.

Productivity tools constitute a third major software category between the system software and application system categories. The term is not firmly established, however, and some operating system documentation refers to such general-purpose software as "applications."

Of course, you can use a productivity tool to build part of an application. When you use a spreadsheet processor, for example, to create a spreadsheet model, it is the model, not the spreadsheet processor itself, that becomes part of your application. Although the spreadsheet processor is directly involved in running your application, it itself knows nothing about that application and is not considered part of it.

See also *application system* and *system software*.

program

1. To develop software; see *programming.*

2. An executable unit of software; see *complete program.*

program environment

The set of values of the run parameters used by a program.

In MS-DOS the user can specify values for a run parameter in two ways:

- By a parameter on the command that invokes the program.

- By a SET command that defines the name and value of an environment variable. (Although MS-DOS terminology refers to these global data items as variables, they are usually constant during program execution.)

The method by which a program gains access to command-line parameters and environment variables is different for each programming language. Most compiler manuals provide this information.

Other operating systems provide similar facilities.

In addition, the program environment includes any other status information that may affect a program's behavior, such as the following:

- The active drive and active directory for retrieving and storing files

- The path for retrieving executable programs

- Any device reassignments (for example, those established by MS-DOS ASSIGN, SUBST, or MODE commands)

- The amount of memory available

It is good practice to ensure that a program leaves its environment as undisturbed as possible. If a program must change the active directory, for example, it should restore the original active directory before returning control to the operating system. (Some widely used software products fail to observe this convention.)

programmer

Anyone engaged in programming, whether as a professional position or in support of academic, professional, or personal activities.

See also *chief programmer, designer, lead programmer, programmer-analyst,* and *systems analyst.*

programmer-analyst

An individual who can perform the duties of both a systems analyst and a programmer. (Some organizations also call their best programmers "programmer-analysts," in an attempt to confer a more prestigious title.)

programming

The creative process of developing a computerized solution to a well-defined problem.

Programming usually includes the following four activities:

Design	Selection of tools, languages, and standards; specification of outputs, functions, algorithms, and inputs; decomposition into major modules
Coding	Preparation in a programming language of the sequence of statements to implement functions, procedures, algorithms, and so on
Testing	Bug detection and correction, validation, and performance tuning
Maintenance	Diagnosis and repair of bugs that arise in production operation, addition of new features and enhancements, and updating of tables and other data hard coded into the source code

The problems a programmer is called on to solve range from complete application system specifications prepared by a systems analyst, to an individual module specification prepared by another (or the same) programmer.

See also *maintenance programming* and *unit test.*

programming language

A formal notation and set of conventions for expressing a strategy, procedure, or algorithm for using a computer to solve a class of problems.

See also *nonprocedural language, procedural language,* and *generations, programming languages.*

programming language generation

See *generations, programming languages.*

PROLOG

A programming language based on formal (symbolic) logic and used widely in artificial intelligence applications. The name, coined by its French developers, comes from *programmation en logique* (programming in logic).

PROLOG uses backward chaining to determine whether a goal or query is satisfied by a combination of facts ("data base") and inference predicates ("rule base"). The language also employs sophisticated matching to find one or more sets of values that, when substituted for variables in the rules, make the inquiry true. Such values are usually the answers or results the user seeks.

See also *nonprocedural language* and *predicate.*

prologue

In a high-level language, the code generated for execution as a program is entered. Depending on the programming language, the prologue may allocate memory, initialize local variables, and establish exception-handling procedures.

See also *epilogue.*

prompt

1. A message on the screen that requests a reply from the user.

2. To issue such a prompt.

See also *command prompt, dialog box,* and *popup window.*

protected mode

A hardware state in which individual jobs are prevented from storing data into any area of memory (or virtual address space) currently assigned either to another job or to the operating system itself.

Protected mode capability is essential for reliable multiprogramming. It was supported by most third-generation computers and has been available on most desktop computers since the Intel 80286.

See also *real mode*.

protection exception

An error caused when a program refers to an address in memory (or in virtual address space) that lies outside its own area. See *protected mode*.

These errors, usually caused by a program bug, result in a transfer of control to the operating system, which can then terminate the offending job with an explanatory message to the user. In early versions of Microsoft Windows, protection exceptions often led to a crash of the whole system.

See also *UAE*.

protocol

A formal agreement in the form of a set of rules regarding message exchange. Although the term has been applied to communications between program units, it is most correctly applied to communications between distributed hardware devices.

Common protocols include BSC (Binary Synchronous Communications), SDLC (Synchronous Data Link Control), TCP/IP (Transmission Control Protocol/Internet Protocol), Kermit, and XMODEM.

prototype

A demonstration version of a proposed application system or software product, especially one that mimics the user interfaces without the underlying processing logic. The prototype replaces those parts of a written specification that define the content and layout of system outputs and inputs.

The purposes of the prototype are the following:

- To clarify to a prospective user community the nature of the proposed new software and how the user community will use the software

- To confirm early in a software development project that the project team is solving the right problem

The growing availability of more powerful tools for rapid development of sophisticated user interfaces has made prototyping increasingly practical. The effort required to prepare an input-output prototype is often little more than the effort required to prepare equivalent written specifications.

 A slick prototype can sometimes divert the users' attention from missing content or functionality. Many cautious application system development organizations encourage both prototyping and careful review of written specifications of all system outputs and inputs.

Prototyping is sometimes confused with incremental development, in which the initial version becomes the first production version and forms the basis for additions and enhancements. Because a prototype is often unsuitable as a basis for flexible enhancement or acceptable performance, it is rarely retained in the eventual production software.

pseudocode

Any nonstandardized or proprietary representation of a programming language. For instance, a programmer may use plain-English pseudocode to describe programming procedures before they are actually implemented. A compiler may also translate source code into a proprietary pseudocode during compilation.

pseudo-op

An assembly language statement that does not represent a machine language instruction (or a macro), but instead gives to the assembler information that enables it to perform such operations as defining constants, setting symbolic values, or choosing options.

PSP—program segment prefix

A 256-byte control block immediately preceding an MS-DOS program in memory, describing the status of the program during execution, including pointers to the allocated memory segments.

public class member

In object-oriented programming (OOP), a data item or function that can be referred to anywhere in the program. In contrast, a private class member can be used only by objects of the same class in which it was declared.

See also *accessor function.*

public domain

Software for which ownership has been transferred to the public. It has no ownership or distribution restrictions.

See also *freeware.*

pulldown menu

A window that appears from the top of the screen downward.

A pulldown menu is activated when the user selects the menu title from the main menu bar. The user can use a mouse or the cursor to highlight the available pulldown menu options. When the desired option is highlighted, the user double-clicks the mouse or presses Enter.

See also *popup window* and *list box.*

push (stack operator)

An operation that places an element on a stack. Push and pop are the primitive stack operations.

See also *pop* and *stack.*

QBasic

An interpreter for BASIC, distributed with MS-DOS (Version 5 and later) and intended as a replacement for BASICA.

QBasic is a major break with the decade old BASIC language for desktop computers. It removes several long-standing restrictions, extends the language in the same direction as popular compilers like Microsoft's QuickBASIC, and provides an integrated environment for program editing and testing. Certain incompatibilities with BASICA may require modification of some older programs.

qualified name

A name of a data item or program object accompanied by the names of higher-level structures that contain that data item or program object. Name qualification may be required for the following reasons:

- To resolve ambiguity

- To override a default

For example, consider a C program containing these two structures:

```
struct    inventory {
    char part_number[8];
    int  on_hand_quan;
    int  on_ordr_quan;};

struct    order {
    char customer_id[10];
    char part_number[8];
    int  quantity;};
```

A simple reference to part_number would be ambiguous, and therefore an error would be detected at compile-time. Instead the programmer must specify a qualified name, either inventory.part_number or order.part_number.

All programming languages that support data structures also support name qualification and require it when it's logically needed. Many languages use the dot notation to implement name qualification. For example, in the preceding example, inventory.part_number and order.part_number both use the dot notation.

Note these two special cases:

- C++ supports two distinct kinds of qualification:

  The member operator (.), which can be used to distinguish items with the same name within structures known in the same block.

  The scope-resolution operator (::), which can be used to distinguish items with the same name declared in different blocks.

- COBOL reverses the normal highest-to-lowest order by using the keywords IN or OF, as in the following example:

```
PART-NUMBER IN ORDER
```

In some situations, a programming language may require a "fully" qualified name reference, in which the programmer must specify all levels in the naming hierarchy even if they're not logically necessary to resolve ambiguity.

See also *block.*

quality assurance

1. A formal review of the deliverables produced in a phase of an application system development project, in order to validate compliance with applicable standards and to detect certain kinds of flaws.

2. An organization responsible for conducting such reviews, often abbreviated "QA."

See also *walkthrough.*

Quattro Pro

Borland International's spreadsheet processor for various operating platforms.

See also *Excel* and *Lotus 1-2-3.*

queue

A dynamic data structure in which items are added to one end and removed from the other end. Also called a *FIFO* (first-in, first-out) list.

See also *deque, list,* and *stack.*

QuickBASIC

A popular BASIC compiler from Microsoft.

Compared to the earlier interpreted version of the language (BASICA), this compiler provides significant improvements, including the following:

- Support for structured coding

- Subroutines and functions with parameters

- Elimination of the requirement for a statement number on every line

On the other hand, several incompatibilities—especially in the handling of exceptions, such as the printer not being ready—may present obstacles to converting older BASIC programs to QuickBASIC.

QuickC

A C compiler from Microsoft, compatible with larger, more expensive C compilers, but providing fewer features. QuickC for Windows, a special version that operates within the Windows environment, is used to develop Windows application programs.

quicksort

A method of internal sorting.

Like merge sort, quicksort uses a recursive divide-and-conquer strategy. To sort the N items stored in S[j] through S[j+N-1], you follow these steps:

1. Choose a "pivot" element at random; for example, S[p] = P.

2. Compare each element with P to determine k, the number of items less than P. Place P in its final position S[j+k] and partition the array by swapping elements until all items less than P precede P, and all items greater than P follow P.

3. Recursively invoke quicksort on each of the two partitions, S[j] through S[j+k-1] and S[j+k] through S[j+N-1].

The number of comparisons varies between an average of n log n and a worst case of n^2, according to the original ordering of the items. Because of its low overhead, quicksort is sometimes preferred over methods that have better worst-case performance in theory.

See also *internal sorting* and *merge sort*.

radix

The base of a number system.

The conventional decimal system uses 10 as its radix. Others commonly used in computing are binary (base 2), hexadecimal (base 16), and less often, octal (base 8).

In writing constants in bases other than 10, it is customary to specify the base either by writing it in parentheses, as in 235(hex), or as a numeric subscript, as in 235_{16}.

RAM—random-access memory

See *memory*.

random-access memory

See *memory*.

range

In a spreadsheet, the same as *block*.

Although experienced spreadsheet users have no difficulty understanding either term, the newer term *block* is less likely to be misinterpreted. Depending on context, a reference to a range can also mean the range of values of a function or a graph.

See *block structure*.

range name

See *block name*.

raster

A graphic or video image represented by a matrix of dots; also, a technique that uses dots to create fonts or graphic images. Bitmap (BMP) or PCX files created by Windows Paint or other "Paint" programs are called raster graphic images. In contrast are vector graphics, which are images a computer-aided design (CAD) program creates by using lines to connect points.

In television, the term refers to the visual image.

rational number

A quantity that can be represented exactly as the ratio of two integers.

See also *real number* and *irrational number.*

R:Base

A relational database management system (DBMS) from Microrim, Inc., for MS-DOS and networks.

Like competing products—such as Paradox, dBASE IV, and Access—R:Base provides an application generator, query processing, and a programming language.

readability

The degree to which one can read and understand source code.

See also *pretty print* and *structured coding.*

read-only memory

See *ROM.*

read-only storage

1. A permanently recorded portion of memory from which a program can fetch data, but into which programs cannot store or update data. See *ROM.*

2. Any storage medium that can be read from but not written to.

README file

A text file accompanying distributed software, meant to be read before the software is set up or installed. The text may explain the other files in the package and convey instructions for proceeding.

A README file is useful mainly for conveying information specific to a particular software release. Therefore, such information may be only temporarily accurate, and not intended as a permanent manual for subsequent releases.

real data type

A data type that approximates the value of a real number.

Some languages use the keyword FLOAT to implement this type, because arithmetic operations on this data type are usually implemented in the system's floating-point instruction set. Real data items are used to represent fractional quantities as well as numbers that vary greatly in magnitude.

The maximum and minimum values and the number of digits of precision are implementation-dependent. Programming languages and hardware architectures often provide variants of the real type so that the programmer can choose the representation best suited to the problem at hand and the constraints imposed by available machinery.

A common source of programming error is to assume exact values for real approximations. It is not likely that $1/3 * 3 = 1$. Tests based on this assumption will fail, producing sometimes subtle errors.

See also *double precision* and *numeric data type*.

real mode

A computer hardware state in which a program can refer to any address in memory.

Real mode operation avoids the overhead and complexity of both paging and multiprogramming, but it lacks the flexibility those concepts provide. It is practical, therefore, mainly for very small computers running one job at a time, perhaps in some specialized or dedicated application.

On the Intel 80×86 family of computers, real mode operation limits the amount of memory that a program can utilize to 1M.

See also *protected mode*.

real number

Any number obtained as the solution of an algebraic equation. The real numbers include both rational numbers and irrational numbers.

See also *real data type.*

recalculate

To update the values in a spreadsheet by applying all the formulas.

As spreadsheets get large, significant performance degradation arises from repeatedly recalculating every formula throughout the model whenever anything changes. In addition, in specialized situations the results may differ depending on the order (by rows or by columns) in which the formulas are evaluated.

Spreadsheet processors let the user control whether recalculation will be automatic or manually initiated, and in which order. Manually initiated recalculation is usually triggered by a single key, F9 being used in several products.

When automatic recalculation is disabled, printing a spreadsheet containing inconsistent information is all too easy. Forgetting to initiate recalculation just before printing is a common cause of erroneous output from spreadsheet models.

Special care is required in developing sophisticated macro programs. A logically correct process may fail simply because a value didn't get updated. As a general rule, spreadsheet macro programs that contain any loops or iteration should explicitly control any necessary recalculation.

record

1. A group of related fields.

2. In relational terminology, a row of a table.

3. A mode of communications, word processing, and spreadsheet programs in which a macro or script is recorded as its keystrokes are entered, for later playback or editing.

record blocking

The practice of combining multiple logical records into a single physical record, to reduce both storage space on magnetic media and elapsed time for input-output (I/O) operations.

On magnetic tape, gaps between physical records are needed to allow for the starting and stopping of the tape drive. These gaps are long compared to short data records, so that a large number of short records will consume much more tape than an equivalent small number of blocked records, as shown in the following diagram:

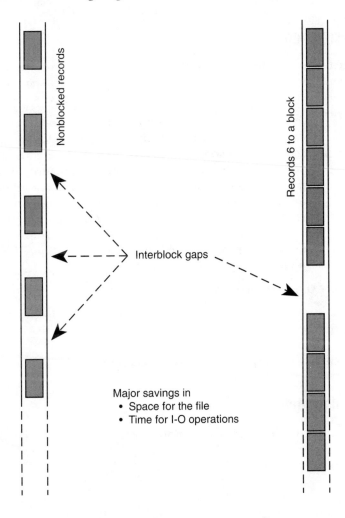

Record blocking on magnetic media.

The same consideration applies to magnetic disk, but with the added complication that the length of the track and, on many types of disk, the fixed length of a sector may make some block sizes much more efficient than others.

Savings in both space and input-output time usually offset both the increased memory requirements for larger buffers and the processing overhead devoted to blocking and deblocking records. Because elapsed time is the most relevant performance measure, record blocking is most useful in operating environments that don't support multiprogramming. In multiple-user operation, input-output inefficiencies in one process make additional processing cycles available for other users.

record description

A specification of the content and layout of a type of record, usually in a form suitable for input to a compiler or a data dictionary system.

When many program modules share knowledge of a particular type of record, you can't afford to let each module contain its own copy of the statements describing the fields within those records. To do so would be prohibitively expensive, and error-prone whenever you change the record structure. Instead, you should maintain a single master copy of each record description in a central library, then use the compiler's source text inclusion facilities to merge it into the source code. To support such a library, an organization must establish appropriate standards for such things as field names, terminal punctuation, level numbers, and bracketing within a record description.

See also *COPY* and *header file*.

recursion

See *recursive definition* and *recursive function*.

recursive definition

A definition that includes one or more instances of the term being defined.

Recursive definitions are used extensively in theoretical mathematics and symbolic logic. You can define positive integer exponentiation, for example, in terms of multiplication, as follows:

$$a^0 = 1$$

$$a^n = a * a^{n-1}, \text{ for } n > 0$$

Note that a recursive definition must always have at least one special case (in this example, n=0), and that the case must be encountered eventually during the recursion's expansion.

Recursive definitions are also a powerful tool in defining language syntax (see the example under *Backus-Naur form*).

recursive function

An implementation of a function or other module that invokes itself.

Although you can implement almost any function recursively, severe performance penalties may outweigh any apparent advantage in simplicity or elegance. Recursive implementation is advisable mainly for algorithms that have the following properties:

- The function or algorithm is simply and compactly expressed by a recursive definition.

- Part of the algorithm is nested to an unpredictable maximum depth.

- The program would otherwise have to keep track of numerous intermediate results, perhaps using arrays of undetermined dimension in which the recursive implementation needs only simple scalars.

Such functions arise frequently when you manipulate dynamic data structures, parse statements in a language, evaluate expressions, implement search strategies, or perform internal sorting.

Recursive techniques are not limited to modules that can be packaged as functions. Many languages and other tools enable you to recursively implement defined *macros, subroutines,* and even *data structures.*

Some older programming languages (such as COBOL and FORTRAN) don't support recursive functions or subroutines at all. In such languages, if a module tries to invoke itself either directly or through an intermediate module, either the compiler will detect the attempt as an error, or the attempt will lead to a loss of control during execution.

Even if a language supports recursion, certain programming techniques can cause it to fail, notably the use of static storage or explicit memory allocation not related to the program's block structure.

REDEFINES

A COBOL data attribute declaring that a data item is to share memory with another, previously declared data item.

Although subject to numerous restrictions, REDEFINES serves much the same function for COBOL as unions for C, EQUIVALENCE for FORTRAN, or DEFINED for PL/1. In addition, its use is mandatory for generating a table with constant values.

redirection

A mechanism for causing either of the following:

- Writing standard output from a program not to the default device (screen or printer) but to a file that can be read by other programs

- Moving the standard input from an existing file to a program

In UNIX and MS-DOS commands, redirection is specified by less-than (<) or greater-than (>) signs. For example, to save the listing of the directory on drive B (for transmission or for input to a program), you would enter the following MS-DOS command:

```
DIR B: > DIRLIST.TXT
```

To avoid having the system stop for console verification of a delete-everything command, you would enter this DOS command:

```
DEL B:*.*  < YESREPLY.TXT
```

See also *command prompt* and *pipe.*

re-entrant

A property of a subroutine (or a complete program) that permits its use by two or more concurrently executing tasks.

To be re-entrant, a routine must maintain completely separate copies of any data associated with each invocation. This in turn requires that data areas in memory be either allocated dynamically or inherited from the invoking higher-level routine. If, in a multiprogrammed operating system, a program wanted by multiple users is not re-entrant, the operating system must load a separate copy of that program each time it is invoked. The savings in space and bookkeeping is usually considered worth the slight execution overhead of re-entrancy.

Many compilers generate re-entrant code, either as their normal output or as an on-request option.

See also *resident program*.

register

High-speed storage circuits in a computer, used for addresses of data or instructions and for operands of some instructions.

The Intel 8086 computer has the following 16-bit registers:

Register Name	Use
AX	Primary accumulator
BX	Base register or accumulator
CX	Index register or accumulator
DX	Input-output (I-O) address or accumulator
BP	Base pointer
SI	Source index
DI	Destination index
SS	Stack segment
SP	Stack pointer
DS	Data segment
ES	Extra segment
CS	Code segment
PC	Instruction counter (program counter)

In the newer 80386 and 80486 processors, some of these registers were widened to 32 bits, designated EAX, EBX, and so on, and additional registers support new features such as protected mode operation.

relation

See *binary relation.*

relational database

A database model in which only tables are used to organize database storage. Usually, each table represents a file, but relational database physical storage techniques may vary from product to product. The objective of a relational database is to facilitate ad hoc requests for information.

Use of the relational model, and the relational database that employs the model, is the primary method of database organization employed today. This database technology replaces the older hierarchical and network database models used in the 1960s and 1970s.

Relational tables are linked together by unique key attributes that the tables have in common. Once this link is created, the relational database system uses those key fields to create a relational view, which enables users to create ad hoc queries and reports, make updates and edits, and perform other database operations.

Having to keep track constantly of these relationships among several tables decreases the performance of the relational database. To solve this problem, relational database vendors provide indexes that are built and maintained for each of the key attributes used for linking tables. Such indexes may be maintained within the database file or in separate files.

The relational model is easier to understand than the more complex hierarchical and network database models, and therefore it requires less time to train users and programmers to use the model. The relational model simulates the way in which database systems were designed before relational databases existed. The model provides a more natural development environment, because little or no translation from the logical database design to the physical is required. For example, consider the following relational database tables:

```
Customer(Customer_Number, Customer_Name, Customer_Address,
    Customer_State, Customer_Zip)

Sales(Customer_Number, Product_Number, Quantity_Puchased)

Product(Product_Number, Product_Description, Product_Price)
```

In the first table, the unique attribute or key, `Customer_Number`, links the `Customer` table to the `Sales` table, which contains the same key attribute. Each table may contain a different number of tuples (records). However, for every customer in the `Customer` table, all the sales made to that particular customer can be found in the `Sales` table. The same concept holds true for the `Sales` table and the `Product` table. They are related or linked by `Product_Number`, so by using the `Product_Number` you can determine the `Product_Description` and the `Product_Price` for a particular sales order.

Edgar Codd developed the relational database concept in 1970, but relational technology was not widely accepted until the early 1980s. Most database systems currently used on computers support this relational model. Although the method of physical data storage may differ from database vendor to database vendor, the relational concepts are the same from product to product. Structured Query Language (SQL) is the standard language used to access a relational database, and is usually supported by most relational database vendors. Examples of relational systems that run on microcomputers include dBASE IV, FoxPro, and Paradox.

See also *SQL*.

relational operator

An operator that compares two values or expressions. The relational operators most commonly used in programming and the symbols that represent them in most programming languages include the following:

Operator	Symbol
Equals	=
Not equal	< > or != or ~=
Greater than	>
Less than	<
Greater than or equal	> =
Less than or equal	< =

Programming languages such as Pascal that include a set data type also provide an operation to test whether an element is a member of a set.

See also *binary operator*.

relocatable

The characteristic of a representation of machine language code that is independent of the actual addresses it will occupy.

Object modules and, in modern operating systems, executable programs are usually in relocatable form, so that they can be loaded into any area of available memory. This form requires, in addition to the machine code itself, some supplementary information to indicate which fields must be incremented by a base loading address or otherwise adjusted when the program is loaded for execution.

remote job entry—RJE

Submittal of batch processing jobs from a location other than the data center which is to run the jobs on its computers, and transmittal of hard copy results back to the remote location.

RJE was one of the earliest forms of teleprocessing to be used in large organizations. In the 1960s, RJE facilitated the consolidation of multiple small data centers, and was thus a key contributor to the growth of large-scale data processing. It persists today mainly through job submittal gateways in networks or time-sharing systems.

report

A file containing a set of related outputs from an application system, designed to be understood easily by people. A report can either be printed on paper (hard copy) or viewed on a display device.

Reports constitute the principal results from most traditional business application systems and many other kinds of commercial and scientific applications.

Widespread dissatisfaction with the amount of detailed coding needed to implement or change a report in COBOL (without the Report Writer Feature) stimulated the development of many current high-level report generator tools.

Although reports come in limitless variety, most traditional business application system reports have the following structure:

- A summary section, often just a single page containing grand totals

- A detail section consisting of a number of columns of information, with appropriate control breaks and subtotals

It is considered good practice for each page to contain as headers or footers the name of the report, the page number, the date, and any column identifiers needed to understand the content.

report generator

Any of a number of specialized languages or other tools designed to make it easy to extract information from a database and present it in an attractively formatted report.

resident program

A program that remains in memory even when it is not executing, usually to be able to respond quickly when it is invoked.

See also *TSR*, *.DLL*, and *kernel*.

resolution

A measure of sharpness or fineness of detail displayed on printers and display screens. Resolution is given in displayable pixels for screens, and in dots per inch (dpi) for printers.

response time

The time interval in an online system between a user's action (such as entering a transaction, pressing a key, or clicking a mouse button) and the system's visible response to that action. (Displaying a clock or a "wait" indicator is not considered a response.)

In most high-volume online and time-sharing systems, the average and maximum response times are the principal criteria in evaluating system performance. In multiple-user or shared database applications, response time may vary widely depending on the number of users competing for system resources.

restartable job

Any job that can safely be run repeatedly if interrupted before completion.

Most report printing jobs are restartable. However, a job that updates master files or databases usually is not, and a misguided attempt to restart it can result in considerable harm.

Some operating systems recognize a code indicating whether a job is restartable. Then, in the event of a power failure or an operating system crash, such jobs can be automatically requeued for execution.

retention

See *file retention.*

return

A statement in many procedural programming languages that terminates execution of a module, transfers control back to the calling module, and (optionally) specifies the function value.

In many languages, the execution of a return statement in a main module terminates execution of the whole program and returns control to the invoking operating system or other control program.

 NOTE In the early 1970s, when structured coding was new, some writers and lecturers warned against coding more than one return statement in a module—the second half of the "single entry/single exit" rule. Although limiting modules to a single entry point has strong advantages, avoiding multiple returns does not necessarily enhance readability or maintainability. A simple return statement is often the neatest way out of a nested construct. See the example under *binary search.*

return code

See *condition code.*

reusable module

A program module that can be used in more than one complete program.

A library of useful, already tested modules can help to significantly reduce the cost and time required for developing both system software and application software. To take advantage of such a library, the program designer must practice modular programming in the highest degree, cleanly separating the functions of the specific application from the abstract, generalizable functions. Exploiting libraries of reusable modules has been common practice for many years in scientific programming, but has been used by only a minority of business applications programmers, partly because of the monolithic programming tradition that originated with early versions of COBOL.

Object-oriented programming (OOP) has recently revived interest in reusable modules, because it encourages separation of concrete and abstract characteristics through encapsulation.

Revelation

Revelation Technologies' database management system (DBMS), which provides query processing, report generation, and a BASIC-like proprietary programming language.

reverse Polish notation

The postfix form of Polish notation.

rewind

To position a sequential file at the beginning, ready to read or write the first record.

For a file on magnetic tape, rewinding is a physical operation. For a file on a direct access medium such as a disk, the operation involves only resetting a record position counter.

REXX—restructured extended executor

A structured programming language combining the flexibility and power found in procedural language with the capability to control operating system functions found in a command language.

345

REXX supports SAA (IBM's System Application Architecture), and is distributed with IBM operating systems, including OS/2 on desktop computers.

RGB monitor—red-green-blue

A monitor that accepts separate signals for the primary colors red, green,
and blue, to produce various colors on the screen.

rich text format

See *RTF*.

RJE

See *remote job entry*.

rollback

To restore an earlier state of a database, either by loading a backup file or by
undoing the effect of one or more recent update transactions.

See also *database management system*.

ROM—read-only memory

A semiconductor memory that contains programs or data that can be read
but not modified. ROM is not volatile; it maintains its contents even after
loss of power.

A familiar example of a ROM system is Intel's BIOS (basic input-output
system). The computer reads information stored in ROM to perform BIOS
operations, but cannot actually modify the BIOS.

root

The origin point of a tree.

root directory

The highest-level directory on a disk volume. In MS-DOS and similar systems, the root directory is unnamed.

rotation

1. In graphics, a mathematical transformation of the coordinates of each pixel in a graphics image, to give the effect of having displaced the image by some angle about the center of its axis system.

2. Less commonly, a "circular shift" operation in which the elements of a vector or machine register shifted out one end reenter at the other end. For example, a three-position left rotation of 100010101 gives 010101100.

round

To approximate a number to the nearest predefined precision. For instance, if an application works with monetary units, you may want to round numbers to two decimal places.

RPG—report program generator

An early nonprocedural language from IBM, used to design and generate reports.

Currently, RPG is used widely on IBM AS/400 computers. MS-DOS versions of RPG are also available, enabling users to port RPG programs to desktop computers.

See also *report generator*.

RTF—rich text format

Microsoft's extended version of IBM's DCA (document content architecture), a set of standards to facilitate interchange of documents containing text and graphics.

rule base

In an expert system, the set of inference rules on which the system is to reason its way to a problem solution.

Pure facts or assertions about an entity are considered part of the expert system's database rather than its rule base, even though they may be coded and internally represented in a similar way. The actual rules are usually of the following form:

IF *condition* THEN *assertion*>

Note the important difference between such a rule and the common if-then-else construct of procedural programming languages: Both test a condition, but in a rule the assertion isn't an action to be performed but rather a new fact or rule in the chain. That new fact may in turn cause conditions in other rules to become true, causing those rules to "fire."

See also *chaining of rules, expert system,* and *inference engine.*

SAA—system application architecture

A set of standards introduced by IBM in 1987 to promote a consistent user interface for programs written for mainframe computers, minicomputers, and desktop computers, at least within the IBM product line.

SAA includes the following components:

- The CUA (common user access), a graphical user interface (GUI) derived from object-oriented programming (OOP) concepts. OS/2 implements CUA on desktop computers.

- The CPI (common programming interface), providing a standard application programming interface (API) for all platforms.

See also *SNA* and *API*.

scalar

Any data item that is not an array (that is, any data item that has no dimension).

In applied mathematics, scalars are usually numbers, but in computer science the concept is generalized to include all data types, including composite items (structures).

A language-dependent ambiguity arises with character strings. Most languages (BASIC, COBOL, PL/1, spreadsheet processors, query processors, and report generators) support strings as a scalar data type, while some (notably C and Pascal) define a string as an array of single characters. Many program designers consider character strings to be scalars, regardless of language, encapsulating any knowledge of an underlying array within object-oriented class definitions or other localized modules.

scanf

A C and C++ library function that enables you to input formatted information. For instance, the following program line waits for the user to input a floating-point number, which is then assigned to the variable Age:

```
scanf("%f",&Age);
```

Virtually every C or C++ library available contains the scanf function.

scheduler

A component of an operating system that selects jobs to be run and launches their execution.

A simple scheduler may just initiate batch jobs from a queue (FIFO) or initiate interactive jobs as requested by an online user. A more sophisticated scheduler may try to optimize throughput or meet fixed deadlines.

scientific notation

A conventional representation for printing real numbers especially very large or very small numbers, as a mantissa (usually between 1.0 and 9.999) and an exponent (power of 10). Thus, 1234567000000 is written as 1.234567×10^{13}.

Most modern computer hardware implements floating-point arithmetic on real variables by using a strongly parallel, internal data representation. Floating-point numbers have an exponent part (usually eight bits) and a mantissa (24 or 56 bits).

scratch file

See *temporary file.*

scratchpad

A storage area (either memory, a register, or disk file) used for very short-term storage of intermediate results.

See also *buffer.*

scroll

To move text or images vertically (or less often horizontally) through a screen or through a window.

Many programs support user-controlled scrolling, in which the user manipulates either a scroll bar or cursor keys to view different parts of a file, a list, or an image. The effect is as if the window itself were moving over a large, stationary document.

scroll bar

A control facility, especially in a graphical user interface (GUI), that enables the user to scroll information on the screen by using a pointing device such as a mouse.

A scroll bar has an up arrow on the top, a down arrow at the bottom at each end, and a block in the middle called the scroll thumb. The user can either click on the up or down arrows to move the screen slowly in either direction or drag the scroll thumb quickly to a position corresponding to a position in the file or list being scrolled. Many list boxes provide scroll bars, enabling the users to move through lists that are too long to fit in the window.

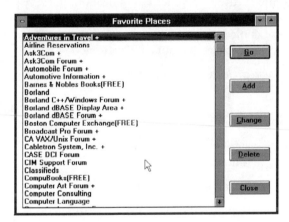

A list box incorporating a scroll bar.

SCSI—small computer system interface

An ANSI standard interface between a microcomputer and a peripheral device; pronounced "scuzzy."

SDLC—system development life cycle

The sequence of phases followed by a system development project, usually including one or more systems analysis phases, a design or architecture phase, a programming phase, and an installation phase.

search

1. Narrowly defined, the process of finding (in a file, table, list, tree, or other container) a data item that matches a given (argument) data item or that satisfies specified criteria.

2. More broadly defined, the process of finding a solution to a problem that involves making a series of consecutive choices.

Although the two kinds of searching may initially seem dissimilar, many of the same strategies are employed. An expert system may traverse a series of choices like examining nodes in a tree, even though no physical tree is actually constructed in memory.

Although the "brute force" method of examining every possibility is theoretically always available, it is impractical when the number of choices and combinations of choices is large. Efficiency in searching results from minimizing the number of choices that must be examined.

See also *backtracking, binary search, chaining of rules,* and *hashing* .

second-generation computer

A computer system manufactured in the late 1950s and early 1960s, characterized by the following:

- Solid state (transistor) circuitry

- Magnetic tapes as the main auxiliary storage medium, although disks are also available

- Overlapped input-output (I-O) channels with asynchronous interrupt capability

- Magnetic core memory of up to more than 128K

- On large machines (such as the IBM 7090, Univac 1107, and CDC 3600), the first operating systems (which processed a single batch job at a time) to manage system resources and provide a standard interface between the hardware and application programs

- Powerful macro assemblers and compilers for new languages (such as ALGOL, COBOL, LISP, and FORTRAN IV)

Large-scale second-generation computers operating at throughput up to 10 times faster than the earlier vacuum tube computers generated a need for the first widely-accepted operating systems. Because of the lack of memory protection in most second-generation hardware, these operating systems did not support multiprogramming, but in many other respects they resembled current operating systems.

See also *generations, computers.*

sector

The smallest unit of data that can be written or read to a disk.

The surface of the disk is divided into circular tracks, and tracks are further divided into sectors. During the disk format procedure, the operating system places empty sector images on the disk, preparing the disk to accept information.

On a given disk, all sectors have the same size, usually between 512 bytes and 8K, depending on the capacity of the disk. Floppy disks usually have a sector size of 512 bytes, while fixed disks typically have sectors of 4K or 8K.

Although the actual size of a file stored on a disk may be smaller than the sector size, the operating system always stores information on an even sector boundary. This can confuse users, because some disk utilities show the file size rounded to the nearest sector, while a DIR command in DOS shows the actual byte size of the file.

See also *cluster.*

seek

The operation of moving the read-write head on a disk drive to a designated track.

Some programming languages (BASIC, C library functions, and of course assembly language) support program control of seek operations, independent of actual data transmission. Such low-level control, however, serves little purpose except in unusual situations requiring extremely fast input-output (I-O).

See also *latency.*

segment

1. In a segmented-memory model, a contiguous block of memory. The size of the segment depends on the size of the offset addressing register.

2. In networking, any definable portion of the entire network.

segmented-memory model

A model in which memory is divided into pieces, and each byte is referenced by a memory segment or an offset.

The Intel 8086 employs segmented memory addressing; however, other systems do not. A given address may represented by many different combinations of segment and offset, and segments may overlap.

Using conventional addressing notation, you express a given address in hexadecimal, inserting a colon (:) between the segment and the offset, as in the following examples:

```
0040:0418        B000:0200        0A40:FFFE
```

See also *flat-memory model*.

self-checking number

See *check digit*.

self-defining name

A name that conveys unambiguously the meaning of a data item.

Self-defining names serve two purposes:

- To enhance program readability
- To eliminate the need to explain the meaning in a data item definition, thus avoiding clutter in a data dictionary

A common pitfall is that some names which initially appear to be self-defining later turn out to have some unforeseen ambiguity. This pitfall can lead to serious discrepancies between a new application system and the expectations of the end users, and these discrepancies are often discovered late in the system development life cycle (SDLC) when changes are difficult and costly. The following names, for example, may be self-defining in context:

QUANTITY ORDERED	(of a PRODUCT in an ORDER)
DATE OF BIRTH	(of an EMPLOYEE)
YEAR-TO-DATE GROSS SALES	(for a REGION)

However, the following examples, although appropriate as data names, would require definition in a data dictionary:

PAYMENT DATE	(Due? Sent? Received?)
DATE HIRED	(Originally? Most recently?)
TEMPERATURE	(Of what? When?)

semaphore

An integer variable shared by two or more concurrently executing tasks in order to synchronize access to a resource.

In the simplest form of semaphore, two operations, wait and signal, are sufficient to provide synchronization. A task that wants to gain control of some resource can wait for it to become free, as shown in the following pseudocode example:

```
WAIT:
    DO WHILE (semaphore >= 0);
      (do nothing);
    END;
    semaphore = semaphore + 1;
```

Then to release the resource, the task simply executes the following:

```
SIGNAL:
    semaphore = semaphore - 1:
```

More sophisticated implementations avoid wasting central processing unit (CPU) time in looping.

See also *coroutine* and *multitasking*.

sentence

In COBOL, a statement or sequence of statements.

One of COBOL's design goals was to faciliate programming in "plain English." Consequently, its designers adopted terminology from linguistics, giving the language the unique flavor of having paragraphs, sentences, and clauses. Modern programmers don't pay much attention to those terms, except for an occasional use of NEXT SENTENCE (the null executable statement).

 A COBOL sentence actually can contain multiple statements. The programmer marks the end of a sentence by a period. However, using a period where it is not required is dangerous, because it terminates all open conditional and loop constructs. Therefore, modern COBOL programmers should avoid using periods wherever possible.

sequential file

A file in which the records can be accessed in the sequence of their positions in the file.

Because of physical constraints, all files that are stored on a purely sequential medium, such as magnetic tape, are sequential files. A file stored on disk or some other directly addressable medium may be either a sequential file or a keyed file.

Because of limitations of some hardware devices, it is customary to consider a write operation as always writing the last record in a file. That is, if you have just written the 9th record on an output file, the next write operation will write the 10th record. Any 11th, 12th, or subsequent records, even if originally present, are inaccessible.

Sequential files are naturally suited to many kinds of batch processing.

serial data

Data transmitted one bit at a time.

Serial transmission is used for all intracomputer data transmission via networks, while parallel transmission is used for communication between functional components of larger systems.

Serial transmission is slower than parallel transmission, and, depending on the cost of transmission facilities, may be more expensive overall because additional circuitry is required in the serial ports.

See also *serial port*.

serial number

A unique identifier recorded on a disk under MS-DOS and some other operating systems. The number is recorded when you format a disk.

serial port

An interface between a computer's input-output (I-O) circuitry and a serial device. Personal computers typically have two or more serial ports, used for a modem, a mouse, or less often, a printer.

Serial ports contain buffers and circuitry, usually a UART (universal asynchronous receiver transmitter), that convert a byte to a series of bits and add parity and framing bits. The receiving serial port reverses the process and presents the reconstructed byte to the receiving computer's I-O system.

server

See *client-server architecture*.

set

An unordered collection of data items.

Sets play a central role in the foundations of mathematics as the primitive structure from which other concepts (numbers, relations, functions, operations, arrays, and so on) can be built. Much of the power of set theory comes from infinite sets, which, of course, have no direct computer representation. Therefore, compared to other types of data structure, sets are used infrequently in programming. A few languages, notably Pascal, support finite sets as a built-in data type.

Note that a set differs from a one-dimensional array in being unordered and without duplicates. The following all define the same three-element set:

> {Boston, Chicago, San Francisco}

> {Chicago, Boston, San Francisco}

> {Boston, Chicago, Boston, San Francisco, Boston, Boston}

Although you must write the items in some order, no element is defined as the first of a set. (An unordered collection with duplicates is a *bag,* also supported by Pascal. The first two examples define the same bag; the third defines a bag with six elements.)

One way to define a set is to enumerate its elements or members, as in the preceding examples. Another is to specify a property or predicate that the set's elements must satisfy, as in the following examples.

> {x: x is an employee & salary(x) > 20000 & age(x) < 36}

In this example, the set consists of all employees 35 or under who earn more than $20,000.

> {x: x (mod 3) = 0}

This set consists of all integers divisible by 3.

Defining a set by the properties of its elements is central to query processing and certain operations on relational databases.

Associated with sets are the following:

- The relational operator, subset; for example, S ∩ T means that every element of S is also an element of T.

- The relational operator, element; for example, x E S means x is an element (or member) of S.

- Operators *union, intersection,* and *complement* (see separate entries).

SET

An MS-DOS command that assigns a value to a global, named variable. A program running under MS-DOS can interrogate the environment to determine whether a variable, of a specific name, has been defined. If so, the contents of the variable can be used to modify program behavior or to set other internal parameters.

Environment variables are typically set, using the SET command, in batch files—particularly in the AUTOEXEC.BAT file. For instance, the following command line defines the DIRCMD environment variable and sets it to the value /OE:

```
SET DIRCMD=/OE
```

Under MS-DOS, this variable is used to define the subsequent behavior of the DIR command.

SHARE

A user group for large-scale IBM computer systems.

One of the oldest user groups, SHARE was founded in 1956 by a group of organizations that had ordered the new 704, a first-generation computer especially suited to scientific computing. Since then, SHARE has adopted the use of each successor IBM mainframe as qualifying an organization for membership. SHARE's purposes were to provide the following:

- A forum for exchanging ideas and experiences related to the administration and use of large-scale computers

- A repository for distributing software (the SHARE Library) developed by member organizations

- A unified voice in dealing with IBM

Later, as companies began to see software as a valuable resource, the SHARE Library became less relevant, and SHARE's emphasis shifted to its role as a pressure group on IBM, expressing the collective desires of the members for enhancements to future hardware and software.

More than most user groups, SHARE has managed to maintain a high degree of independence from its vendor. As a voluntary organization, its viability depends on the continuing participation in committees and working groups of capable individuals representing member organizations. Many significant innovations originated in or because of SHARE, which continues to exercise major influence over the evolution of large-scale operating systems, programming languages, and other system software.

See also *GUIDE*.

shared resources

A device shared by several users on a multiuser system or a network.

For example, if an expensive laser printer is connected to a network, the users connected to the network can each send output to the shared laser printer. File servers contain disks that several users can share, and mainframe computers can enable several thousand users to share a single processor.

shareware

Software distributed over public networks or by other means, and provided to users free of charge so that they can try it before buying it.

After deciding to keep a shareware program, the user is expected to forward a fee to the developer. In exchange for this payment, the developer often provides additional documentation and free upgrades to the product. PC File, PC Write, and PC Talk are examples of popular shareware programs.

Although shareware is available to the public, the developer retains ownership and may pursue its rights under copyright law.

See also *freeware*.

sharing violation

In a multiple-user system, an attempt to access a resource (for example, a file, a database record, or a device) that is locked by another user or program.

For example, if a user on a workstation connected to a network attempts to retrieve a file from the file server and another user has already locked that file in order to update it, then the first user will receive a sharing violation message.

Shell sort

A method of internal sorting.

Shell's algorithm uses a variation on the familiar but inefficient simple exchange (see *bubble sort*) method. Instead of comparing immediately adjacent elements, it starts by comparing and swapping elements that are half the length of the array from each other. The algorithm then narrows the interval in successive passes, until a final pass in which adjacent elements are compared. The expectation is that an element that is a long way from its eventual position will approach that position more quickly than if only immediately adjacent pairs are swapped.

The number of comparisons varies from an average of $n^{3/2}$ to a worst case of n^2.

See also *internal sorting, merge sort,* and *quicksort.*

shift (bits)

A family of machine instructions that displace the bits of a word, word part, or register by a specified number of positions, right or left.

Shifting a binary integer left by *n* positions is equivalent to multiplying the integer by 2^n. C is the major procedural programming language that directly supports shift operations.

See also *rotation.*

side effect (of a function)

A change in the value of either a function parameter or a global variable during execution of a function module.

A true function, in the mathematical sense, yields a value. In a program function, that value is set by a return statement, by assignment to the function name (FORTRAN), by evaluation (LISP), or by some other language-specific technique. The invoking program can then use that value in any context in which an expression of the same type is allowed.

In addition, most programming languages allow a function module to assign a value to a parameter or non-local variable. However, such side effects can greatly impair program readability and maintainability. Careful programmers avoid them except where a side effect is directly related to producing the returned value. A function, for example, that returns the next item from a queue, the next record from a sequential file, or the next character from a string might also delete that item from the queue or advance a corresponding pointer.

In object-oriented programming (OOP), encapsulation provides a disciplined way of handling such side effects.

 The results of a void function in C are not considered side effects. See also *void function.*

signal

See *semaphore.*

signed integer

An integer interpreted as either positive or negative. In binary representations, the first bit or a word conventionally represents plus (0) or minus (1), and the remainder of the word represents its magnitude.

A computer can interpret a binary integer of N bits either as a signed quantity between $2^{-(N-1)}$ and 2^{N-1}, or as an unsigned quantity between 0 and 2^N. Both interpretations are useful in programming.

See also *complement* and *integer* .

SIM—Society for Information Management

A professional society for senior executives in the field of information systems.

Founded in 1968 as SMIS (Society for Management Information Systems), SIM now has local chapters in major cities worldwide.

simulation

1. Execution of programs written for one type of computer on another type of computer by means of an interpreter program. (Simulation is sometimes called *emulation,* especially if special hardware or microcode is used.) Simulation is most often used to run application software written for either an obsolete computer that is no longer available or a newly designed computer that hasn't been built yet.

2. Use of a mathematical model to analyze the behavior or properties of an object or a system.

single precision

The smallest internal floating point (real number) representation for a given computer architecture.

Commonly, a single-precision quantity is a word (or a pair of words) containing a one-bit sign and a fixed number of exponent bits, with the remaining bits representing the fraction or magnitude.

SmallTalk

A proprietary object-oriented programming (OOP) language developed by Xerox, and noted for pioneering many language and user-interface concepts currently used in other object-oriented programming languages.

SmallTalk is currently available from two vendors: DigiTalk, Inc. and Parcplace Systems.

SNA—systems network architecture

An IBM interface standard that defines the relationship between other system component standards developed by IBM.

sneaker net

The sharing of software or data files among multiple workstations by simply carrying disks or tapes from one workstation to another as needed. This is an insider's slang term best avoided in writing and presentations.

Compared to a local area network (LAN), this method of file sharing offers low cost, high capacity, and unlimited flexibility, but slow speed and very little version control or assurance of file integrity.

Society for Information Management

See *SIM*.

software

The components of a computer system other than hardware. Software includes not only programs, but also the documentation and permanent data needed to use the programs.

Until the mid-1960s, the term *software* was used mainly in the limited sense of programs supplied by the computer manufacturer, and was not generally applied to application programs. In modern usage, however, software includes all programs used on a computer. These programs fall into these three categories:

- Application software
- System software
- Productivity tools

software development tool

Any software that is directly used primarily by programmers or which performs a function normally considered part of programming.

Such tools range from simple utilities (see *pretty print*), to complex "workbenches" with integrated editors, compilers, screen generators, and debugging aids, to very-high-level application generators (see *CASE*).

A bewildering variety of software tools exist, and so far, few standards exist for the interfaces among them. Organizations can easily run into difficulty trying to get multiple tools to work together smoothly.

sort-merge utility

A software product for reordering records in a file according to the sequence of values of one or more embedded key fields.

High-volume external sorting can consume significant time even on the largest mainframe computer configurations. Consequently, vendors of sort-merge utility products tend to focus on efficiency rather than functional differences to establish their competitive position. All such programs support the following:

- Designation of multiple key fields, each in ascending or descending order.

- Recognition as key fields of all basic data types and their usual data representations in that platform

A sort-merge utility can be invoked either as a separate process (or job step) or from an application program. The COBOL SORT verb provides linkage between an application program and the available sort-merge utility. Many other programming languages provide an equivalent capability through library subroutines.

The external sorting capabilities provided by query processors and small database management systems (DBMS) are not the same as a sort-merge utility. By taking advantage of those products' specific file structures and indexing schemes, they are often very fast for modest-sized databases, but not necessarily suitable for very high-volume applications or other file structures.

sorting

Arranging data items in ascending or descending sequence; often arranging records in the sequence of one or more key fields within them.

See also *external sorting* and *internal sorting.*

source code

A sequence of statements in a programming language. Source code is written by a programmer, and can be read by human beings and processed by a compiler (an assembler or interpreter).

See also *object code* and-source code library.

source code compatibility

The capability to compile a program on two or more platforms and achieve substantially the same results.

Two operating platforms having different architectures cannot run the same object code because they lack object-code compatibility. They may nevertheless provide source-code compatibility in one or more standard programming languages for a given program, if the following are true:

- Compilers for each platform comply with the official language standard.

- Data formats supported on each platform accommodate the requirements of the program.

source code conversion

See *conversion, source code.*

source code library

A group of source code files.

Each file in a source code library can contain either of the following:

- One or more modules that can be compiled to produce an object module.

- A program fragment that can be merged with other source code files by means of an include (C, PL/1) or a COPY (COBOL) statement. A library containing only such program fragments is called an *include library* or a *copy library.* Compilers for some programming languages, especially C and C++, provide an extensive library of standard data declarations, function declarations, macro definitions, object-oriented class definitions, and so on, to support and enhance the language. See also *header file.*

spaghetti code

Computer program code in which the sequence of instructions lacks a coherent structure or is hard to understand. The term derives from the fact that if you drew the corresponding flowchart it would contain a messy network of crossed flow lines.

Spaghetti code usually contains many goto statements that direct the reader to another part of the source code listing. Such code is difficult to follow and to maintain. Although in many cases such programs may function correctly, spaghetti code is considered extremely undesirable.

See also *goto-less programming, maintenance programming, readability, structured coding,* and *structured programming.*

spawn

To create a new job (or task) within an executing job (or task). The original job and the spawned job then proceed independently.

See also *multitasking* and *multithreaded.*

specification

A precise description of the required behavior of a proposed piece of software.

Such software can be anything from a complete application system to a single program module. Although the documentation techniques and structure appropriate for each kind of specification differ widely, almost all software specifications contain the following:

- A precise description of the exact output (results) to be produced

- A definition of any formulas, decision rules, or required algorithms to be used in producing the output

- A precise description of the exact input required

- No description at all of how the software is to be built or of any purely internal techniques that do not affect the results

A programmer or programming team is considered to have met its obligations when it has produced operational software that satisfies all agreed-on specifications and constraints.

See also *data item definition, structured design,* and *structured analysis.*

SPOOL—simultaneous peripheral operation on-line

To use auxiliary storage as a staging area for information being transmitted between a program and a slow peripheral device, especially a printer.

On a multiprogrammed operating system or in a local area network (LAN), there are almost always fewer actual printers than concurrent jobs or processes to be printed. The operating system, therefore, cannot allocate a printer to an individual job for the duration of that job.

Even in single-user environments, in which only one job is run at a time, the wide disparity between a fast central processing unit (CPU) and a slow printer can cause enormous inefficiency, alternating periods during which the computer is slowed to the speed of the printer with periods during which the printer is idle.

To smooth out these peaks and provide efficient resource utilization, SPOOLing systems do the following:

- Intercept each job's attempts to print, redirecting the output to a virtual device assigned exclusively to that job

- Write the data to be printed to a "SPOOL file" on auxiliary storage (or a special hardware buffer) associated with the particular virtual printer

- Asynchronously (as a background process or on a dedicated server) print the contents of the SPOOL files on physical printers, managing the queues according to FIFO or other appropriate priority rules.

Early SPOOLing systems were equally concerned with input devices—punched-card readers—used in batch processing. Because such devices are now rarely used, most people think of SPOOLing exclusively in connection with printing.

 Because of the current exploitation of multiple type fonts and graphics, you can no longer assume that the physical printer is the slowest link in the printing process. Even a simple word processor may now take longer to format a finished document than a printer takes to transfer it to paper.

spooler

A system software component, sometimes augmented by special buffering hardware, to manage SPOOLing.

sprite

In graphics, a group of pixels that can be manipulated independent of a background image, supported by special hardware that greatly reduces the amount of programming required for games and simpler forms of animation.

SQL—Structured Query Language

A database-oriented language used to access a relational database.

SQL is supported by most major relational database management systems (DBMS). It can be used directly by a user making a query, or embedded in program code written in a general-purpose programming language such as COBOL.

The following is an example of SQL statements:

```
SELECT FIRST_NAME, LAST_NAME, SALARY FROM EMPLOYEE
WHERE SALARY > 50000
ORDER BY LAST_NAME
```

The output would list the employees having a salary greater than $50,000, and order the list according to the employee last names.

SRAM—static random-access memory

A type of random access memory (RAM) that does not require periodic refreshing to retain the data it contains, as long as power is maintained.

SRAM is faster but more costly than DRAM (dynamic random access memory). It also is used less often than DRAM, typically for high-performance caches.

See also *DRAM*.

stack

A data structure that stores data in a LIFO (last in, first out) fashion.

Stacks are often used to store parameter information associated with procedure calls. As a called procedure in turn calls other procedures, parameter information is pushed onto the stack. When a called procedure terminates, it pops this data off the stack as part of its return task.

stack segment

In an Intel computer, a portion of memory used as a stack for holding subroutine parameters and results as well as other short-term data accessed in last-in first-out (LIFO) order.

See also *code segment* and *data segment*.

369

stage

To move from a less-expensive (usually offline or slow access) auxiliary storage medium to an expensive (online or fast access) medium.

Staging may occur either manually or as a result of some automatically triggered procedure. A common example in large-scale computer operations is the fetching of tape reels from a library a few minutes before a job needs them on the computer.

See also *migrate.*

stand-alone program

A program loaded directly on computer hardware by a bootstrap loader, and run without the use of an operating system.

Many hardware diagnostic programs must operate in a stand-alone mode. Another example of a stand-alone program is the BASIC interpreter that was installed in read-only memory (ROM) on the early IBM personal computers.

standard input

The input stream associated with the user's keyboard.

See also *standard output.*

standard output

The output stream associated with the user's display device.

Having a standard input and output stream relieves the programmer from having to declare, open, and close named files for such routine functions as entering run parameters, displaying error messages, or examining intermediate debugging values.

Programmers customarily use the standard output stream for logging information describing the progress of the run. Any module at any level can write to the standard output, perhaps to flag some unusual occurrence, to display intermediate results, or to report on the status of a long calculation. Therefore, any report that you want to produce in a particular format should be written in its own separate file rather than in the standard output stream.

statement

The smallest construct in a programming language that can cause a processor for that language to take some corresponding action.

A statement in a programming language serves roughly the same role as a sentence in English. It represents a complete thought, but it may make sense only in the context of the other statements around it.

In procedural programming languages, statements are either declarative or executable. A declarative statement, such as the following, gives information to the compiler:

```
short int  line_ctr;
```

An executable statement, such as the following, specifies an action to be taken by the program:

```
if  (line_ctr > page_size)
    start_new_page(report);
```

A statement that is executed immediately after being recognized (by the operating system, by an interpreter, by a query processor, and so on) is often called a command.

See also *assignment statement*, *.COM*, *command*, *control statement*, and *sentence*.

statement label

A symbolic name associated with an executable statement in a program.

Statement labels are used as the target of goto or branch instructions. Because such branching is strongly discouraged under the conventions of structured coding, well-written programs coded in a modern procedural language need few if any statement labels.

See also *goto-less programming*.

statement number

An all-numeric form of a statement label, used in FORTRAN and BASIC. Because statement numbers have virtually no meaning except for sequencing, they are considered even more harmful to program readability than mnemonic statement labels.

Many versions of BASIC require a statement number on every line, even for lines that are never referred to. The original purpose might have been to teach the stored-program concept by mimicking machine-language addresses.

See also *goto-less programming*.

static data item

1. A data item allocated and possibly initialized at compile time, not during program execution. In some programming languages (including COBOL and FORTRAN), all data items are static.

2. In PL/1 and some implementations of BASIC, a keyword that preserves the value of a variable local to a procedure between invocations. Using static data conflicts with both recursive and reentrant programming, and is discouraged in structured programming because it is prone to error.

3. In C++, a data item shared among all objects of a given class. Such data items may be useful for keeping track of objects in the aggregate; for example, the number of objects of the class that currently exist.

4. As applied to random access memory (RAM), see *SRAM*.

stepwise refinement

An approach to developing a complex program by adding detail in successive iterations.

The programmer begins by sketching the broad outlines of the program logic, either in pseudocode or in an actual programming language:

```
DO WHILE more transactions;
  get valid transaction;
  process a transaction;
END;
generate reports;
```

At the second iteration, the programmer expands the references to undefined actions, like this:

```
DO WHILE more transactions;
  good_transaction = FALSE;
  DO UNTIL good_transaction;
    get  a transaction;
    edit a transaction;
    good_transaction = (error_count = 0);
  END;
  log transaction;
  update data base;
END;
print management summary;
print inventory detail;
```

Note that the structure of the program is unchanged. The programmer simply added detail.

The programmer continues this process until the program contains only legal statements in the actual programming language being used or until all lower-level modules are defined.

See also *modular programming, pseudocode, structured programming,* and *top-down.*

storage

Any device or medium that can hold data for later retrieval.

The term usually refers to nonvolatile storage devices such as magnetic disks, optical disks, and magnetic tapes.

See also *auxiliary storage* and *memory.*

storage volume

1. A unit of physical storage (such as a disk pack, hard drive, magnetic tape, or even a floppy disk).

2. A logical unit of storage. This type of volume is not bound by the physical limitation of the device and may span several storage devices. For example, Novell enables you to address several hard drives on the server as one volume of storage.

See also *disk drive.*

stream I/O

Transmission of a specified list of data items between memory and a sequential file in external (character string) format.

Output streams are often associated with printers and display screens, and input streams with keyboards. BASIC, C, FORTRAN, Pascal, and PL/1 support stream input-output (I/O) with straightforward, built-in statements or standard library functions. COBOL, however, does not, and instead requires the programmer to construct and manipulate line images as records.

See also *format statement.*

stress test

The process of testing an application system or a computer configuration under a very heavy processing load; also called *volume test.*

This process helps hardware manufacturers and software vendors determine how the product will operate under these conditions before the product is released.

See also *system test* and *acceptance test.*

string

A data type comprising a sequence of characters (or less commonly, a sequence of bits).

Languages vary widely in their tolerance and support of the string type and in the way it is implemented. Libraries of string functions are provided for C, whereas BASIC provides several built-in facilities to handle the string type.

See also *ASCIIZ character string* and *variable (or varying) length string.*

strong typing

A programming language's strict enforcement of rules for ensuring compatibility of data types.

When a program uses a value (a constant, a variable, or an expression) of one type in a context in which the compiler expects a variable of some other type, the compiler must do one of the following:

- Flag the usage as an error, and reject the program.

- Generate if possible the code required to convert the value to the expected type; for example, the compiler may have to convert an integer value to floating-point.

- Let the program use the unconverted value.

Strongly typed languages, such as Ada and Pascal, emphasize the first option. Proponents of strong typing like the protection it provides against many kinds of programming errors.

Assembly languages, on the other hand, let any instruction store any kind of data in any location (as described in the last option previously listed). Other languages (notably C and COBOL) also permit certain kinds of undetected mismatches, but in most situations they try to apply the second option described.

Most programming languages provide both implied conversions and explicit coercion (or casting) operators.

structure chart

A diagram showing the hierarchy of modules in a complete program and the data items passed among them.

structured analysis

A methodology used by systems analysts to document the specification or "model" of a new or existing application system or software product. Structured analysis results in the following benefits:

- The prospective end users can easily grasp exactly what a proposed new application system will do, and either approve it or request changes.

- The software developers (designers and programmers) will understand exactly what they must build.

- The systems analysts can easily modify and manipulate the specification in response to both user requests and new insights.

Structured analysis specifies not only the documentation itself (see *structured specification*) but also a recommended sequence of activity for producing it. For a project that will replace an existing application system with a new one, structured analysis requires the preparation of the following sequence of four system specifications:

- A physical model of the current system, showing not only what occurs but also who performs each function, how (automated or manual) each function is accomplished, and what organizations are involved in each function.

- A logical model of the current system, derived from the previous model with all "who," "how," and "where" information removed. What remains describes in abstract terms what functions occur and any rules, policies, algorithms, or formulas that apply to those functions.

- A logical model of the proposed new system, derived by changing the previous model to reflect the new features and changes that the users require.

- A physical model of the new system, derived by adding to the previous model the "who," "how," and "where" information that relates the system to the real environment.

See also *data-flow diagram.*

structured coding

The use of disciplined detailed coding techniques aimed at making programs easy to understand and easy to change.

The core of structured coding is the use of standard constructs for controlling the program flow. In theory, any possible procedural logic can be expressed by a combination of only these three constructs:

- Sequence: the normal progression from one statement to the next

- Iteration (or looping): executing a group of statements repeatedly. See *do while, do until,* and *for.*

- Selection: executing one of two or more groups of statements, based on some condition. See *if-then-else statement.*

Another important aspect of structured coding is attention to readability. Appropriate use of indentation, page breaks, and white space can contribute greatly to a reader's ability to grasp a complex program.

See also *goto, goto-less programming, modular programming, pretty print,* and *spaghetti code.*

structured design

A formalized approach to the design of a program. Structured design typically involves the rigorous application of predefined standards, tests, and benchmarks to the design process.

structured English

A pseudocode used by systems analysts to specify rules or policies, often as part of a structured specification.

Structured English combines the rigor and clarity of a programming language with the expressiveness and flexibility of English. Although structured English has no formal rules, it typically draws from the following kinds of elements:

- Names of data items defined in the data dictionary

- Flow constructs for looping (do while, do until, for) and alternative selection (if-then-else)

- The usual numeric and Boolean operators and expressions

- Any unambiguous English phrases or sentences that the intended audience will understand, especially descriptions of business functions

The following is the same example used to illustrate the entries for *decision table* and *decision tree*:

```
IF   yearly_sales to customer > $10000
THEN IF    good_payment_history
     THEN  give priority;
     ELSE  IF  (date of order - date of customer_record) > 20
years
          THEN give priority;
          ELSE treat normally;
ELSE treat normally;
```

or equivalently

```
IF   yearly_sales to customer > $10000
AND   (good_payment_history
       OR date of order - date of customer_record) > 20 years)
THEN  give priority;
ELSE  treat normally;
```

structured programming

A methodology for developing reliable, easy to maintain programs.

Since the "structured revolution" of the early 1970s, writers have proposed many variations on the basic structured programming discipline. Most structured programming methodologies include these three components:

- A very high degree of modular programming

- A top-down or stepwise-refinement sequence for developing modules

- Structured coding

Some structured programming methodologies also include some or all of the following components:

- A project team organization based on a chief programmer
- Data-driven programming
- Exploitation of reusable modules
- Use of tables to simplify program logic.
- Use of macros to subordinate detail
- Interactive development driven by one or more CASE tools

structured specification

A set of documentation, resulting from structured analysis, that describes a proposed or existing system; also called a "model" of the system.

Normally systems analysts write a structured specification for two audiences: the end users and the software developers. It typically includes at least the following components:

- A brief overview and summary to orient the reader
- Specifications of the system outputs
- A data dictionary defining all the data items referred to anywhere in the specification
- Specifications of the system inputs
- A set of hierarchically structured data-flow diagrams showing the relationships among the inputs, outputs, and data items
- A set of logic specifications for each process on any data-flow diagram that is neither obvious nor expanded in a lower-level data-flow diagram.

subdirectory

In a hierarchical file system, a directory that is a subordinate to another directory.

In MS-DOS, you create subdirectories by using the MD or MKDIR command. To gain access to files in subdirectories, you can either specify the complete path, including the directory and subdirectories, or change the active directory to the desired subdirectory. For example, in the following hierarchy, SQL and SAMPLES are subdirectories of DBASE4:

```
                    \DOS
(root) \
                    \DBASE4
                                   \SQL
                                   \SAMPLES
```

Therefore, to gain access to files in those subdirectories, you must use the complete path, as follows:

\DBASE4\SQL\ or \DBASE4\SAMPLES

subroutine

A programming module designed for repeated use during the normal course of a program. For instance, a programmer may design a subroutine to update a display screen or to write a record to a disk file. This routine can be called whenever this function is required.

Subroutines eliminate the need to repeatedly code the same functions in different parts of a program. Effective use of subroutines makes program development more efficient and reduces the time required for program maintenance.

subscribe

In Macintosh System 7, to link into one file (the subscriber) another file (edition). Subscribing is similar to object linking and embedding (OLE) in Windows.

supervisor call

A synchronous interrupt (or trap) that a program initiates to request a service from the operating system.

See also *interrupt* and *int86*.

SVGA—super video graphics array

An enhanced form of VGA that provides the capability to display a higher resolution and a wider range of colors than does VGA technology.

SVGA can produce a resolution of 1024×768 or greater. For a system to function with enhanced capability, both the video adapter and the monitor must support SVGA.

switch

A Boolean variable, usually one that represents a run option or the occurrence of some event.

Many second-generation computer systems actually included physical console switches that a program could test. At the start of a job, the computer operator would set the appropriate switches to reflect desired run options; for example, switch #5 might represent "print the detailed inventory list." The term was thus well-established in business data processing, and remains within that community the most commonly used term for Boolean variables.

Sybase

A relational database system from Sybase, Inc., based on the client-server architecture.

Sybase operates on UNIX, DOS, and several other operating systems and hardware platforms. It includes a SQL Server, SQL Toolset, and a client/services interface.

symbolic constant

Input to a macro or preprocessor compile phase, in which program constants are equated to preprocessor variable names. The preprocessor substitutes the constant text for the preprocessor variable, retaining the advantages of efficient execution and localized definition of constants.

sync bits

Bits used to start timing circuits to synchronize serial transmission. In asynchronous (async) transmission, each character representation is preceded by a start bit (which starts receiving clock circuitry) and ended by one (or less commonly, two) stop bit(s). In BSC (binary synchronous communications), each block is preceded by one or more special characters (called the SYN character) that cannot occur within a block of data.

The term is a contraction of *synchronization bits.*

synchronous transmission

A data transmission method that requires an external clocking signal to maintain synchronization between sending and receiving equipment. Each block of bits transmitted is preceded by one or more special characters (SYN) that the receiving equipment recognizes as a clock synchronizing signal.

Synchronous equipment is more complex and expensive than asynchronous equipment. However, synchronous equipment is more efficient for large amounts of data because it must send the SYN characters only at the beginning of each block, not with each character.

syntax

The rules specifying the form of the statements used in a given language, and how the statements may be combined into programs. Any violation of these rules is called a syntax error.

system

A set of physical or logical facilities that perform a certain function when working together. The term can denote any of the following:

- An application system

- A computer configuration, comprising the central processing unit (CPU), devices, and the operating system

- An operating system

System/360, System/370

A series of third-generation computers that IBM first introduced in 1964 and 1970, respectively. The main difference between the two is that System/370 supports virtual memory.

The 360 and its still-available successors exerted such a huge influence on the direction of computer technology and systems for two decades that they came to be viewed as the "mainstream" of data processing. The emergence in the 1980s of less expensive desktop computers (including IBM's own PC) brought the era of mainframe dominance to a close.

See also *DOS, MVS,* and *VM/370.*

System 7

The operating system for the Apple Macintosh desktop computer. This popular operating system features multitasking and extended built-in help.

system application architecture

See *SAA.*

system date

The current calendar date, held in memory by the operating system.

Almost all operating systems and programming languages support facilities that provide access to the system date.

See also *system time.*

system development life cycle

See *SDLC.*

system error

A severe error that forces the operating system to stop all activity.

A system error may be caused either by a hardware malfunction in the central processing unit (CPU), memory, or other vital component or by a bug in the operating system itself.

See also *crash*.

system input

Data entered into an application system.

System input refers specifically to data from outside the system. It includes both of the following:

- Data entered by a human operator through an input device, such as a keyboard or a scanner. See *editing program*.

- Data from another application system.

Files created earlier by the same system are not considered system inputs. They are master files or databases of the application system.

See also *system output*.

system output

Information produced by an application system. The term denotes specifically data sent outside the system.

System output includes both of the following:

- Information intended for users and displayed on an output device

- Information sent to another application system

Archive files, master files, and databases created or updated by the system are *not* considered system outputs.

See also *system input*.

system test

A test that involves all components of an application system, including not only the software but also the manual procedures performed by actual users.

Before a system test is conducted, the programmers should have performed thorough integration tests to validate the correctness of each complete program or job. The system test will then encounter few program bugs except for problems related to the user interface or other high-level functions.

Normally programmers or systems analysts should not be present to assist the users, because a system test is supposed to reveal whether the users can cope with the system. They should, of course, note any problems the users encounter, and take corrective action that can include software changes, documentation (including online help) improvements, or more thorough user training.

See also *beta test, stress test,* and *acceptance test.*

system time

The time of day currently held by the system clock.

On an MS-DOS machine, you can retrieve the system time by using the TIME command, and most programming languages provide time functions that enable programmers to retrieve the current time.

See also *system date.*

system unit

The cabinet or section of a computer that contains the central processing unit (CPU) and its support circuitry. Often, this cabinet contains the system's random-access memory (RAM).

systems analysis

The process of determining in detail the information-systems needs of an organization and preparing a rigorous specification of a new or modified system to meet those needs.

Compared to design and programming, systems analysis is less concrete. It's often difficult to determine whether a problem solution is correct or when it is complete. Some aspects of systems analysis are amenable to systematic methods and automated tools. Structured analysis and various CASE products, helpful as they are, assist more in documenting and manipulating the results than in actually performing systems analysis.

The activities normally considered a part of systems analysis include the following:

- Interviewing managers, potential system users, and other key people in the affected organization. The objective is to understand their perceptions of the problem to be solved or the opportunity to be exploited.

- Examining procedures, forms, manuals, correspondence, and other documents, and observing activities, so that you understand the current business or other processes.

- Defining the exact problem that might be solved (or opportunity that might be exploited) by a new or modified system.

- Documenting the user organization's requirements for a solution to that problem and any constraints that apply to a solution.

- Specifying in detail a new or proposed system to satisfy those requirements.

- Assisting the user organization in analyzing the costs, benefits, and risks of implementing a new system, and determining whether it is justified to proceed.

- Training the organization's personnel to use the new system.

- Participating in acceptance testing, parallel testing, and startup of the new system.

Note that designing computer programs and designing databases are not activities of systems analysis but rather of system design.

systems analyst

Anyone engaged in systems analysis, either in a full-time position or a part-time role.

Some systems analysts have a programming background, whereas others have a background in one or more business areas. Systems analysts may report either to a central information systems organization or to a user organization. It is desirable for a systems analyst to have knowledge of both computer technology and the user-organization's business area. Programming skills, however, are not required to do systems analysis.

In some organizations, the same people do both systems analysis and programming. Successful programmer-analysts clearly differentiate between the two roles, performing systems analysis part of the time and programming part of the time, but never trying to perform a mixture of the two.

There are few courses or standardized academic curricula to prepare one to become a systems analyst. Consequently, practitioners demonstrate a huge range of skills and competence levels.

See also *designer* and *chief programmer.*

system software

The set of programs to support the operation of one or more computers, and to support the development on those computers of other programs. The term commonly is interpreted to include the following:

- Operating systems and related major utility programs
- Compilers and interpreters for programming languages
- Other software development tools
- Teleprocessing monitors
- Database management systems (DBMS)

See also *application software* and *productivity tool.*

systems programmer

A programmer who develops and maintains system software, or who assists others in using system software.

For a large computer center (a mainframe or a network), systems programmers are less likely to write new system software than to provide help in diagnosing problems with the operating system or some other hardware or software component. The role is highly specialized, and calls for the highest level of technical expertise, interest in learning new things, and coolness in a crisis.

Because of confusion between the terms "systems programming" and "systems and programming" (a name many organizations use for their application system developers), some organizations have chosen other names for this role, such as "technical support." With the growing specialization of system components, these roles are evolving into subspecialties such as network administrator and communications analyst.

table

1. An array, especially one used for storing and retrieving data items.

2. In relational database terminology, a file.

table element

See *element, table.*

table lookup

The process of finding the item in an array (usually one-dimensional) that matches a search argument. The result is the index (or position) of the matching item. That index can then be used to retrieve corresponding items from other tables.

Common table search methods include the following:

- Linear (or sequential) search

- Binary search

- Hashing

See also *binary search, hashing,* and *search.*

tail recursion

Self-invocation by a subroutine or function in its last step.

Tail recursion is potentially more efficient than general recursion, because it doesn't require the saving and restoring of values of local variables and parameters. Many LISP and PROLOG processors, as well as some optimizing compilers for other languages that support recursive functions, can recognize tail recursion and avoid generating redundant code to save and restore the local environment.

tape

A sequential auxiliary storage medium that consists of a long strip of magnetic material which can record data when moved across the write head of a tape drive. One side of the tape is coated with a ferromagnetic material that can record information.

The declining cost of more flexible disk storage has nearly eliminated the use of tape for master files and temporary files, except for extremely high-volume batch processing. Today tape is used mainly for archive files and backup files.

task

1. An independently executing program and its data; also called a *process*.

   A task that doesn't depend on or know about any concurrently executing task not under its control is called a *job* or *job step*. Most tasks initiated by a human user or operator are jobs.

   See also *multitasking*.

2. In project management, the smallest unit of work to be assigned— usually to an individual—and tracked. A well-defined task produces a definite, tangible result or "deliverable."

   A few project management systems refer to tasks as *activities*.

TCP/IP—transmission control protocol/Internet protocol

A set of standards for communicating among dissimilar computers, developed and supported by ARPA (Advanced Projects Research Agency) of the U.S. Department of Defense.

See also *FTP*.

techie

A computer programmer or software technician who has a strong command of the details of hardware and system software. In many organizations, this term now has a pejorative connotation, designating a technician who lacks communication skills and a sense of proportion and who, therefore, can't be trusted to exercise mature judgment.

Although *techie* has appeared occasionally in the trade press as a term of praise, many computer professionals consider it demeaning, and it is best avoided. Earlier synonyms "bit twiddler," "computer jock," and "computer nerd" were similarly considered offensive when applied to a programmer.

See also *hacker.*

teleprocessing monitor

A system software component that provides an interface between application programs and online users at remote terminals.

A teleprocessing monitor is commonly used in transaction processing. It handles the communication network protocols and the different kinds of terminals, relieving the application program from having to know about such details of the physical environment. A widely used example is IBM's CICS.

See also *CICS* and *transaction.*

template, diagramming

See *diagramming template.*

temporary file

A file created and used in a job (job step or process) and discarded at the end of that job; same as *scratch file* or *work file.*

The continuing increase in available memory has eliminated the need for all but the largest temporary files. Programs now can store data records in arrays or other internal data structures rather than writing them to a file and reading them back. This not only improves performance, but in many cases also simplifies program logic. Some of the expected performance gain on smaller machines, however, may be lost in the behind-the-scenes input-output operations required for virtual paging.

Temporary files are still needed, of course, for really huge data requirements or where a program must avoid imposing any limit at all on the size of the input. Sorting a large file, for example, often requires the use of temporary files.

See also *virtual memory*.

terminate and stay resident

See *TSR*.

termination

Returning control from an application or utility program to the invoking operating system (or other higher-level process).

In many modern procedural programming languages, the usual way of terminating execution is a return from the main module. That is, when the flow of control reaches either a return statement or the end of the main program, control is transferred back to the operating system. Languages that support this kind of termination include ALGOL, Ada, C, Pascal, and PL/1.

Some languages also provide a facility for terminating execution from any active module. These facilities include the following:

Language	Statement
BASIC	SYSTEM or END
COBOL	STOP RUN
FORTRAN	CALL EXIT
PL/1	STOP

test driver

A program written for the purpose of testing another program, usually a subroutine.

Test drivers are a basic tool of bottom-up testing, in which programmers make sure that each module works correctly before using it in any higher-level modules. A typical test driver exercises the routines being tested by presenting it with a set of test data that covers the special cases and combinations of cases.

Some test drivers are discarded after the module passes all tests, while others are retained for possible use in testing future versions of the same routines. In either case, because the test driver never becomes part of an actual production program, most organizations do not hold test drivers to the same standards of coding and documentation as other programs.

text-based graphics

The creative use of a PC's (or a terminal's) line-drawing and special characters to give a character-oriented display the appearance of a graphical interface.

These displays can be created very efficiently on modestly priced graphics adapters and monitors. The need for text-based graphics will diminish as windowing environments become more widely used.

then

See *if-then-else construct*.

third-generation computer

A computer system manufactured between the mid-1960s and the late 1970s, characterized by the following:

- Integrated circuitry

- Magnetic disks as the main auxiliary storage medium, accompanied by the continuing use of magnetic tape

- Magnetic core memory of up to 512K (in 1966), eventually expanded to several megabytes

- Sophisticated operating systems supporting multiprogramming, SPOOLing, and online users

- Virtual storage supporting address spaces of up to 16M per user
- Database management systems (DBMS) and more sophisticated programming languages (PL/1, APL, Ada).

IBM's long-lived System/360 dominated the third generation.

See also *generations, computers*.

throughput

Any measure of the amount of work done by a computer system in a given period of time.

Throughput depends on the processing speed of the computer, its configuration of peripheral devices, the efficiency of the operating system, and the characteristics of the application workload. It is often used to evaluate configurations being considered as potential upgrades.

See also *benchmark test* and *efficiency*.

tick

See *clock tick*.

.TIF

MS-DOS file name extension identifying information in tagged image file format (TIFF).

TIFF—tagged image file format

A standard format developed by Aldus and Microsoft for efficiently storing graphic images.

timebomb

Disruptive behavior coded into a program, usually intentionally, to be activated at a certain time—for example, the end of the year, Friday the 13th, or Michelangelo's birthday. Timebombs may be coded into production programs, or introduced as computer viruses.

The introduction of some timebombs is inadvertent, due to incomplete testing procedures rather than malice. Financial programs often fail at year-end, and there are dire predictions of chaos caused by program logic errors at the turn of the 21st century.

timeout

An action performed at the expiration of a time limit.

To avoid infinite loops or indefinite delays in abnormal situations, timeouts are essential. For example:

- After the system prompts the user for a password and the user fails to respond within a reasonable time, the system can assume that the user is no longer available and should terminate the log-on request.

- When a device driver initiates an input-output (I/O) operation and the operation isn't completed within a reasonable time, the program can assume that the device is offline or malfunctioning and should issue a message to the operator.

- In initiating a batch processing (or any noninteractive) job, the operating system may set a time limit. If the job is still running when the timeout occurs, the system can assume that the program is malfunctioning and should forcibly terminate it.

timer

A hardware counter used to measure intervals of time, especially for setting timeout intervals.

time sharing

The simultaneous online use of a large computer by multiple users through individual terminals.

Before the availability of powerful desktop computers, time sharing provided the most practical way of gaining interactive access to computing power for developing programs or solving problems. Several successful commercial time-sharing services provided such access for users whose organizations were too small to support their own mainframe computer. In the 1960s, colleges and universities such as Dartmouth and MIT developed their own time-sharing systems, which later influenced the direction of hardware, software, and programming languages.

token

1. An electronic "signature" used to control communication discipline on some computer networks. The token is passed among the nodes of the network—a node must have the token before it can send a message. A node that has a message to send captures the token, sends its message, then releases the token to circulate. This method prevents message collisions, but may induce significant overhead.

2. The most basic object recognized by a text-parsing routine. Examples of tokens include variable names, reserved words, and operators. In this usage, the term is of most interest to compiler writers and language developers.

toolbar

A graphical strip appearing across the top of the screen in a graphical user interface (GUI) containing icons that represent functions the user frequently invokes.

For example, to print a document from a word processor, the user can either select the appropriate menu options or click on the printer icon displayed on the toolbar. Both operations produce the same results.

A toolbar.

top-down

In design or development, beginning with the highest-level view of the whole system or problem, dividing the problem into two or more smaller problems, and then recursively applying top-down design or development to each of those smaller problems. *Top-down* is the opposite of *bottom-up*.

Top-down software development can mean either of the following:

- Top-down design of a whole system or a complete program, followed by bottom-up coding and testing of the modules that were identified in the design.

- Integrated top-down development, in which each module may be coded and tested as soon as it is identified during the course of top-down design.

See also *stepwise refinement* and *structured programming*.

trace

A program-debugging technique used to observe the program flow and its impact on variable values.

Some languages, particularly interpreted languages, provide extensive tracing facilities, including step-by-step execution and the display of changes in variables designated by the programmer.

Competent programmers can provide their own debugging information, even if the language in use does not. Strategically located display statements, perhaps compiled conditionally, provide highly specific debugging information.

track

One of the concentric circular areas for recording information on a surface of a disk.

See also *cylinder, disk drive, partition table,* and *sector.*

transaction

See *input transaction.*

transaction file

A sequential file containing input transactions for batch processing.

Most often, the transactions are in the chronological sequence of their arrival or entry; the effect is then the same as if the transactions had been processed online as they arrived. In some situations, however, transactions may be sorted in some other sequence to reflect a policy (for example, to allocate inventory so that orders for favored customers are given first priority) or a strategy (for example, to credit all deposits before debiting any withdrawals).

transfer

See *branch*.

transmission

See *asynchronous transmission* and *synchronous transmission*.

transpose

1. An operation on an m by n matrix M yielding an n by m matrix M' in which each $M'_{i,j} = M_{j,i}$. For example, the transpose of

$$\begin{bmatrix} a & b & c \\ d & e & f \end{bmatrix} \quad \text{is} \quad \begin{bmatrix} a & d \\ b & e \\ c & f \end{bmatrix}$$

2. To form the transpose of a matrix.

3. A command in a spreadsheet processor to interchange the rows and columns in a block, analogous to transposing a matrix.

trap

A hardware-generated signal that notifies the operating system of the occurrence of some event or exception.

See also *interrupt*.

Most operating systems allow an application program to intercept some kinds of traps and interrupts.

tree

A structure that defines the relationship between data elements, often used in indexing schemes. The structure is called a tree because the relationships between data elements or the path used to move between data elements are represented in such a diagram as branches of a tree.

trim

An operation applied to a string of text to remove leading or trailing blanks. Trimming is useful in combining text fields in fixed fields, such as name and address components, into a conventional form.

Trim operations may be implemented as library routines or built-in functions, depending on the programming language. In variants of BASIC, the left and right trim operations are LTRIM$ and RTRIM$, respectively.

Trojan horse

A computer program that masquerades as an apparently harmless program, but causes severe damage to the system's files.

Trojan horse programs are typically less subtle than virus programs, but can be as damaging. Like virus programs, Trojan horse programs are almost exclusively a microcomputer phenomenon. The effectiveness of their disruption is enhanced by the frequency with which program files are exchanged among microcomputer users.

truncation

The dropping of any value to the right of the decimal point.

truth value

One of two possible values: true and false.

Various program constructs and data types yield a truth value result, including the following:

- A predicate

- A Boolean operator or Boolean expression

- A switch, indicator, or flag

- A condition

- An option

For some uses, it is more natural to interpret or represent truth values in some other way, such as the following:

True	False
On	Off
Yes	No
Closed	Open
1	0
Present	Absent

TSO—time sharing option

Component of IBM mainframe operating system (MVS) providing access to operating system services from online terminals.

TSO is intended mainly for programmers and others who need full access to MVS. Terminals dedicated to a particular online application system are more likely to go through a teleprocessing monitor system like CICS.

See also *CLIST.*

TSR—terminate and stay resident

A type of program that can remain in memory after it is terminated, then be activated when needed.

See also *resident program.*

Turbo C

An inexpensive and popular C compiler from Borland International, widely used by student, professional, and amateur programmers.

Turbo C provides C program developers with an integrated development environment (IDE) and a menu-driven interface. The compiler also offers a command-line compiler that you can invoke from the DOS prompt. Because of attractive pricing and the growing availability of larger computers, many programmers now buy Turbo C++.

Turbo C++

An inexpensive and popular C++ compiler from Borland International.

Turbo C++ provides developers with an integrated development environment (IDE) and a menu-driven interface.

Turbo C++ supports the older standard C functions, and also provides the additional development facilities to support the standard object-oriented language C++. Turbo C++ is widely used by colleges and universities as a learning environment for C and C++.

See also *Turbo C.*

Turbo Pascal

A full-featured Pascal language implemented and marketed by Borland International. Turbo Pascal first appeared as a language approximately a decade ago, and was immediately and widely accepted because it was easy to use and inexpensive.

Turbo Pascal, as currently distributed, contains not just an implementation of the Pascal language, but also an editor, assembler, compiler, linker, and librarian. The high-end version of Turbo Pascal is marketed under the product name Borland Pascal.

See also *Pascal.*

turnover, production

See *production turnover.*

two's complement

A number in the binary system that is the complement of another.

You form the two's complement by inverting each bit in the binary representation of a number, then adding 1 to the result. For example, 47 decimal is 00101111 binary. Inverting yields 1101000, and adding 1 gives 11010001, the two's complement.

The two's complement form is used to represent negative binary numbers in many kinds of computers. In this usage, the leftmost bit is used as a sign bit, with a 1 designating a negative quantity.

.TXT

MS-DOS file name extension identifying a file that contains only text.

See also *ASCII file*.

type

A Pascal, Ada, and Modula-2 keyword that declares a data type.

One of Pascal's most valuable features is its capability to define data types that mirror real-world objects and then to enforce disciplines in manipulating objects of those types. For example, if you define a new numeric data type for day_of_the_week, specifying a range of 1..7, Pascal will not allow the program to assign 0 or 8 to a data item of that type. Such disciplines help the programmer detect and avoid many common kinds of errors, contribute to program readability, and constitute an essential aspect of object-oriented programming (OOP).

Skilled Pascal programmers exploit this facility at every opportunity.

See also *encapsulation*.

typecast

See *casting*.

typedef

A C language keyword that declares a synonym for the name of a data type.

Note that a typedef does not define a new data type or restrict the range of values, in the sense that type in Pascal does. Typedefs are valuable because they can simplify notation and localize dependency on the choice of a built-in data type. For example, a global definition package (#include file) might contain the following:

```
typedef      short     PAGE_COUNTER;
```

Then you can declare page numbers for printed reports as follows:

```
PAGE_COUNTER     inv_rpt_pageno;
```

If short integer representation later proves to be too small for some reports, you have to change only the typedef line in the source code.

typeface attribute

The characteristics of a particular type font, such as the weight (thickness) of the various parts of the letter, height of ascenders and descenders, and whether the letters contain serifs (small lines crossing the main stroke of the character).

For some typefaces, variants such as boldface, italic, and subscript are considered attributes of a single font rather than separate fonts. Many word processors use the term *attribute* in this way.

typematic

The characteristic of a keyboard that repeats a key that is held down for longer than the time required for a single keystroke.

Typematic keys can greatly speed up underlining and scrolling, but have limited usefulness for most keys. A problem sometimes arises with software that is too slow to keep up with a typematic keyboard, because the user does not see the effect of each keystroke on the screen until several seconds after it is entered, and may therefore hold down the key too long.

UAE—unrecoverable application error

An error message from Microsoft Windows (Version 3.0) indicating that an application program has lost control and cannot continue.

The UAE message gained notoriety among Windows users because it sometimes led to a system crash, bringing down all running applications, not just the one causing the error. Improvements in Windows (Version 3.1) eliminated the UAE error message (see *GPF*), and also reduced the frequency of complete system crashes.

See also *ABEND, crash, exception, fatal error,* and *GPF.*

UI—user interface

A set of standards defining the interaction between a user and a program.

Such standards often specify screen layouts and menu structures for providing access to software functions and operations. The UI consists of the visible features (such as windows and dialog boxes) that represent a system to the user, in contrast to the internal program functions and database facilities.

See also *GUI.*

UMB—upper memory block

The unused sections of upper memory that can be accessed in blocks. You can load drivers and terminate-and-stay-resident (TSR) programs into this area by using UMB providers, such as LOADHIGH= or DEVICEHIGH= from MS-DOS 5.0.

A common use is to put DOS and the mouse driver into the UMB with commands in the CONFIG.SYS, such as the following:

```
DOS=HIGH,UMB
```

```
DEVICEHIGH=C:\DOS\MOUSE.SYS
```

underscore

1. An ASCII character (ASCII 95) that often is used as a surrogate for a space in variable names (because most compilers do not permit spaces in variable names).

2. More generally, a line under a word or group of words, often used for emphasis or to indicate italics with a typeface or printer that does not provide italic characters.

unit of measure

For a numeric data item, an attribute that specifies the quantity represented by 1.

The following table provides examples of units of measure, indicating how the units are maintained internally to the program and represented externally to the user:

Data Class	Common Internal Unit of Measure	Common External (or Alternative Internal) Unit of Measure
Length (or distance)	Centimeters	Miles Light-years Feet and inches
Money	Cents (U.S.)	Dollars ECUs Yen
Temperature	Degrees Kelvin	Degrees Fahrenheit Degrees Celsius
Date	Days	Year, month, and day
Time	Seconds	Hours, minutes, and seconds
Mass (or weight)	Grams	Pounds and ounces Metric tons

See also *attribute, data representation,* and *numeric data item.*

uninstall

To remove software or hardware from a computer system.

If a user no longer needs a software product, wants to move it to a different computer, or simply needs to free fixed disk space, he or she can remove it from the fixed disk or file server disk. Once removed, the program is uninstalled and no longer available on the system.

In most cases, an uninstall procedure is unnecessary. You can simply delete the files and directories from your fixed disk.

Uninstall procedures may be required in the following situations:

- In moving a software product that enforces a copy-protection scheme and that keeps track of the number of times the original installation disk has been used. Before the installation program lets you put the software on another machine, you must remove it from the first machine.

- In restoring an earlier version of a product after you encounter problems running the new version.

union

A binary operation on two sets, yielding the set of all elements that belong to either of the sets. Formally:

$$x \text{ is an element of } A \cup B$$

if and only if

$$x \text{ is an element of } A$$

or

$$x \text{ is an element of } B$$

See also *intersection*.

union (C)

A data declaration specifying two or more alternative structures for an area of storage. To access the structure, the program can simply refer to the name of the union, regardless of which variant a given instance of the union actually contains.

Unions are useful in processing files containing multiple record types. Usually, a common field appears near the beginning of each variant structure, and the value of this field identifies the variant structure.

See also *derived class* and *REDEFINES*.

unit test

Testing of a single module (or small group of related modules), usually done with or immediately following coding.

Unit testing is the first stage in testing new or modified software. Coding and unit testing normally constitute a single task assignment in a project, to be done by the same programmer and tracked as a single activity, such as "develop the XYZ module."

When modules are being designed and coded bottom-up, unit testing must also be done bottom-up. When modules are being designed and coded top-down, unit testing can be done top-down, bottom-up, or a combination. Top-down unit testing is typically simpler and evolves eventually into the next stage, integration testing. On the other hand, bottom-up unit testing is often more thorough, because a test driver is more likely than the real higher-level modules to exercise the full range of values of the module's inputs.

In bottom-up unit testing, a temporary test driver program invokes the module to be tested. Any required lower-level modules will have already been unit tested, and thus can be called by the module being tested.

In top-down unit testing, the module to be tested is invoked by the previously tested, higher-level modules that will actually invoke the module in the finished program. Any required but still unwritten lower-level modules are replaced by temporary dummy modules or module stubs that return a constant or trivial result.

UNIX

A multiuser, multitasking operating system that runs on several hardware platforms, including VAX and Intel.

Developed by AT&T Bell Laboratories in the late 1960s, UNIX was the first large program written in C.

The UNIX operating system consists of the kernel, the file system, and the user interface or shell. The kernel controls all aspects of memory, the central processing unit (CPU), and other component operations. The file system is hierarchical, much like the file system of MS-DOS. The user interface is provided by the use of shells: under UNIX the user can use the standard Bourne shell or the C shell to control file and program command operations. X Window, the standard graphical user interface (GUI) for UNIX, provides a graphical, easy-to-use interface for a complex operating system. Other UNIX GUIs include OSF/Motif and Open Look.

See also *kernel, Motif,* and *X Window.*

until

See *do until.*

upper CASE

CASE (computer-assisted software engineering) tools or techniques used in the first half of the life cycle, which consists of the automated generation of analysis and specification documentation.

See also *lower CASE.*

uppercase

The capitalized alphabetic characters, *A* through *Z.*

See also *ASCII, EBCDIC,* and *lowercase.*

upper memory block

See *UMB*.

upward compatibility

1. The capability of a computer system to run software designed for older computer systems. For example, the Intel 80486 processor is upward-compatible with the 8088 processor, because software written to run on the 8088 can usually operate on the 80486.

2. The capability of programs, documents, or spreadsheets to be used in newer versions of the software (compilers, word processors, spread-sheets, and so on). For example, if a newer 2.0 version of a word processor can edit a 1.0 document, the document is upward-compatible.

Products usually provide upward compatibility, but not downward compatibility.

See also *downward compatibility.*

user-friendliness

The quality associated with software that is designed to be easy to use and easy to learn.

User-friendly software usually provides extensive help features. Context-sensitive help enables the program to determine what the user is currently doing and what help the user needs at the time. User-friendly instructions also result in better usage of the software. Users consider graphical user interfaces (GUIs), and applications running under GUIs, as user-friendly because the interface is attractive and consistent.

Intuitive software, in which instructions and key combinations are presented and executed in forms that the user expects to see, is considered user-friendly. For example, if a user is familiar with pressing the Enter key to exit a text field, a program that requires the pressing of the Esc key would not be considered user-friendly.

validation

Demonstrating that a program works and meets its specifications.

Some writers on structured programming prefer this term to the more common testing or debugging. They feel that it reflects a more positive attitude toward both the purpose and the expected results of testing. Indeed, when good programmers use the best modern tools and techniques, they produce many modules that work correctly the first time they are tried, and there are no bugs to be diagnosed and corrected.

See also *data validation*.

vanilla

Used as-is, without customization or add-ons. This term usually applies to software products.

vaporware

A product publicly announced by a vendor but not yet available.

This term is never used by the vendor, but is applied pejoratively by the user community. Vaporware may be the result of either unintended overcommitment or a deliberate attempt to deter prospective customers from purchasing an already available competing product.

variable (or varying) length records

Records within a file that are not of uniform size. The records in a file may vary in size for the following reasons:

- They contain a varying number of repetitions or occurrences of some data item or group of items.

- They contain text or other fields that may themselves vary in size.

The first reason is becoming less common, as more organizations adopt a fully normalized approach to database design. The second, however, may be increasing, as application system designers try to make new software more user-friendly.

When all the records in a file have the same length, a number of simplifications and economies are possible in computing disk track addresses and managing buffers. Such advantages, however, rarely justify distorting a database design simply to make all records the same size.

variable (or varying) length string

A character string whose length is determined by its current value.

If you declare a character string variable to have a fixed (constant) length, subsequent operations will not affect that length. When you assign a shorter string to the fixed-length string, the new value is padded on the right with blanks; when you assign a longer string, the rightmost characters are discarded. Sometimes this is exactly the behavior you want—for example, such behavior would be useful in filling in fields on a form-image screen. At other times, however, you want the string variable to conform exactly to the size of any string you assign to it.

To conserve runtime overhead, some languages support variable-length strings up to a user-specified maximum. The program allocates enough space for the longest possible value, but keeps track of how much of that space is occupied by the current contents. Other languages, to conserve space, support dynamically growing strings with no user-specified limit.

The following table shows which popular languages directly support each kind of string:

Language	Fixed Length	Varying to a Maximum	Varying with No Maximum
BASIC	No	No	Yes
C	Yes	Yes	No
COBOL	Yes	No	No
Pascal	Yes	No	No
PL/1	Yes	Yes	No

VCPI—virtual control program interface

A DOS extender specification for Intel 80386 and later processors to allow programs to run concurrently with real-mode programs, utilizing memory without conflict.

Developed by Quarterdeck and Phar Lap Software, this specification was widely used in software product development.

vector

An element that can be described only by values for both magnitude and direction. For instance, a finite line can be described as a vector if you know its starting position, length (magnitude), and direction. This enables you to compute its ending point, as well as any other point along the line.

version dependency

Programming that takes advantage of some unpublished or obscure feature of a particular version of an operating system or other software product.

A well-known example of version dependency arose when Microsoft upgraded MS-DOS to Version 4. In the new version, certain addresses in the kernel were different from what they had been in Version 3. Although knowledge of those addresses was not part of the legal interface between programs and MS-DOS, several software products would not work under Version 4 because they had taken advantage of that unofficial knowledge.

See *device-independent* and *implementation dependency*.

VGA—video graphics array

An IBM video display standard first introduced with the PS/2 line of desktop computers.

VGA provides a standard resolution for text and graphics and is currently considered the minimum standard for most Intel-based microcomputers. A VGA adapter and monitor are analog devices, and can support software that uses the older CGA and EGA modes. In addition, VGA can display up to 640×480 with 16 colors. Advanced VGA adapters, called SVGA (super video graphics array) adapters, can display 600×800, 1024×768, and even 1280×1280, with an almost unlimited array of colors.

See also *CGA, EGA, resolution,* and *SVGA.*

VHL—very high-level language

A programming language that is considerably more powerful than a procedural language such as C.

Most VHLs are nonprocedural, proprietary to a particular vendor, and limited to a particular problem domain. They may be integrated with report generators, query languages, or CASE tools.

See also *CASE, nonprocedural language, procedural language, and level, programming language,* and *generations programming languages.*

vi

The standard UNIX-based, screen-oriented (visual) display text editor.

The vi editor is supported on virtually all UNIX versions, and was designed to support C programmers. The vi editor has been widely criticized as being extremely error-prone and not user-friendly, and has now been eclipsed by the newer UNIX editor, emacs.

See also *emacs.*

video

A device that uses a lighted screen, such as a television screen or a computer monitor, to provide viewable information.

video driver

A device driver program for video output.

In MS-DOS, the basic video driver is specified in the CONFIG.SYS file. That video driver supports video operations by most software, but some types of software may require their own special video drivers. Microsoft Windows, for example, uses such a special video driver to support its special graphics display requirements.

video graphics array

See *VGA*.

video RAM

A special type of memory available to video systems on a computer; sometimes called *VRAM*. Video RAM holds a representation of the image that appears on the screen.

Video data is stored as pixel or text data. Video RAM generally resides on a video display adapter board. The more video RAM available to the video adapter, the more information or resolution the adapter can have. Most modern VGA video adapters have at least 512K of video RAM onboard.

virtual base class

In C++, a special kind of base class that lets you avoid certain conflicts that arise with multiple inheritance.

Programmers are often surprised the first time they define classes like the following:

```
class Work
    {char title[40]; . . .};   // Base class
class Dramatic_Work : Work
    { . . . };                 // Derived class
class Musical_Work  : Work
    { . . .                }; // Derived class
class Opera
    : Dramatic_Work,           // Multiply-derived class
      Musical_Work             //   won't work! Inherits two
    { . . .               }; // data items called "title".
```

Fortunately, you can specify that a base class is virtual, which means that its descendants will inherit only a single copy of any of its members, even if they inherit through multiple intermediate classes:

```
class Work
    {char title[40]; . . .};   // Base class
class Dramatic_Work : virtual Work
    { . . . };                 // Derived class
class Musical_Work  : virtual Work
    { . . .              }; // Derived class
class Opera
    : Dramatic_Work,           // Multiply-derived class
      Musical_Work             //    works fine! Inherits a
    { . . .              }: //    single copy of "title".
```

Note that the virtual keyword is specified not in the declaration of Work, the actual virtual base class, but in the declarations of the classes derived from it.

See also *base class, overloading,* and *polymorphism.*

virtual memory

The capability to simulate more memory than actually exists on the computer by swapping portions of an address space between real memory and disk.

The available memory appears very large to the program, even if the real memory is comparatively small. The operating system divides into small portions called *pages* to enable the sections to be swapped more easily in and out of physical memory.

See also *address space* and *paged memory.*

virtual reality

The use of technology to create the illusion that the user is actually occupying an artificial space that he or she can observe and interact with.

The user typically must be fitted with the following apparatus:

- Goggles that simulate three-dimensional, full-field vision, and respond appropriately to the user's head and eye movements
- Gloves that track the user's hand movements to enable the user to touch, grasp, and move objects in the simulated world

To be convincing, virtual reality requires an immense amount of computer power. Furthermore, the extremely complex algorithms needed to simulate many forms of interaction are still the subject of research. It is doubtful, therefore, that virtual reality will have widespread practical application in the 1990s. In limited forms, however, it has already been implemented in arcade games and training devices such as flight simulators and flight combat training equipment.

virtual storage access method

See *VSAM*.

virus

A computer program embedded in another apparently harmless program designed to infect other computers.

When the virus program becomes active, it may exhibit harmless but annoying behavior, or be truly disruptive, destroying other programs or data files. For the virus to take effect, the program containing the virus must be executed; taking stringent precautions against executing programs received from other sources.

Cleverly written virus programs can remain dormant for some period, but contaminate programs generated on an infected machine.

See also *disinfect, infect,* and *Trojan horse*.

VisiCalc

The first commercially available spreadsheet processor, devised by Dan Bricklin.

Developed for the Apple II, VisiCalc is widely credited for Apple Computer's early success and for introducing microcomputers into the business world. The innovative VisiCalc user interface, although crude by current standards, persists as a strong influence in modern spreadsheet programs.

See also *Excel, Lotus 1-2-3,* and *Quattro Pro*.

Visual Basic

An application development system from Microsoft, based on the BASIC language and the Windows operating platform.

Visual Basic lets users develop many kinds of Windows applications without having to understand and use the extremely detailed and difficult Windows programming interface. It uses a graphical interface that lets the programmer "paint" the application and create the complete user interface before writing the program logic.

Using an event-driven model, Visual Basic was a departure from the procedural language model. Objects called *controls* (including list boxes, buttons, and dialogs) are arranged on a *form,* which is a window in which the controls reside. The programmer writes code that responds to events, such as the pressing of a button or the entering of text into an edit control.

See also *GUI.*

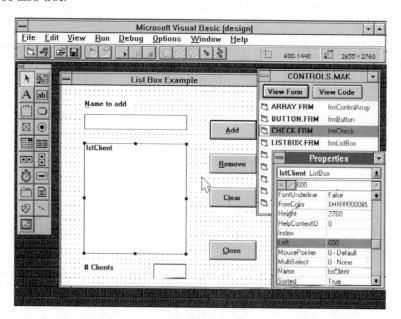

A Visual Basic screen.

VM/370

An operating system that simulates one or more IBM mainframe (System/370 or successor) configurations on a single mainframe. Each of the simulated configurations is called a "virtual machine."

Each virtual machine running under VM/370 looks just like a real mainframe to the software running on it. Each virtual machine can itself run any IBM mainframe operating system: DOS, MVS, or even another instance of VM/370.

Although not as widely used as either DOS or OS/MVS, VM/370 gained acceptance both as an efficient time-sharing system, and as a vehicle for testing new versions of an operating system or allowing occasional use of an obsolete one without disrupting normal operations.

VMS—virtual memory system

The principal operating system for Digital Equipment Corporation's VAX computers.

VMS is widely used in support of academic computing, as well as some mid-range applications. Although VMS is generally admired for its efficiency and ease of use, its future is in doubt due to the emergence of UNIX on the same hardware.

void function

In the C or C++ programming language, any function that does not return a value.

volatile memory

Memory that does not retain stored information after the system's power is shut off. Random-access memory (RAM) is usually volatile memory. In contrast, media (such as the system ROM BIOS) that maintain information when the power is off are nonvolatile.

volume label

A machine-readable label record at the beginning of a tape reel or disk uniquely identifying that tape or disk.

A volume label usually contains a serial number, and may contain information about the manufacturer or the date the volume was put into service. Unlike a data set label, it remains unchanged over the lifetime of the tape or disk volume.

In a computer center that has a large library of magnetic tapes or dismountable disks, the volume serial number is usually the main key to both rack storage and file cataloging.

MS-DOS provides both an unchanging serial number record and an 11-character label record that you can change by using the LABEL command.

volume test

See *stress test*.

VP-Expert

A moderately powerful expert system shell for MS-DOS, developed by Paperback Software.

One of the least expensive tools of its kind, VP-Expert enables users to experiment with artificial intelligence applications and actually build nontrivial expert systems.

See also *inference engine, inference rule,* and *rule base.*

VSAM—virtual storage access method

The largest and most important input-output subsystem under IBM mainframe operating systems.

VSAM was a great advance over IBM's first OS/360 access methods in terms of flexibility and efficiency. The subsystem continues to influence the designs of modern file systems.

VSAM's name is misleading—there's little in VSAM that requires a virtual storage capability. The name might have been chosen simply because IBM announced a major overhaul of its earlier input-output subsystems at the same time it announced its first virtual memory systems.

Many business applications actually use only the VSAM subset that closely mimics the earlier ISAM (Indexed Sequential Access Method). Because ISAM support is available in many PC-based products, you can sometimes easily convert a mainframe application that uses VSAM to a platform that supports ISAM.

VT-100 terminal

A DEC terminal consisting of a CRT (cathode ray tube) and keyboard. The VT-100 is widely used in online systems of the 1980s and is still emulated in many desktop computer telecommunications applications.

See also *3270 terminal.*

W

wait

See *semaphore.*

wait state

A delay that occurs while the central processing unit (CPU) waits for data.

Third-generation computers entered a wait state whenever the CPU had no work to do until an input-output (I/O) operation was completed. Some modern computers also interleave an idle cycle every few clock ticks to compensate for a speed mismatch between the CPU and memory. When the CPU and memory speeds are matched so that memory access is always completed in a single clock tick, the machine is said to have "zero wait states."

walkthrough

Any of several kinds of group review sessions intended to enhance the quality of software under development.

Although programming is a rather private activity between the programmer and the computer, experience repeatedly shows that program quality is greatly enhanced when other programmers get a chance to look at the design or the actual code and discuss alternatives openly. The idea of a walkthrough is to combine the thoroughness of a quality assurance (or standards enforcement) review with the casual and non-threatening feeling of a discussion among professionals.

On an important project, such walkthrough sessions should be held for any critical design decision, even a single data structure, as well as for original algorithms and other critical modules. The programmer-author leads a discussion group of between three to six peers in a session lasting between one to three hours. Everyone in the group is free to make comments, and no one is supposed to feel hurt or offended if the ideas of others prevail.

It's important to distinguish clearly between a walkthrough and a quality assurance review. The walkthrough is held before the major part of the work is done, whereas quality assurance is often a final or after-the-fact review. The walkthrough encourages alternative ideas, whereas quality assurance focuses narrowly on measurable criteria. The walkthrough is conducted internally within the project team, whereas quality assurance may involve staff specialists.

Warnier Diagramming

A set of techniques for specifying hierarchical (or nested) and conditional constructs, such as unnormalized data structures and processing logic.

One of a number of competing techniques that arose in the "structured revolution" of the 1970s, Jean Dominique Warnier's diagrams gained favor among advocates of a highly data-driven approach to analysis and design. Despite the absence of support in leading CASE tools, some systems analysts still prefer it for its compactness and clarity.

wave

A disturbance or alteration, oscillatory in nature, such as light and sound waves, or a sound file in sound or multimedia programs. A sound or wave file typically contains a .WAV extension.

white space

1. The areas of a page that contain no type or graphics. Appropriate arrangement of white space makes headings stand out more prominently, provides space for notes, and generally makes the page visually pleasing and easier to read.

2. Specific to standard C programming, the separations delimiting tokens in the preprocessor.

wild card

A variable symbol in a file name that will match any character in the corresponding position.

In many operating systems (including MS-DOS, UNIX, OS/2, and VAX/VMS), certain commands that operate on directories accept file names containing wild cards. For example, the MS-DOS command

```
COPY B:RPTXYZ?? A:RPTABC??
```

copies a file RPTXYZ94, if it exists on the B disk, to the A disk, naming the copy RPTABC94.

You can code an asterisk (*) to specify a variable number of characters. If you want to delete all the text files in the TEXTFILE directory, for example, you could enter the following:

```
ERASE C:\TEXTFILE\*.TXT
```

To delete all files having names that begin with the letter A, you would enter the following command:

```
ERASE C:\A*.*
```

To delete all files in the active directory, you would enter the following:

```
ERASE *.*
```

window

1. A rectangular area on the screen used as a viewing area.

2. An executing job or task associated with such a viewing area.

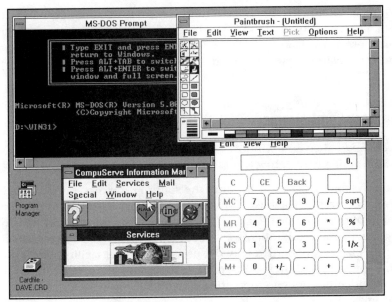

A screen featuring several windows.

Windows

A system software product for MS-DOS, introduced in the mid-1980s by the Microsoft Corporation, that provides an environment for other programs, based the following:

- Multiprogramming

- A graphical user interface (GUI) in which each executing program is associated with its own application window

- Dynamic data exchange (DDE) between two independent programs

- Management of the hardware congifuration, including memory and devices

- Output SPOOLing

Although Windows is not an operating system, users often characterize it as such, because Windows and MS-DOS together provide the range of functions normally considered as those of an operating system. Its main competition comes from complete operating systems, such as OS/2, Windows NT, and UNIX.

Windows for Workgroups

A version of Microsoft Windows 3.1 that provides support for groups of users working cooperatively.

Windows for Workgroups includes the software (drivers, network shell, and so on) required to establish a workgroup network based on the Windows graphical user interface (GUI). This product comes bundled with Microsoft Mail (electronic mail), Microsoft Schedule Plus (a shared electronic calendar), a shared clipboard, a network user-to-user chat facility, and several other multiuser features. It can operate as a stand-alone network, or it can work with other network operating systems such as Novell or Microsoft LAN Manager.

See also *groupware, GUI,* and *Windows.*

Windows NT

An operating system from Microsoft, released in 1993 and intended to compete on large Intel computers and network configurations with OS/2 and UNIX.

Windows NT is not an improved version of Microsoft Windows, but a completely new operating system. It shares with Windows only the name and a similar user interface. Like OS/2, Windows NT supports emulation of applications written for MS-DOS and for Windows.

word

Sixteen bits.

See also *bit* and *fullword.*

word-aligned

Having an address in memory that is divisible by the number of bytes in a word.

For example, suppose a computer has 32-bit words and each byte has an address (see *addressability*). Then a data item stored starting at an address divisible by 4 is word-aligned.

workaround

Any method of circumventing a problem or bug without correcting it.

See also *patch*.

work file

See *temporary file*.

work group

A group of two or more computer users who need to share files and exchange information regularly.

Many such groups work together as a team on a project. Large software development projects are especially suited to a workgroup approach, where various members of the team need to read, edit, compile, and test programs in a coordinated manner.

A local area network (LAN) is the most common vehicle for supporting a work group. Specialized software, such as Lotus Notes and Microsoft Windows for Workgroups, offers additional functions specifically designed to facilitate workgroup interactions.

WYSIWYG—What You See Is What You Get

A property of software in which the output displayed on the user's screen looks very similar to the eventual hard copy or printed output, with respect to page layout, fonts, and graphics. It is considered a desirable characteristic in word processing and spreadsheet software.

The following are the benefits of WYSIWYG:

- It helps the user avoid wasting both time and paper in generating printed output that turns out not to be exactly what was wanted.

- It lets the user interact directly with the software to achieve a desired format immediately, without iterative trial and error.

On the other hand, WYSIWYG has these drawbacks:

- It consumes much computer power, much of which is spent handling details the user may not care about.

- It usually requires duplication of output formatting functions in the program, leading to larger and more complex software.

See also *print preview.*

XGA—extended graphics array

A high-resolution IBM video display standard that features up to 1,024 × 768 resolution and 256 colors. The XGA also maintains support for the older VGA graphics modes, although IBM intends the XGA to serve as a replacement for the older 8514/A standard. The XGA standard faces stiff competition from makers of SVGA (super VGA) video adapters, which also support higher resolutions and color palettes.

XMS—Extended Memory Specification

A Microsoft-developed specification, much like EMS, used in Intel 80286, 80386, and 80486 computers to enable programs to utilize memory above the 1,024 kilobyte addressing limit.

XMS provides a set of predefined functions for allocating and transferring data to and from extended memory. Because allocated memory is protected, "XMS-aware" DOS programs can allocate extended memory without conflicting with other programs.

This specification also allows access to the HMA (High Memory Area), located just above the 1024K line in DOS memory. Only one program at a time can use HMA. The XMS driver normally used is HIMEM.SYS, which comes with Microsoft Windows or MS DOS 5.0 and above. You also can use other memory drivers that provide XMS services. Microsoft Windows 3.X uses XMS as the primary means of memory management.

xor

1. A binary logical operator that is assigned the value true only if one (but not more than one) of its operands is true.

2. One of the class of logical machine instructions that apply the xor operation bit-by-bit to two bits, bytes, or words, producing a result of the same type.

The xor operator is useful for efficiently manipulating bitmapped graphical display regions.

X Window

A graphical user interface (GUI) for UNIX.

The X Window windowing environment uses a graphical workstation, called an X Terminal, and a mouse. Using the client-server model over a network, X Window can display on workstation screens the graphics generated on a server. Sometimes both the client and server portions of X Window can be maintained within the same computer.

Most versions of UNIX support X Window. In addition, DOS-based X Terminals are available to display graphics on DOS workstations connected over a network to a UNIX server.

yacc—yet another compiler compiler

A development tool used to create simple compilers, interpreters, and complex programs.

The developer supplies yacc with a set of rules describing the custom command language and the actions accomplished for each command during computation. This utility is part of the UNIX development system.

Z80

See *Zilog CPU*.

Zilog CPU

The Z80 central processing unit (CPU) from Zilog Corporation used in the popular Tandy (Radio Shack) desktop computers of the 1970s.

The Z80, which was similar to the Intel 8080, usually ran under the CP/M operating system.

See also *Intel CPU*.

ZIP file

A file created and read by compression programs produced by PKware, Inc.

Compressing a file significantly reduces its size, perhaps by as much as 90 percent, depending on content.

This compression reduces software production and line costs for data transmission. Virtually all BBS (bulletin board systems) files are in a compressed format. ZIP files can be produced in a self-extracting executable form, well-suited to software distribution.

See also *PKZIP*.

zone bits

In EBCDIC character coding, the leftmost four bits. See *EBCDIC* for an explanation of the name.

zoned decimal

The representation of a numeric data item as a string of EBCDIC characters, in which one byte is used to represent each digit. By extension, some people also refer to ASCII representation as zoned decimal. *Unpacked decimal* is sometimes used as a synonym.

See also *packed decimal*.

ASCII Code Character Set

ASCII Dec	Value Hex	ASCII Character	ASCII Dec	Value Hex	ASCII Character
000	00	null	014	0E	♫
001	01	☺	015	0F	¤
002	02	●	016	10	►
003	03	♥	017	11	◄
004	04	♦	018	12	↕
005	05	♣	019	13	‼
006	06	♠	020	14	¶
007	07	●	021	15	§
008	08	◘	022	16	–
009	09	○	023	17	↨
010	0A	◙	024	18	↑
011	0B	♂	025	19	↓
012	0C	♀	026	1A	→
013	0D	♪	027	1B	←

ASCII	Value		ASCII	Value	
Dec	Hex	ASCII Character	Dec	Hex	ASCII Character
028	1C	∟	054	36	6
029	1D	↔	055	37	7
030	1E	▲	056	38	8
031	1F	▼	057	39	9
032	20	SPACE	058	3A	:
033	21	!	059	3B	;
034	22	"	060	3C	<
035	23	#	061	3D	=
036	24	$	062	3E	>
037	25	%	063	3F	?
038	26	&	064	40	@
039	27	'	065	41	A
040	28	(	066	42	B
041	29	)	067	43	C
042	2A	*	068	44	D
043	2B	+	069	45	E
044	2C	,	070	46	F
045	2D	–	071	47	G
046	2E	.	072	48	H
047	2F	/	073	49	I
048	30	0	074	4A	J
049	31	1	075	4B	K
050	32	2	076	4C	L
051	33	3	077	4D	M
052	34	4	078	4E	N
053	35	5	079	4F	O

ASCII	Value		ASCII	Value	
Dec	Hex	ASCII Character	Dec	Hex	ASCII Character
080	50	P	106	6A	j
081	51	Q	107	6B	k
082	52	R	108	6C	l
083	53	S	109	6D	m
084	54	T	110	6E	n
085	55	U	111	6F	o
086	56	V	112	70	p
087	57	W	113	71	q
088	58	X	114	72	r
089	59	Y	115	73	s
090	5A	Z	116	74	t
091	5B	[	117	75	u
092	5C	\	118	76	v
093	5D	]	119	77	w
094	5E	^	120	78	x
095	5F	–	121	79	y
096	60	`	122	7A	z
097	61	a	123	7B	{
098	62	b	124	7C	¦
099	63	c	125	7D	}
100	64	d	126	7E	~
101	65	e	127	7F	Δ
102	66	f	128	80	Ç
103	67	g	129	81	ü
104	68	h	130	82	é
105	69	i	131	83	â

| ASCII | Value | | ASCII | Value | |
Dec	Hex	ASCII Character	Dec	Hex	ASCII Character
132	84	ä	157	9D	¥
133	85	à	158	9E	P$_t$
134	86	å	159	9F	ƒ
135	87	ç	160	A0	á
136	88	ê	161	A1	í
137	89	ë	162	A2	ó
138	8A	è	163	A3	ú
139	8B	ï	164	A4	ñ
140	8C	î	165	A5	Ñ
141	8D	ì	166	A6	ª
142	8E	Ä	167	A7	º
143	8F	Å	168	A8	¿
144	90	É	169	A9	⌐
145	91	æ	170	AA	¬
146	92	Æ	171	AB	½
147	93	ô	172	AC	¼
148	94	ö	173	AD	¡
149	95	ò	174	AE	«
150	96	û	175	AF	»
151	97	ù	176	B0	░
152	98	ÿ	177	B1	▒
153	99	Ö	178	B2	▓
154	9A	Ü	179	B3	│
155	9B	¢	180	B4	┤
156	9C	£	181	B5	╡

ASCII Dec	Value Hex	ASCII Character	ASCII Dec	Value Hex	ASCII Character
182	B6	╢	208	D0	╨
183	B7	╖	209	D1	╤
184	B8	╕	210	D2	╥
185	B9	╣	211	D3	╙
186	BA	║	212	D4	╘
187	BB	╗	213	D5	╒
188	BC	╝	214	D6	╓
189	BD	╜	215	D7	╫
190	BE	╛	216	D8	╪
191	BF	┐	217	D9	┘
192	C0	└	218	DA	┌
193	C1	┴	219	DB	█
194	C2	┬	220	DC	▄
195	C3	├	221	DD	▌
196	C4	─	222	DE	▐
197	C5	┼	223	DF	▀
198	C6	╞	224	E0	α
199	C7	╟	225	E1	β
200	C8	╚	226	E2	Γ
201	C9	╔	227	E3	π
202	CA	╩	228	E4	Σ
203	CB	╦	229	E5	σ
204	CC	╠	230	E6	μ
205	CD	═	231	E7	τ
206	CE	╬	232	E8	Φ
207	CF	╧	233	E9	θ

ASCII	Value	
Dec	Hex	ASCII Character
234	EA	Ω
235	EB	δ
236	EC	∞
237	ED	ø
238	EE	∈
239	EF	∩
240	F0	≡
241	F1	±
242	F2	≥
243	F3	≤
244	F4	⌠
245	F5	⌡
246	F6	÷
247	F7	≈
248	F8	°
249	F9	•
250	FA	·
251	FB	√
252	FC	η
253	FD	²
254	FE	■
255	FF	

GO AHEAD. PLUG YOURSELF INTO PRENTICE HALL COMPUTER PUBLISHING.

Introducing the PHCP Forum on CompuServe®

Yes, it's true. Now, you can have CompuServe access to the same professional, friendly folks who have made computers easier for years. On the PHCP Forum, you'll find additional information on the topics covered by every PHCP imprint—including Que, Sams Publishing, New Riders Publishing, Alpha Books, Brady Books, Hayden Books, and Adobe Press. In addition, you'll be able to receive technical support and disk updates for the software produced by Que Software and Paramount Interactive, a division of the Paramount Technology Group. It's a great way to supplement the best information in the business.

WHAT CAN YOU DO ON THE PHCP FORUM?

Play an important role in the publishing process—and make our books better while you make your work easier:

- Leave messages and ask questions about PHCP books and software—you're guaranteed a response within 24 hours
- Download helpful tips and software to help you get the most out of your computer
- Contact authors of your favorite PHCP books through electronic mail
- Present your own book ideas
- Keep up to date on all the latest books available from each of PHCP's exciting imprints

JOIN NOW AND GET A FREE COMPUSERVE STARTER KIT!

To receive your free CompuServe Introductory Membership, call toll-free, **1-800-848-8199** and ask for representative **#K597**. The Starter Kit Includes:

- Personal ID number and password
- $15 credit on the system
- Subscription to CompuServe Magazine

HERE'S HOW TO PLUG INTO PHCP:

Once on the CompuServe System, type any of these phrases to access the PHCP Forum:

GO PHCP
GO QUEBOOKS
GO SAMS
GO NEWRIDERS
GO ALPHA

GO BRADY
GO HAYDEN
GO QUESOFT
GO PARAMOUNTINTER

Once you're on the CompuServe Information Service, be sure to take advantage of all of CompuServe's resources. CompuServe is home to more than 1,700 products and services—plus it has over 1.5 million members worldwide. You'll find valuable online reference materials, travel and investor services, electronic mail, weather updates, leisure-time games and hassle-free shopping (no jam-packed parking lots or crowded stores).

Seek out the hundreds of other forums that populate CompuServe. Covering diverse topics such as pet care, rock music, cooking, and political issues, you're sure to find others with the same concerns as you—and expand your knowledge at the same time.

Que Gives You the Most Comprehensive Programming Information Available!

Introduction to Programming
David Veale & Lisa Monitto

This book explores the fundamental concepts and tools involved in the development of the user's own tools, utilities, and applications.

IBM-compatibles

$19.95 USA
1-56529-097-6, 400 pp., 7³/₈ x 9¹/₄

More Programming Titles from Que

Advanced Assembly Language
Microsoft Macro Assembler & Borland Turbo Assembler
$39.95 USA
1-56529-037-2, 720 pp., 7³/₈ x 9¹/₄

Borland C++ 3.1 Programmer's Reference, 2nd Edition
Latest Versions of Borland C++ and Turbo C++
$29.95 USA
1-56529-082-8, 900 pp., 7³/₈ x 9¹/₄

C Programmer's Toolkit 2nd Edition
Turbo C, Quick C, & ANSI C
$39.95 USA
0-88022-788-5, 350 pp., 7³/₈ x 9¹/₄

Clipper Programmer's Reference
Clipper 5.01
$29.95 USA
0-88022-677-3, 800 pp., 7³/₈ x 9¹/₄

DOS Programmer's Reference, 3rd Edition
Through DOS 4.0 - 5.0
$29.95 USA
0-88022-790-7, 1,000 pp., 7³/₈ x 9¹/₄

Network Programming in C
Book + 2 Disks!
$49.95 USA
0-88022-569-6, 650 pp., 7³/₈ x 9¹/₄

Paradox 4 Developer's Guide
Paradox 4
$44.95 USA
0-88022-705-2, 800 pp., 7³/₈ x 9¹/₄

UNIX Programmer's Quick Reference
AT&T System V, Release 3
$8.95 USA
0-88022-535-1, 160 pp., 7³/₈ x 9¹/₄

UNIX Shell Commands Quick Reference
AT&T System V Releases 3 & 4
$8.95 USA
0-88022-572-6, 160 pp., 7³/₈ x 9¹/₄

Using Assembly Language, 3rd Edition
Microsoft Assembler & Borland's Turbo Assembler
$29.95 USA
0-88022-884-9, 900 pp., 7³/₈ x 9¹/₄

Using BASIC, 2nd Edition
GW BASIC & BASICA
$27.95 USA
1-56529-140-9, 584 pp., 7³/₈ x 9¹/₄

Using C
Microsoft C Version 6, Turbo C++, & QuickC Version 2.5
$29.95 USA
0-88022-571-8, 950 pp., 7³/₈ x 9¹/₄

Using Turbo Pascal 6, 2nd Edition
Through Version 6
$29.95 USA
0-88022-700-1, 800 pp., 7³/₈ x 9¹/₄

To Order, Call: (800) 428-5331
OR (317) 581-3535

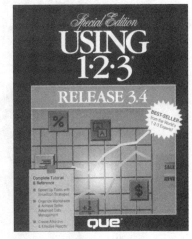

Count on Que for the Most Up-to-Date Information on Integrated Packages

**Using Microsoft Works
for Windows, Special Edition**
Douglas Wolf

This book provides plenty of timesaving tips and hints on sharing information between Works' modules. A comprehensive reference and tutorial, this book will give you everything you need to know about Microsoft Works.

Version 1

$24.95 USA
0-88022-757-5, 550 pp., 7³/₈ x 9¹/₄

**Using Microsoft Works:
IBM Version**
Douglas Wolf

Through Version 2

$22.95 USA
0-88022-467-3, 444 pp., 7³/₈ x 9¹/₄

Using Q&A 4
David Ewing & Bill Langenes

Version 4

$27.95 USA
0-88022-643-9, 550 pp., 7³/₈ x 9¹/₄

Q&A 4 Quick Reference
Que Development Group

Latest Version

$9.95 USA
0-88022-828-8, 160 pp., 4³/₄ x 8

Q&A 4 QuickStart
Que Development Group

Version 4

$19.95 USA
0-88022-653-6, 400 pp., 7³/₈ x 9¹/₄

Que's Using Enable
Walter Bruce

All Versions Through Enable/OA4

$29.95 USA
0-88022-701-X, 700 pp., 7³/₈ x 9¹/₄

Using Lotus Works 3.0
J. D. Watson

Release 3.0

$24.95 USA
0-88022-771-0, 500 pp., 7³/₈ x 9¹/₄

Using PFS: First Choice 4.0
Katherine Murray

Through Version 4.0

$27.95 USA
0-88022-969-1, 600 pp., 7³/₈ x 9¹/₄

Using PFS: WindowsWorks 2
Deanna Bebb

Through Version 2

$29.95 USA
1-56529-073-9, 500 pp., 7³/₈ x 9¹/₄

To Order, Call: (800) 428-5331
OR (317) 581-3535